Claude and Madeleine

EDWARD MARRIOTT is the author of three acclaimed
works of non-fiction: *The Lost Tribe*, which was shortlisted
for the 1996 Thomas Cook Travel Book Award and the
John Llewellyn Rhys Memorial Prize; *Wild Shore*;
and *The Plague Race*. He lives in London
with his wife and two sons.

Edward Marriott

Claude and Madeleine

A True Story of War, Espionage and Passion

PICADOR

First published 2005 by Picador as *Claude and Madeleine: A True Story*

First published in paperback 2006 by Picador
an imprint of Pan Macmillan Ltd
Pan Macmillan, 20 New Wharf Road, London N1 9RR
Basingstoke and Oxford
Associated companies throughout the world
www.panmacmillan.com

ISBN-13: 978-0-330-41917-8
ISBN-10: 0-330-41917-X

1 3 5 7 9 8 6 4 2

A CIP catalogue record for this book is available from
the British Library.

Printed and bound in Great Britain by
Mackays of Chatham plc, Chatham, Kent

All Pan Macmillan titles are available from
www.panmacmillan.com
or from Bookpost by telephoning +44 (0)1624 677237

Milla

'We were all a little bit mad on that ship. That was the way the captain wanted us: to be tough guys like him, to care about nothing.'

Auguste Roulland, former crew member of HMS *Fidelity*

'[In Claude Péri] we have a man of great courage, determination and loyalty, although somewhat unorthodox in his methods.'

Admiral Percy Noble, Commander-in-Chief Western Approaches, in a letter to the Secretary of the Admiralty, 11 January 1942

'Madeleine Bayard was one of the war's most romantic figures. Claude Péri was the finest warrior I have ever known.'

Major-General Albert Guérisse DSO, KBE, known during the war as 'Pat O'Leary'. From June 1940 to April 1941 he was HMS *Fidelity*'s First Officer

PROLOGUE

IT IS MORNING, early January, and I am driving. It is cold, barely above freezing, and a pale metal sun gives a silvery cast to the terrain. I'm heading east, and when the road rises the wind knocks the car and the wheel trembles for a moment in my hands.

The land seems asleep: after the inrush of Edinburgh commuter traffic the Fife coast road, once out of Kirkcaldy, is empty. Highland cattle stand heads-down and motionless in fields a-shimmer with ice, frozen puddles icing-sugared with snow. Driving feels almost like sailing: the car a boat, riding a low swell of hills, the North Sea horizon lost to mist. And then I hit Leven – granite-grey, the milk float tinkling down the main street – and the spell is broken.

The directions are good: the house – 'the only one with ivy' – is white and freshly painted, one of a truncated terrace that sits right on the road. I park the car, pull my coat around me. The wind has died and there is no sound. The hills have gone, and across the flat fields the sea feels close: just across that stretch of rubbled plough, maybe, or behind that far stand of winter-stripped trees.

AN OLD MAN opens the door. The house feels upside down: bedrooms are on the ground floor; kitchen and sitting room upstairs. There's a lever-arch file on a coffee table. From the windows the fields are the colour of stone, disappearing into mist.

He's seventy but, passionate and angry, seems suddenly younger. He sits with the file on his knees and tells me about his brother, whose ship was torpedoed in the Atlantic on New Year's Eve 1942. His brother was twenty-one; there's a photograph of him on the wall: a faint buzz of moustache, barely even a man with his rounded cheeks and soft cloudless eyes. His brother was ten years older than him and his last memory is of him on leave, visiting the family at home in Belfast. During breaks from previous postings, his brother had brought presents of Mexican sombreros, stunt guns from China, beads from Malaya. This time, though, there were no gifts. He seemed different, unable to sit still for long. He told his father, 'The captain says that this is one journey we won't come back from.'

We get up and walk towards the window. Near the photograph of his brother is one of a ship. The hull is patchy, streaked with oil, dotted with irregularly spaced portholes. It looks as if it has just returned from an arduous voyage and now, in calmer water approaching dock, with a strip of land just visible behind the superstructure, it is going to get the overhaul it has long needed. 'HMS *Fidelity*,' he says, touching the photograph with the tip of one finger. 'That's her.' Sixty years have passed and still he's grieving. I wonder what has happened to prevent him being able to lay his brother to rest, and as I'm thinking this he begins to answer it.

For a year after his brother's death his parents, along with other bereaved relatives, wrote letters to the War Ministry asking for information. 'Each time they made enquiries they were blanked; the government didn't want to know. At one point it was even claimed that the ship never existed.'

It took a small ad in a naval newspaper for more to emerge. 'I was inundated. I had literally thousands of phone calls, letters and other enquiries from people whose fathers, brothers and husbands had, as they put it, "disappeared" on this ship.' Each person had a little extra to add, but all asked the same questions: Where was the ship heading when she was lost? Why all the secrecy? Was there really a woman on board? And was she only there because the captain, her lover, had insisted?

As I sought out others – men who'd served on the ship, others who'd lost family members – a picture emerged of an Allied ship unlike any other, whose captain, like most of his crew, was French and whose female cipher officer – also French, a former spy, his lover – was the only woman to have served on a British fighting ship during the war.

CLAUDE PÉRI and Madeleine Bayard met in Vietnam in the 1930s, gathering information on the communist underground for the Colonial Ministry in Paris. They became experts in the use of plastic explosive and, with war looming, were sent back to Europe. By the end of June 1940, their nation having capitu-lated to the Germans, they had cut their ties with France. They changed their names and became British secret agents. Somehow – for reasons I was yet to discover – Claude managed swiftly to secure the highest-level access to senior British government figures and, refitting 'his' ship, he got pretty much everything he asked for. Including – uniquely – his beloved Madeleine, disguised as a Wren, as his cipher officer.

The more I learned about Claude and Madeleine, the more I wanted to know; the more, indeed, I wished I'd known them. They seemed designed to appeal to one's deepest long-ings for passion and adventure: he volatile yet charming; she blonde, feline, a markswoman. And yet it seemed that British intelligence, initially delighted to have them, later attempted to erase their very memory. What was it about Claude and Madeleine, I wanted to know, that had been felt to be so special and yet so dangerous?

This is their story. It is for all those who were left behind.

VIETNAM, 1936

MADELEINE PARTED the shutters. She'd been woken from her siesta by the noise. Outside was a sight she and her husband had long dreaded: a hollering crowd working its way towards their house, men with ravenous eyes and veins on their forearms thick as electrical cable. Approaching the white picket fence that circled the garden, a small group of men broke from the rabble and pushed through the gate, muscling the guards aside.

Madeleine's husband locked the front door, telephoned the local garrison and pulled Madeleine towards the office at the rear of the bungalow. The two of them heard hammering fists, then the high-treble splinter of timber as the door was flattened on its hinges. The intruders banged through the house, screaming in voices that Madeleine – despite three years of learning Vietnamese – understood only in part. And then the briefest hiatus, a sweet silence, as the men saw the locked office door and gathered themselves for the final assault.

There had been a risk of this, Madeleine knew, ever since they had taken over the rubber plantation in the early 1930s. The inequality was palpable: she and her husband inhabited surroundings that were spacious and luxuriously furnished, and which were daily kept immaculate by a team of servants, secretaries, cooks, gardeners and 'boys'. Their workers laboured ten-hour days cutting forest and planting rubber saplings, rising at four in the morning to cook their rations for the day, and starting work at six. A contemporary account of a worker on a similar plantation describes physical punishment that was harsh and routine: questioning an order could result in the offender being forced to pull down his underpants for a beating, or hit across the feet with a rattan cane 'until the soles were in ribbons'. Many attempted escape. Those captured were dealt with by the plantation soldiers, who were ordered to 'tramp on [the escapees'] ribs with their nail-studded boots. Standing outside I could hear the sound of bones snapping. When they had finished trampling them, they beat them another round with canes, then shackled them in a darkened building.' There they were left to die. By the mid-1930s, in plantations across the country, resentment was building, and attacks on managers and supervisors were becoming increasingly common.

THE MEN WERE inside the bungalow now. They'd brought rope. They bound Madeleine's husband, forced Madeleine against the desk, and took turns to rape her. As she crouched shivering in the corner, hands over her head, eyes screwed too tight for tears, one of them held a pistol to her husband's head. Looking up, finally, a long time later when all was quiet, she saw his blood, like exploded paint, shot across the plantation map.

LATER THAT AFTERNOON Claude, a part-time French-government intelligence agent, was driving alone. He saw the smoke first, rising into the clear afternoon sky. He turned through the plantation gates. The place appeared deserted, no workers anywhere. He stopped his car near the workers' huts, which had been burned to almost nothing: only the charred spikes of corner posts remained. In the distance, smoke from a cooling cookfire rose into the blue. As Claude stood there in the silence, making jottings in his notepad, he could hear nothing from the surrounding forest, neither birdcalls nor the yip of monkeys.

He walked on. Ahead of him stood the manager's bungalow, strangely intact. He picked his way over the flattened fence, through trampled flowerbeds, and stood a moment on the threshold. Thinking he had just caught the merest sound, he strained to listen. Nothing. He moved inside to find stoved-in tables, chairs with their legs ripped off, crockery and glass smashed across the floor, thick and percussive as gravel. There was a bathroom suite with an enamel claw-footed tub, and in the bedrooms the sheets lay untouched, *voilages* still drawn.

The door to the office was half-closed, and hanging loose from its topmost hinge. As he stepped cautiously into the room, Claude smelled excrement. Then he saw the body slumped at the desk, back of the head matted and treacly. Flies rose, settled again. As Claude opened his notebook to write, he saw a movement under the table. He bent down slowly: a woman, knees at her chest, bare feet, blonde hair fallen into her face. He spoke to her gently, but received no response. It took him an hour to get her to the car. It would be another day before she spoke a word.

HANOI, VIETNAM, 1908 TO 1919

CLAUDE ANDRÉ MICHEL PÉRI was born in Hanoi on
7 April 1908, second son of François-Michel Péri, head of the
new Indochinese military telegraphic service. For the previous four years François-Michel Péri – thirty-seven years old,
still with his first wife – had travelled the country setting up
wireless transmitters, using technology patented by Marconi
just a few years before.

Claude's father was a powerful man, contradictory and
charismatic, a broad-shouldered one metre sixty-seven, whose
pioneering use of wireless telegraphy in Indochina would earn
him the Légion d'honneur. He was a man about whom few felt
neutral. His career service record describes him, at different
points, as conscientious, zealous, energetic and 'acutely' intelligent, as well as impressionable, disorganized, pretentious,
overrated and superficial, with 'little taste for desk work'.

He married three times. His first marriage, to Jeanne
Costabel, mother of Henri and Claude, foundered after he was
unfaithful. The second time around it was his wife, Augustine-
Amélie Arnauld, who found herself drawn to another. His
third wife, Marcelle Boucher, was his junior by three decades
– thirty-one, to his sixty. They wed on 10 July 1931, during
his retirement in Paris. He died seven years later, amid the
burgeoning rumours of war.

Henri's widow today recalls Claude's father as 'meticulous,
curious about everything, but rather authoritarian'. From
photographs, this authoritarian streak is immediately striking

– upbrushed, tightly clipped moustache, collar starched, eyes an intense glacial blue.

During Claude's childhood, Hanoi was the administrative capital of the new French colony, and a town upon which the Europeans – from the moment the first troops entered in 1873 – had swiftly stamped their identity. Built on a raised plain between the West Lake and, to the east, the Red River, Hanoi was the former royal capital of Vietnam, and in the closing years of the nineteenth century, as the colonists tightened their grip, every vestige of the ousted regime was razed. The old quadriform regal citadel – containing 'endless courtyards', 'incomparable' apartments and 'large stone arcades' bordered by 'extraordinarily thick walls' – was destroyed. In its place, laid out in grids along terracotta-sand roads, came naval and infantry barracks, artillery depots and a military prison. Though the token pagoda was left standing, by the time Claude was born in 1908 the imposition of the colonial aesthetic was complete – broad boulevards reminiscent of Haussmann's Paris, the white-stone neo-classical buildings of the new administration, street after street of spacious villas for the *fonctionnaires*.

It was a striking and impressive colonial capital, replete with concert hall, theatre, even a monumental cathedral, St Joseph's. These structures exuded confidence: the railway station, with its colonnaded entrance and clear sweep of driveway, seemed more like a Loire Valley chateau than anything so mundane as a transport hub. From photographs, one senses an air of ordered leisure: the ivory plush of cushions on the rickshaws lined up along Rue Paul Bert, the wide clean-swept pavements along which a pair of strolling pyjama-trousered Vietnamese officials have been captured on celluloid.

The crowning architectural achievement, though, and one with which the Péri family were to become well acquainted, was the Governor-General's palace. Erected between 1901 and 1906 on the twenty hectares of confiscated Vietnamese land which had once housed the regal pagoda, and overlooking an expanse of West Lake with its flocks of scudding teal and clatter of electric-white storks, the bulk and detail of its construction 'emphasized the "sacred authority" of the ruling regime'. As a cultural statement, the palace was uncompromising: from the ascending banks of steps to the marbled and highly polished interior, the one-tonne chandeliers and staterooms bordered with gilt armchairs, the message was that this was the seat, even the source, of power.

The opening years of the twentieth century – as the darkly clustered labourers sweated in the red dirt of the foundation trenches and the colonial palace rose skyward – were also the time of François-Michel Péri's most fertile and creative period. Married in the autumn of 1902, aged thirty-one, he spent much of the next year, and a considerable amount of his own money, conducting radio experiments. He did these in his own time – weekends, holidays, hours snatched from his duties as a second lieutenant – and was so successful that the Governor-General promoted him within a year to a new post: head of 'télégraphe sans fil' for Indochina, with special responsibility for setting up radio links between Hanoi and points along the Indochinese coast.

He worked swiftly. By 1905 he'd erected three sixty-metre masts – in Hanoi, Phu Ly, and the coastal town of Hong Gai – and overseen the construction of adjacent bungalows to house staff and equipment; he can be seen in official photographs posing proudly – legs astride, hand on hip – or leaning with proprietorial nonchalance against newly painted iron railings.

When, on 31 August, a typhoon exposed the radio masts' fragility, Péri retreated to his workshop in Hanoi. He emerged six months later with another invention: mobile transmitters and receivers, spring-suspended on boxed-in agricultural chassis, which bumped through the paddies on wooden-spoked wheels, pulled by horses. Péri and his team – four or five European soldier-engineers and three times that many Vietnamese assistants – took tents, food and rifles and camped out in the fields, whispering into the static for days on end, surrounded by astonished villagers.

He worked ceaselessly, and there are references in his military record to his resultant ill-health. In 1913, with Claude now five, and Henri nine – and after an intense five-year period which saw him scout back-country Laos for suitable transceiver sites, earn commendations for his leadership during the 1909 counter-revolutionary operations, and set up three more permanent radio posts – he suffered a collapse. How crippling, or to what degree physical or psychological, is unclear, but it was concerning enough for his friend Albert Sarraut, the Governor-General, to mention in his 1914 recommendation to the War Minister in Paris that 'the swift set-up of the Hanoi station, carried out during a period of intense heat, imposed on this officer an exhaustion which has gravely affected his health'.

It is likely that, even on the rare occasions he was at home, Péri cut a distant figure as a father. Records show that the family lived for at least some of Claude's early childhood in Rue Pavie, a street of two-storey colonial villas in the newly built French neighbourhood to the south of the city. There was at once an ambassadorial grandeur and something inescapably French-provincial about these residences, with their gated compounds and uniform green shutters, in which the families of bureaucrats, bank managers and opium agents spent their days cloistered from the heat outside. These homes were serviced by teams of servants, horse-drawn carriages, nannies and cooks. And, in the early years of the colony, a shortage of European women – just two hundred in Hanoi in 1900 – led to thriving prostitution. When a conventional family nucleus did happen to coalesce, the early evenings of the adults were spent enjoying cocktails – '*l'heure de l'absinthe*' – and, for women and children, summers were passed at the Tam Dao and Sa Pa hill stations, as if Hanoi were no more foreign than Nantes, or Clermont-Ferrand.

During the year of Claude's birth, his father was absent from the family for prolonged periods. The following year, 1909 – with Péri now head of military radio, and the army fighting rebels in the mountains north of Hanoi – saw even more sporadic, unpredictable and short-lived home visits. So began the pattern of Claude's infancy and early boyhood: an absent father, a fractured family life, his everyday needs – food, sleep, exercise – overseen by young Vietnames women, his mother a fragrant and exotic presence, pale dresses in high-ceilinged rooms, forever tantalizingly out of reach.

Claude was four years younger than Henri and, though details are scant, it is clear that from the start they were both fiercely independent. Both boys also had a bellicose streak, and it is likely that Claude learned at least some of his close-combat skills at the hands of his elder brother – at the age of eight, Henri came home from his school, Hanoi's Collège Paul Bert, to relate how he'd ended up in a playground fight with his friend Omer Sarraut, the Governor-General's son. Like a latter-day heavyweight, Henri had claimed victory by sinking his teeth into Omer's ear.

The siting of the family villa at the southern edge of

Hanoi, a mere ten-minute walk from the sandy banks of the Red River, where the colonial streets gave way to clusters of Vietnamese workers' huts, encouraged the boys' hunger for exploration. Claude was a gifted linguist, and these first glimpses into the smoky interiors of Vietnamese houses – the pungent scent of frying *nem* rolls or the sight of steam rising from soup cauldrons of hot-pepper *pho* – were also his introduction to the spoken language. Yet his place in society was never in doubt, and as his father became an ever-closer ally and friend of Albert Sarraut, so the Péri boys began to spend increasing amounts of time with the Governor-General's children: Henri with Omer, Claude with Omer's younger sister Lydie. The journey across town from Rue Pavie to the Sarraut palace overlooking West Lake was one which stated and reaffirmed the status quo with every mile: the broad-shaded sweep of Boulevard Gambetta; the capacious Charrière department store on Rue Paul Bert, stocked with Paris fashions and pots of imported foie gras; the racetrack, where society would gather at the weekend.

In family mythology, Claude is the more feral of the two brothers, the more adventurous and less rule-bound. An anecdote of his early daring has survived, dated by his nephew Bernard Péri to between 1917 and 1919, making Claude about ten years old. At this point, nearing the end of the First World War, Claude had seen neither his father nor his brother in years: Péri senior had been posted to Lyon at the start of 1913, to set up and run its wartime military radio-communications base, and a year later Henri too had taken the steamer from Saigon, bound for boarding school in France. At around this time Claude's mother had also sailed for Europe, leaving Claude alone in the empty villa. And so it was, playing one day with the Governor-General's children in the palatial official residence, that he and Lydie Sarraut, having heard that the Vietnamese Emperor Khai Dinh was in residence, decided to smuggle themselves unseen into his state rooms. On tiptoe, they banged through one heavy mahogany door after another, getting lost, growing hotter and more nervous as they neared their quarry. Rounding the last corner, they clasped their hands over their mouths to muffle the screams as they found themselves facing the Emperor himself, smiling as he emerged from his siesta. Khai Dinh, the true statesman, turned it to his advantage. To mark the occasion when two young spies almost made it to the inner sanctum, he presented both their mothers with gifts. Jeanne Costabel Péri received a silver vase, decorated with a rampant dragon, talons outstretched, jaws spewing flame: symbol of old, pre-colonial Hanoi.

PARIS TO VIETNAM, 1911 TO 1932

IF HANOI at the start of the twentieth century was a town sure of its place and position, then Paris – its mother city, and, on 21 February 1911, birthplace of Madeleine Victorine Bayard – had never been more exuberant. Of any period in the city's history, this, the Belle Époque, was its most unrestrained and grandiloquent. From the completion of Gustave Eiffel's tower for the 1889 Exposition, through to the outbreak of war in 1914, Paris flourished and expanded economically and artistically as never before. With the development of the Métro from 1900, a thickening web of road links between Paris and other major centres, growing numbers of bicycles and the introduction of the Orient Express and *wagons-lits*, people began to travel on a scale previously inconceivable. Confidence abounded: by the end of the nineteenth century, Paris was an unparalleled venue for culture, with more than two hundred *café-concerts*, *bals musettes*, *ginguettes* and *cabarets artistiques*. Fauvism, Cubism and Surrealism were born there; concert halls trembled to the sound of new symphonies by Ravel, Debussy and Satie; and in the capital's galleries curators were hanging the latest works from Matisse, Dufy, Bonnard and Picasso.

The years that saw Claude's father carve out his radio innovations in the Far East were, in Paris, a time of equally momentous advances. In 1895, Louis Lumière showed the first moving picture; fourteen years later came Louis Blériot's pioneer airplane crossing of the English Channel. Telephones, books, newspapers, the postal system: all were embraced and expanded. By the eve of the Great War, France had become the world leader in automobile production, manufacturing forty-five thousand cars a year.

Strolling along the boulevards, Parisian confidence found orchidaceous, bodily form. Fashion historians highlight 1909 as the moment that designers – electrified by the first appearance on the Paris stage of the Ballet Russe, with its corsetless costumes, vibrant colours and intoxicating Oriental flavour – finally abandoned the puffed sleeves and flounces of Edwardian dressmaking and created a modern style that is still echoed on today's catwalks. This was the year in which Coco Chanel began her Paris career, and that Jeanne Lanvin, Madeleine Vionnet and Paul Poiret all embarked on their most distinctive work. Fashion magazines were launched – three in 1912 alone – and a glance through their pages is enough to sense the reverence with which the new fashions were treated. 'Certainly fashion is a more serious thing than is believed,' wrote Lucie Delarue-Mardrus in *Le Journal des Dames et des Modes* on 10 September 1912. 'So, ladies, be stylish. It is a great civic duty. Though Notre-Dame is a cathedral, it is nonetheless *une dame*. May your exterior be also the cathedral of your soul.'

For socialite women to be able to turn themselves into walking artworks, battalions of support workers were required, and it was into this twilight world of gas-lit garrets, the all-hours hum and rattle of the sewing machine, that Madeleine was born. Her mother, Adèle Suzanne Bayard, was a thirty-one-year-old seamstress; her father's identity is unknown.

Illegitimate children were far from uncommon in the Paris of that time – in 1913, twenty-four per cent of all births in the city were to unmarried women – but in Adèle's case it was not just a matter of wedlock. Hospital records state that by the time Madeleine was born, Adèle had not had sexual relations for some five months: there was, one may assume, no partner, husband or boyfriend. Certainly there is a yawning blank on Madeleine's birth certificate where a father's name would normally go; and moreover she was given her mother's name, Bayard.

Madeleine was Adèle's fifth child, born at a quarter past eleven in the morning on Tuesday 21 February 1911 in the Maternité Baudelocque, the city's best-equipped delivery hospital. With Adèle's troubled childbearing history, the Baudelocque would have been the natural choice, the safest option, for although her fourth child, a son, was born healthy in August 1902, her second and third children – a girl and a boy – both died in infancy. The infection that struck them down – at just twenty-two months, and six months – was tuberculous meningitis, a microbacterium that, in turn-of-the-century Paris, thrived among the working classes, breeding fastest in overcrowded apartments with poor ventilation and sanitation.

At some point between the births of her third and fourth children – in February 1900 and August 1902 – Adèle developed an infection in her uterus, and had a section removed. By the time her next son was born she decided to make some changes: where her ill-fated second and third babies were given to wet nurses, allowing Adèle to return immediately to work, she breastfed the new boy herself. By the time his younger sister Madeleine was born, he had grown into a robust nine-year-old. Adèle's first child, a girl, was already fifteen years old by this time, and under treatment for an unknown condition at the Berck-sur-Mer hospital.

Madeleine's was a fractured family, without much of a model for how things might have been done differently. The Bayards were also very poor, and their parlous health history says much about their inner-city living conditions, the dank smoky interiors in which Madeleine grew up. By the time Madeleine was born, all of Adèle's immediate family were dead: father at forty-one from a lung infection; mother at sixty-five from stomach cancer; brother and sister at thirty-nine and forty-one respectively. For Madeleine, there would be no father, no grandparents, no uncles nor aunts, no cousins. She did, however, have a sister, Paulette Gabrielle, two years her junior, and the two girl grew up together in a claustrophobic apartment at 8 Rue Volta, in the third arrondissement, a five-minute walk from the Conservatoire des Arts et Métiers and the newly completed Arts et Métiers Métro stop. Then, at the age of five, Madeleine gained a stepfather, Paulette's father Pierre Nard, a typographer by trade, who'd been recently drafted into the army. For Adèle, the wedding was the moment to draw a line in the sand. The person she had been before would no longer exist: Adèle Suzanne Bayard became Adèle Henriette Nard. From Madeleine's earliest years, reinvention was part of the fabric of family life.

Yet there is a darker shadow that hangs over Madeleine's childhood. A single-line reference in her military dossier records the fact that Adèle 'acknowledged' her daughter at the fourth-arrondissement *mairie* in May 1912, when Madeleine was some fifteen months old. The precise meaning of this remains opaque, but such an act would not have been necessary had Madeleine always been looked after by her mother. For Adèle to have had to stake an official claim to her daughter in this way means the two must have been separated for a considerable length of time. Alone, without any support, with a nine-year-old son to raise and a teenage daughter in hospital, the prospect of having to look after a baby would have spelled destitution. In order to continue working – to be able to live – Adèle had given up Madeleine at birth. In May 1912, having met Pierre Nard, and so finally being able to view a more secure future, she had tracked down the infant Madeleine and taken her back.

Number eight Rue Volta, Adèle's marital home, was most likely her husband Pierre's apartment, though it would have been rented, rather than owned. Before moving there, records show that Adèle lived in rooms a mile or so to the south, at 86 Quai de l'Hôtel de Ville, a narrow five-storey house on the Right Bank. From the confines of her bedsit, she could look through windows furred with candle-smoke and condensation clear to Notre-Dame, Sainte-Chapelle and at least three of Paris's pale-stone bridges. Across the cobbles in the street below clattered horse-drawn cabs, bearing men and women sporting fashions that Adèle herself, as one of the city's army of overworked and underpaid home-based seamstresses, had stitched together.

Working as a seamstress was debilitating and breadline: a government survey in 1911 interviewed one homeworker who claimed to earn just four hundred and twenty francs a year for ten hours' daily labour – at a time when annual rent was one hundred and eighty francs and the estimated minimum wage about nine hundred. This shortfall meant that most seamstresses were married women supplementing their husbands' earnings or single women still living with family. Adèle, though, was single, with no living relatives; through desperation, with no extra hours in the day to take a second job, it is possible that she would have been driven to prostitution, as were many women in similar circumstances. And when her baby was born – the father unknown, the circum-stances of conception forgettable or worse – how easy it must have been to wish, at least in some measure, that this had never happened; to hand the infant over to an orphanage, persuading herself that the carers would provide the mother-ing that she could not.

The gruelling quality of the garment work – and the often sexualized view that men took of these *'petites couturi-ères'* – found expression in contemporary advertisements. *'L'ouvrière'*, a colour lithograph selling iron treatments for anaemia, depicted a bare-armed, ivory-skinned seamstress fallen decorously asleep over her sewing machine, a curl of blonde hair lying the length of her cheek. Less subtle was the claim made by Dr Eugène Gibout in a case-study of a seamstress patient published in the Paris hospital bulletin in 1866. 'These [sewing] machines,' his study concluded, 'are powered by two pedals, one for each foot . . . these different movements produced a considerable genital excitement that sometimes forced her to suspend work, and it is to the frequency of this excitement and to the fatigue it produced, that she attributed her leucorrhea, weight loss, and increasing weakness.'

Yet no degree of sexual enervation managed to prevent seamstresses vigorously protesting their working conditions with a series of strikes during the opening years of the twentieth century. The strikers were Adèle's more visible colleagues, the workshop-based *couturières*, and in Febru-ary 1901, through the summer of 1910 and the winter of 1911 to 1912, thousands of workers 'dropped their thimbles and needles', in the words of one reporter, picketed workshops, skirmished with police and marched by the thousand down the boulevards of central Paris. If the strikers failed in cutting working hours and fixing a minimum wage, they nevertheless succeeded in heralding a new militancy, and in forging a powerful sisterhood.

As a home-worker, though, Adèle was on the periphery of the sorority, and her friends – such as the inner circle who witnessed her wedding in March 1916: Juliette, a thirty-year-old milliner, Marguerite, a twenty-nine-year-old usherette, and Augustine, a fifty-year-old laundry worker – would likely have been so too. These were friendships that Adèle, like most working-class women, cemented in the neighbourhood cafe and upon which, with no family, she relied heavily. By the time she met Pierre Nard, her friends had stood by her through a series of crises: the arrival of her first five children, born to different fathers; the infant deaths; the floods of January 1910 – the worst in a hundred and fifty years – which submerged the ground floor of her block on Quai de l'Hôtel de la Ville, forcing her to literally swim for her life.

War came when Madeleine was three years old and, to begin with, in France as in England, the prospect of combat was welcomed. 'War refashions everything anew,' declared Abel Bonnard with unintended irony. 'We must embrace it in all its savage poetry.' In Paris, there were mass injections against typhoid; it was hard to walk a single block without being assailed by walls of identical posters hollering of the need for vaccination. Sugar, bread and dairy products were rationed; cafe owners were forbidden from serving milk or butter; 'meatless days' were introduced – by July 1918, the daily meat ration was two hundred grams. As 1919 dawned, a working-class family like that of Adèle and Pierre Nard, unable to afford meat, milk, butter or sugar – which were now three times as expensive as they had been five years previously – would have been subsisting on little but bread.

For Madeleine, in addition, there was the troubling, inchoate knowledge that she didn't quite belong, that she wasn't a Nard like her sister Paulette, and that the man to whom her mother was married was not her father. There was certainly favouritism: on her mother's wedding certificate, a comprehensive document which lists not only those present but also the secondary purpose of the ceremony – the '*légitimation*' of two-year-old Paulette – there is no mention of Madeleine. She was five, easily grown-up enough to have joined them, and yet she seems to have been excluded. In these circumstances, perhaps it was only natural that she began to look elsewhere for affection, approval and a sense of purpose and belonging.

WARTIME IN PARIS was grittier than the years of conflict as experienced by Claude in Hanoi. For him, the dominant impressions of war were absence and solitude: the three years his father was away, the disappearance of Henri to boarding school, his mother's extended stays in France. Here in Vietnam there was no rationing, little – bar the absence of fighting-age men, conscripted back to Europe – to suggest the gravity of the conflict being waged in the mud of northern France. By contrast for Madeleine, as a small child in Paris, the war was imminent, the enemy at the ramparts. In 1918, when she was seven, German artillery had advanced to within ninety miles of the capital; Zeppelins, sluggish with explosives, drifted silently above the Seine; a million Parisians fled to the countryside; Madeleine, her family and others too poor to relocate, jammed tight as piano keys along Métro platforms as the klaxons emptied the streets overhead and caped *hirondelle* policemen cycled the blacked-out boulevards. Children grew up witnessing feats of ingenuity and opportunism: Passy's Parc de la Muette planted with potatoes; beans and carrots pushing up between the chestnuts in the Jardin du Luxembourg; on one occasion, men casting off in boats into the river in search of fish stunned belly-up by an exploding shell.

School continued regardless and Madeleine was educated in a system into which, over the previous four decades, huge funds had been channelled. Three hundred primary schools – bulwark against a national rate of illiteracy, in 1850, of 44 per cent of women and 28 per cent of men – were built in Paris between 1870 and 1914. They were monumental civic edifices, mostly in three red-brick storeys, similar to the English Victorian model. Madeleine sat on a wooden bench, pencil poised above a flat-topped wooden desk, one of a class of forty-eight, as her teacher scratched the alphabet onto the blackboard. On the walls were ten-foot-high maps: Europe, with France at the centre; Africa, her French colonies in red; the Far East, Indochina aglow, China and Thailand and Burma melting into the periphery.

WHAT MADELEINE never picked up at school was any sense that France's colonial project in Indochina was anything but benign, Hanoi's French administrators anything less than dedicated, humane and visionary. In Hanoi, however, this was not an impression even the most committed jingoist would have gleaned. The largely journalistic and intellectual anti-colonial protest of the war years was being supplanted by a more active rebellion, and Claude's teenage years – until he took ship in 1925 at the age of seventeen for his navy training in Toulon – were shot through with menace. In rubber plantations, rice fields and coal mines, French profits depended on cheap indigenous labour, resentment of which was fuelling the

independence movement. Paul Doumer, Governor-General
from 1897 to 1902, and chief architect of the exploitation,
had transformed Indochina's economy in the five years of his
premiership, erecting roads and bridges and creating monop-
olies to market alcohol, salt and opium, but in the process
had also laid the foundations for seven decades of conflict.
By the end of 1902, he would claim, with no mean justifica-
tion, that 'Indochina began to serve France in Asia on the
day that it was no longer a poverty-stricken colony, reduced to
begging for alms from the motherland. Its strong organization,
its financial and economic structures and its great power are
being used for the benefit of French prestige.' In his memoirs,
he unambiguously recalled his intentions. 'When France
arrived in Indochina, the Annamites were ripe for servitude.'

Claude, as one of the ruling class, grew up surrounded by
this kind of rhetoric, learning – as was the colonial custom
– to address all Vietnamese as '*tu*', regardless of status, thus

'A little Paris of the tropics': Hanoi, 1930

reducing them to the level of children or servants. But as he began to travel – already, in his teens, a keen big-game hunter – he noticed too the grind and poverty, the splayed feet, bent backs, hungry eyes. At one Michelin rubber plantation, twelve thousand out of forty-five thousand workers died of malaria, dysentery and malnutrition between 1917 and 1944. The coastal coal mine at Hong Gai – which produced an annual two million tons by 1927 – was owned by the Société Française des Charbonnages du Tonkin, a syndicate which, as an American journalist remarked, laid claim to 'everything from the bowels of the earth to the slightest sprig of grass that may force its way through the coal dust'.

Claude spent his teenage years – as pioneering postwar tourists began to amble through the streets of Hanoi – at the newly opened Lycée Albert Sarraut, a secondary school reserved for the French and the children of wealthy, cooperative Vietnamese. The curriculum was heavily classical, and Claude also took classes in Vietnamese. It was a more sophisticated package than that which was offered to normal Vietnamese, whose learning, in the words of Sarraut, was not intended as a means to social betterment: rather it should 'permit the child to learn all that will be useful to him to know in his humble career of farmer or artisan to ameliorate the natural and social conditions of his existence'. The texts used for reading instruction reinforced the colonial hierarchy: according to one primer, Vietnamese houses were 'pressed against one another [and are] dark and unhealthy with poor ventilation. In French towns, on the other hand, the houses are well planned, large, tall with several storeys. [They have] many windows which allow air and light to enter the rooms.'

By the time Claude left for Toulon in 1925, he was quitting a society that had become entrenched and polarized,

where talk of revolution among Paris-educated Vietnamese
– returning home and seeing anew the inequalities suffered
by their countrymen – was intensifying. Most prominent
among the early-1920s activists was Nguyen An Ninh,
some eight years older than Claude, who was born into an
intellectual, well-to-do family, and educated, like Claude, in a
Franco-Vietnamese *lycée*. After taking a law degree in Paris,
he returned to Vietnam and founded a robust French-language
newspaper, *Cloche Fêlée*, the Cracked Bell, wherein he wrote
pieces on political injustice, the slavery of the Vietnamese
and press censorship. By 1925, he was advocating armed
uprising. 'When a race is trapped to the point of having a
choice only of death or slavery, to face death is the more
courageous. Violence should be condemned where it is not
necessary. But there are cases where it must be resorted to
because it is the last resource.'

As yet, though, such movements operated clandestinely.
To the outsider, Hanoi gave every impression of being the
archetypal well-oiled colonial capital. To Harry Franck, an
American travelling through Indochina with his family at the
time, life was ordered, easeful, and surprisingly technologi-
cally advanced: 'electric street cars – found nowhere else in the
colony – railways in four directions, many automobiles, both
of the taxi-cab and private limousine variety, several excellent
hotels; in short, it is a little Paris of the tropics, with some
advantages that even Paris does not have'.

This was fulsome praise from an American, for 1920s
Paris – as Madeleine entered her teenage years – was proving
a powerful magnet for US writers and artists. With one dollar
buying more than twenty-six francs in early 1920, it was also
possible for the likes of F. Scott Fitzgerald, Ernest Heming-
way and Man Ray to be free to create with few of the financial

pressures they had faced back home. For Parisians, though, with no such currency advantage, the early 1920s offered little respite from the privations of the war. Prices had quadrupled since 1914, unemployment was severe, and pensions were close to worthless. In the Métro, signs urged commuters to surrender their seats to the '*mutilés de guerre*', the same bandaged and limping veterans who had staggered through Paris during the 14 July 1919 peace celebrations, their eyes glassy and distant.

The Olympic Games, held in Paris in 1924, marked a moment of change for the city. The vigour of a recovering economy found artistic expression in the official posters: a trio of male athletes, stripped to the waist, right arms raised in a salute that presaged Nazi Germany a decade later, gaze fixed on a heroic horizon. The following year, a lavish exhibition in the heart of Paris made the new era explicit, proclaiming France's emergence from hardship. The Exposition Internationale des Arts Décoratifs et Industriels Modernes, featuring exhibits from France and twenty-one other countries, stretched from the Grand Palais and the Cours de la Reine on the Right Bank, across the Seine on the Pont Alexandre III, and culminated in a vast cloistered court on the Left Bank's Esplanade des Invalides. It was an unashamedly elitist confection, featuring a Pavilion of Diamonds, a hall of French perfume and exhibitions of Baccarat crystal and Christofle silver. The closest that a working-class fourteen-year-old such as Madeleine was likely to get was an attic view across the roofs of the Marais of the dazzling acres of night-time floodlighting.

Charles A. Lindbergh's arrival in the skies of Paris on 22 May 1927, however, carried no two-franc-fifty entry fee. Madeleine, then aged sixteen, along with the rest of the city witnessed the triumphant conclusion of the American mail pilot's pioneering transatlantic flight, a million faces turned towards the sky. It spoke to her of freedom, of the possibility of life elsewhere. Yet now, as she enters early adulthood, the details of her early adulthood are scant. No records from this period survive. All we know – because she would later tell of it – is this: that she was courted in Paris by a Frenchman, the manager of an Indochinese rubber plantation and that, sometime in early 1932, they married, and she returned with him to Vietnam. Here, as the anti-French rebels grew in strength and number, she played the role of colonial wife. She dressed with a cool elegance, as if she were still in Paris, in designs she improvised using Vietnamese silk and the same sewing machine upon which her mother had taught her the *couturière*'s craft. For long weeks she was alone. Her mother stopped writing. Some nights, looking through the screen door, straining her eyes in the raucous tropical night for the flash of a tiger's eyes, she swore she glimpsed men with rifles and machetes in the undergrowth, waiting.

TOULON TO VIETNAM, 1925 TO 1937

CLAUDE VOLUNTEERED for military service in Toulon in the summer of 1925. Seventeen years old, he enrolled in the École de Télégraf sans Fil, bowing to his father's wish that his son study in the field in which he was pre-eminent. Yet, after just two years, Claude was already moving in his own direction, and he signed up for submarine training. His photograph album from this period contains a shot of him before a table of radio equipment, headphones clamped over a head of wild curls, the supervising officer at his shoulder. Claude's eyes are turned towards the camera, but it is hard to read his expression. There seems to be something out of character, a hint of uncertainty in the raised eyebrows, wide-open eyes, the flash-bleached face. Certainly it is the only photograph that hints at self-doubt, and it is likely that this was specific to submarines: the following year, according to his brother's widow, 'he played crazy, simulated mental illness, pretended to be psychotic. He was completely disgusted by submarines, felt suffocated in them.' His ruse was successful: he was judged unfit for service and thrown out of the submarine service in October 1928.

His working life in the following few years was peripatetic. Three months as a radio operator on a merchant ship, SS *Émilie*, were followed by eight as a secretary in the Chamber of Deputies in Paris. There seems little logic in the choices he made, though one senses a need for change, a hunger for novelty. In 1930, aged twenty-one, he was back at sea again, and photographs show him on board a number of different vessels: in white jacket and trousers and leather deck shoes, hands jammed into jacket pockets, posing for the camera with a cigarette hanging from the corner of his mouth; akimbo in a deckchair, gossiping with another young officer; on board the *Cap Saint Jacques* in March 1930, perched on the edge of a teak sunlounger upon which a woman stretches out in a sleeveless dress, eyes fixed on Claude, a finger touching her lips. The same woman features in another photograph, this time alone: standing in front of the ship's lifeboat, she pushes her hair up from her neck, smiling. Nowhere is there much indication that these were arduous missions: captions list Singapore, Colombo; there are group shots on beach-fronts, the cross-hatching of coconut palms in the distance; and, in what was fast becoming the pattern of Claude's early adulthood, there is another woman. Beneath a picture of her leaning towards a white-uniformed Claude, trying to catch his eye, head almost on his shoulder, is Claude's handwriting. '*L'hirondelle . . .* ' Swallow.

For all his travels, though, Indochina was calling to him, and sometime in the early 1930s Claude headed for Saigon. Within a year he had set up office as an insurance agent on Boulevard Charner in the ivory-stucco heart of colonial Saigon, its white-gloved traffic police semaphoring bicycles along magnolia streets. This, says his nephew Bernard, was his 'day job', for Claude's 'passion' for tracking tiger and elephant was fast providing him with a second income as a hunt organizer. He bought a sawmill near Kratie – now Krâché, in Cambodia, some hundred miles up the Mekong River from Phnom Penh – and was granted a licence to hunt rogue elephants.

Contact with family was increasingly seldom. His father

Claude, the young hunter, in backcountry Vietnam in the mid-1930s

lived in Paris with his new wife; his brother Henri, a career soldier, was serving in French Somalia, then in northern Vietnam; and the last time he'd seen his mother was in 1930, before he returned to Indochina. A photograph of her from this time – probably taken by Claude – shows a woman with sad anthracite eyes and an uncertain half-smile. It is a face that seems to emanate stoicism and disappointment; there is a pallor to her skin, as if she's recently been crying.

In 1935, Claude and Henri took a holiday together, the first time the brothers had seen each other in eight years. Having rendezvoused at Angkor, they spent much of the time hunting elephant, and well into his old age Henri would recount one episode in particular from these weeks. Driving one night on a back road near Claude's sawmill, they were forced to pull over when a leopard emerged blinking in the headlights. Dazzled, the animal froze. Claude grabbed his rifle and stepped out of the car, telling his 'boy' to focus the hunting searchlight on the leopard. Henri covered his brother, standing up through the car roof, carbine trained on the glinting eyes. The boy, though, was scared, and failed to turn on the light. The leopard, now able to see Claude, leapt for the undergrowth. Claude's fury – palpable enough when, on top of the missed scalp, the car initially refused to start – became volcanic when the scenario repeated itself, this time with a colossal tiger in place of a medium-sized leopard, a little further down the road.

Volatile, passionate, seemingly fearless, committed to an oftentimes monochrome moral landscape of rights and wrongs, Claude, like his father, was already a man who triggered extreme emotions in others. On Friday 12 June 1936, a disagreement with a stranger in Le Papillon, a Saigon bar, led to Claude and one Monsieur Fraissard, an engineer, choosing to decide the matter with a handgun duel. The duel made all the Saigon newspapers, with *La Presse Indochinoise*, the first to report the incident on 14 June, cryptically referring to Claude as 'M Probable' and Fraissard as 'M Possible'. The duel, deadpanned the paper, was the result of a 'gentle exchange of words, in a fashionable restaurant, between M Possible the brilliant quinquagenarian and M Probable the young fiery-blooded bear'. The official statement, signed by four witnesses and surgeon Dr Roton, the 'Directeur du Combat', offered little supplementary explanation. The two men, it said, ran into each other at midday. Fraissard raised a subject which led Claude, who deemed it *'offensive'*, to call for an apology or *'réparation pars les armes'*. At five that afternoon Fraissard and Claude, in the presence of witnesses, attempted – and failed – to come to an accommodation, a process that was repeated at eleven the next morning. By five in the afternoon this flurry of diplomacy had only succeeded in escalating the animosity, and the two men marched out on to a deserted airstrip, pistols in hand. Both fired and missed. Encouraged by their witnesses, they were then 'reconciled'.

The substance of Fraissard's original supposed slight has not survived, but the fury of Claude's response certainly raises the possibility that his accuser had hit on something. Around the same time, elections to the colonial legislature were taking place, and Henri Péri's childhood playmate Omer Sarraut, now a Saigon lawyer and close friend of Claude's, was standing. In the middle of the election campaign, Claude, lobbying for Sarraut, was charged with electoral corruption. The evidence was flimsy – a ballot paper with an 'X' against Sarraut's name, on the reverse of which was a list of figures. These had been totalled and signed 'Durban', the name of Claude's fellow campaigner. The accusation, which was backed up by witnesses in court, was that Claude had been buying votes for Sarraut.

On 5 August 1936, Omer Sarraut wrote to Claude, and the depth of his affection – to say nothing of his fury at Claude's accusers – is manifest. 'Whatever happens, *mon vieux*, you know that you can count on me . . . The courage and dedication you have exhibited will not be forgotten . . . Believe me, despite all their dirty schemes, their time-delaying tactics, we will finish *par les avoir*, by defeating them.'

By the time the case came to court, there were few in Saigon who didn't have an opinion, rare the *heure d'absinthe* that didn't feature at least one tussle over the guilt of the young insurance agent and the degree of association of his chum, the former Governor-General's son. Though Madeleine had not yet met Claude, she would by now certainly have been aware of him. Newspapers began dubbing the case *'L'affaire Péri'*, always alongside the same photograph of Claude looking stern, somewhat sleep-deprived, but sombrely respectable in white shirt, jacket and tie. Under cross-examination, prosecution witnesses did their best to bolster the evidence. A

L'Impartial 7 Avril 1937

M. Péri a été acquitté

Au Palais

AUX APPELS CORRECTIONNELS

M. Péri a été acquitté

La Chambre des Appels Correctionnels a siégé hier matin sous l'habituelle présidence de M. Garrigues.

M. l'avocat général Coppin, de retour à la colonie depuis peu, occupait le banc du ministère public.

Ainsi que nous l'avons annoncé brièvem nt hier, M. Péri, qui, en première instance, avait été condamné à 8 jours de prison ferme et à mille francs d'amende, a été acquitté purement et simplement par la Cour d'Appel.

L'affaire, nous l'avons dit, à cette même place, la semaine dernière, avait été longuem nt plaidée par Me Réveille et Me Giacobbi d'une part et par Me Couget de l'autre.

Les juges de la Cour, se rendant aux arguments exposés avec leur conviction et leur talent habituels par les deux brillants défenseurs de M. Péri, ont infir mé le jugement de première instance, motif pris que les dépositions des témoins paraissaient singulièrement suspectes, que cer taines étaient contradictoires et que par ailleurs le fameux bon Durban ne saurait constituer une charge contre M. Péri.

Nous félicitons très sincère ment M. Péri de cette heureuse solution : le jugment de 1re ins tance étant d'ailleurs si étrange que la Cour ne pouvait manifestement le confirmer.

Comme nous l'avons dit hier brièvement, M. Péri a été acquitté par la Cour.

On trouvera le compte-rendu des débats en 2e page.

Phnom Penh garage owner remembered Claude telling him, *'J'ai une vingtaine d'électeurs à faire.'* Two other men claimed he'd proposed that a vote for Sarraut was simply 'an easy way of earning money'.

Found guilty, and sentenced to eight days in prison and a fine of one thousand francs, Claude appealed his case. In front of the assembled appeal-court judges, he roused himself to indignant, flowing polemic. 'My crime?' he pleaded. 'Only to have helped a friend, to have backed his campaign with passion, fervour and assiduousness. Despite threats to my life, I have hunted down cheating candidates and now, after a thousand setbacks, find myself here.' The judges agreed and – pausing briefly to note the 'singularly suspect' motives of the prosecution witnesses, their conflicting submissions and the shakiness of the 'Durban' evidence – Claude was acquitted on 6 April 1937. It was the right decision, affirmed Saigon's *L'Impartial*. 'We sincerely congratulate M Péri on this happy solution.'

VIETNAM, 1936 TO 1937

IT WOULD BE HARD to devise a better training ground for a female intelligence agent than that in which Madeleine unwittingly found herself in the mid-1930s. Married to the manager of a large rubber plantation, she was witness and party to the kind of everyday and casualized brutality that was making revolutionaries of ordinary workers all over Indochina. Later, she would seldom speak of this time; as with so much else in her life that had caused her pain, she tried to erase the memories. So we know only the bones of the story: how she came to be in Vietnam and, later – though here there are inconsistencies – how she met Claude.

Accounts of life on such plantations as Madeleine lived on with her husband have been published, notably Tran Tu Binh's memoir of life during the late 1920s on Michelin's Phu Rieng plantation. 'Every day one was worn down a little bit more,' he writes. 'Cheeks sunken, teeth gone crooked, eyes hollow with dark circles around them, clothes hanging from collarbones. Everyone appeared almost dead, and in fact in the end about all did die.'

Tran Tu Binh, who was born in 1907 in a peasant village in the Red River delta of northern Vietnam – and who after the Second World War would go on to become a Communist Party luminary, being appointed Ambassador to China in 1959 – was one of more than seventeen thousand contract labourers who arrived from northern Vietnam to work on rubber plantations in the south in 1927 alone. To Tran Tu Binh, the theme of the next three years was one of 'a bitter test of wills between exploiter and exploited'.

The French lured workers with promises that were soon exposed to be hollow, forcing them to sign contracts in French, a language most of them did not speak, before shipping them down the coast from Haiphong to Saigon. Advertisements had promised 'three square meals a day, with beef and fish; that there would be seven kilograms of rice a month, and two suits of work clothes a year'; free medical care and, at the end of their three-year terms, ten piastres 'to pay for their immediate needs'.

Female workers, he claims, were systematically raped; mosquitoes, ox-flies and fighting ants were a continual menace; those who did not perish at the hands of their overlords were likely to be claimed by malaria or dysentery. And over all this carnage – a monthly death toll, according to Tran Tu Binh, of one hundred workers – presided the manager: in Tran Tu Binh's case the notoriously brutal Triair, a former captain in the Foreign Legion. The manager was exalted, 'the prince of the plantation [whose house was] off-limits like the private chambers of a king . . . He also had several private cars – one he might use around the plantation, another to go off on trips, yet another for the family to use when they went out on pleasure drives.'

In 1929, a new manager – Soumagnac, a thirty-year-old 'tall and quite handsome' former French air force captain – was appointed at Phu Rieng, one of about twenty-five such plantations that cut a twenty-mile swathe through the rainforest from the South China Sea to the Mekong River in Cambodia. By now, open revolt was looming, hastened by the sexualized form of exploitation favoured by Soumagnac. According to Tran Tu Binh, Soumagnac selected 'handsome, strong and young men' as servants, upon whom he would then force himself. 'The wife took after her husband. Soumagnac's wife was only about twenty-one or twenty-two years old, devilishly beautiful and unbelievably passionate ... [She] made the servants and cooks come up to satisfy her.'

Throughout late 1929 workers argued over plans for a strike; and at the start of the Vietnamese lunar new year on 30 January 1930 – a symbolic moment of spiritual renewal – the workers at Phu Rieng abandoned their posts. Soumagnac barricaded himself in his bungalow and waited for the storm to blow over. Three days later, he awoke to find hundreds of workers surrounding the building, their sharpened machetes catching the early sunlight, chanting and stamping till the air rose pale with dust. Panicking, he telephoned for troops, but these proved little match for the strikers' fury: seven soldiers were disarmed, and the entire platoon beat a flustered retreat. Soumagnac, fearing for his life, agreed to every one of the strikers' demands: no more beatings or docked pay, an eight-hour day, maternity pay for female workers, exemption from taxes and compensation for injuries sustained at work. Riotous festivities ensued: opera, a torchlit banquet, bonfires of office files, speeches late into the night. The eventual arrival of backup soldiers may have brought an end to the Phu Rieng uprising – Tran Tu Binh, a ringleader, was sentenced to five years on Con-Son prison island – but in Communist Party cells across the colony talk was suddenly of how close the strikers had come, and how their example might be emulated in every other rubber plantation, wherever injustice existed.

CLAUDE MARRIED for the first time on 13 August 1935. Nothing is known of his wife, Raymonde Fouche. He was now twenty-seven, still working as a Saigon insurance agent, and fast becoming a reckless romantic, as headstrong in love as he was in business, hunting and politics. Within months, however, his attention had drifted, and two years later his only child – a son, André – was born to another woman. André's mother, Do Tikem, was Vietnamese, and to this day the Péri family is uncertain of the exact nature of her relationship with Claude. What they are agreed upon is that the woman for whom Claude left Raymonde, Marguerite Paire, was unable to have children. Immediately after Do Tikem bore Claude's son, he was handed to Marguerite, who, like Claude, came from a long-established colonial family. In her case, though, there was money to accompany the status: she owned 'several plantations, a bar, a coffee shop', according to Claude's sister-in-law Madame Henri Péri.

To a less charismatic and persuasive man, sustaining such a juggling act would have been impossible. But Claude, who by now had seen his own father breeze through three marriages and the same number of divorces, had learned opportunism first-hand, and from the earliest age. His was a family where relationships that became difficult were most often abandoned, where negotiation, diplomacy and the assumption of emotional responsibility were qualities that were neither prized nor much practised.

And then he met Madeleine. Despite the lack of documentation at this point in their story, what does seem to be clear is that, by the late summer of 1937, Claude and Madeleine had become two of the first recruits of the newly inaugurated Deuxième Bureau – the intelligence section – of the French government's Colonial Ministry. Aware of an increasing threat to its colonial territories – in the Far East from an expansionist Japan, and in North Africa from a similarly bellicose Third Reich – French Colonial Minister Marius Moutet in

June 1937 created for the first time a dedicated Colonial Ministry intelligence section, under whose control was Claude and Madeleine's employer: the Service de Renseignements Impérial. And, though their immediate bosses were based in Hanoi, the section head – and a man with whom Claude and his brother Henri had long been friends – was Raoul Salan, later to become one of France's most distinguished military figures. When Edouard Daladier took over as premier in April 1938, and Moutet was replaced by Georges Mandel, Salan was promoted to SRI chief.

Salan, eight years older than Claude, was already a long-serving colonial soldier, and it was in Saigon – on leaves of absence during his 1934 to 1937 Indochina posting – that the two men became close. Salan – who would later become France's most decorated soldier, and whose career would encompass stellar achievement, with stints as the head of French forces in Indochina and Algeria, as well as a six-year prison term for leading a violent military campaign in 1962 to prevent Algerian independence – was, like so many others, drawn by Claude's vitality, the aura of possibility and lawless fun that surrounded him. He was also, as his memoirs make clear, plain fond of him. From Claude's point of view, there could have been no better champion: Salan was powerful, and rising fast. His influence was also international: within a year of joining the SRI, he'd developed what he described as 'excellents rapports' with Britain's Secret Intelligence Service. Of Madeleine, Salan's memoirs reveal nothing, but it is not hard to imagine at least a flutter of uncertainty as Claude introduced her, making it plain that he had no intention of working without her. Or maybe this appealed to Salan, immediately able to see that a couple operating undercover – lovers, moreover – might be able to gain access to places a lone agent could not, and to arouse less suspicion. Possible, in short, to masquerade more effectively, to inveigle better information and – should it come to that – wreak more damage.

Both Claude and Madeleine, on different occasions, told conflicting stories of their first encounter and of their first months together. Claude liked to recount how he had 'rescued' Madeleine, and from this grew a literal knight-in-shining-armour narrative in which Claude, who by now was working part-time as a French-government intelligence agent, stumbled upon the aftermath of the plantation uprising in which Madeleine's husband had been shot dead and Madeleine raped and abandoned.

Or it happened another way, and this was Madeleine's version, an alternative narrative that better preserved her dignity. There are holes in the chronology, though: for a start, no bridge between the time she fled the deserted plantation and her dead husband and the moment she and Claude exchanged passwords on a hot day in the autumn of 1937 in a remote upcountry village. In her version, a beggar, his features shrouded by a threadbare cowl, sits at an intersection. He has been there for hours, his bowl empty, when a woman appears before him. She is tall, and clearly not Vietnamese: pale ankles show beneath her skirt. She drops him a coin. The beggar raises his head, murmurs a line from *Hamlet*. The woman responds. He stands, and follows her down a dusty alley. And so begins their collaboration and their tryst.

There are no records of their recruitment, nor of their motivations, though Madeleine's desperate circumstances would have made it hard for her to refuse Salan's approach. Before long, they were singled out for dangerous assignments. Their training included the use of high explosives. Claude later told how, in the approach to Christmas, the two of them detonated a warehouse full of Japanese military supplies in occupied southern China.

Ever since Japanese warplanes dropped incendiary bombs on Shanghai on 29 August 1937 – triggering war between the two nations – Paris had become convinced that Indochina would be the next target. Extra intelligence agents were hurriedly recruited, and in this work Claude finally found an occupation suited to his maverick temperament. And in Madeleine – whose learned toughness, lack of attachments and familiarity with uncertainty made her a near-perfect spy – he found someone close to a soulmate.

On 21 January 1938, Claude's father died, aged sixty-seven. When the news reached Claude from Neuilly-sur-Seine, he immediately began preparations to leave for France. To safeguard the future of his son André, and despite the fact that he'd not yet divorced Raymonde Fouche, he married Marguerite Paire on 28 February, just two days before he set sail. There was little romantic about the occasion, according to Claude's nephew Bernard. 'He married her so that she could legally take care of André.' Claude's attention was elsewhere: on the com-ing war, on his bereavement and on Madeleine, whom he would be leaving behind.

By the time his ship docked at Marseilles some two weeks later, Claude was buzzing with a new idea, one that promised to combine freedom and adventure with espionage work and continued contact with Madeleine. At François Péri's memorial service in Neuilly, in the western suburbs of Paris, Claude set the details of his plan before Raoul Salan. Amid coffee and cigar smoke, he laid out a classic undercover itinerary. He would travel alone by car through Nazi Germany, Turkey, Syria, Iraq, India and Thailand, he told Salan, in the guise of an ethnographer working for the Musée de l'Homme in Paris. Finally he would arrive back in Saigon. During the journey he would file reports to Salan, noting political tensions, military build-up and the moods of the different populaces.

Salan agreed, and the Colonial Ministry provided him with a cover: Claude would be on a 'scientific mission' to film

wild animals in their natural habitat and to capture 'a certain
number of live specimens' for the Natural History Museum.
Family friend Roger Sainteny – who became a senior de Gaulle
minister as well as husband to Claude's childhood playmate
Lydie Sarraut – lent him a car, an ageing and somewhat
boxy-looking matt-black Ford. Sitting at his father's desk in
the Neuilly apartment, Claude began petitioning for funds,
but not before executing a canny manoeuvre, the donation
of his entire collection of Far Eastern sculpture, jewellery,
earthenware, embroidery and weaponry – some hundred
and sixty-four items – to the Musée de l'Homme. Goodwill
established, he wrote to the Caisse Nationale de la Recherche
Scientifique for a grant of fifty thousand francs: twenty thousand to cover food, automobile maintenance, petrol and oil;
ten thousand for clothing, tents and arms; and another twenty
thousand to buy a moving-picture camera and films. With
the help of Lydie's brother Omer, now based in Paris at the
Interior Ministry, he arranged meetings with senior personnel
at the Foreign Ministry. By the middle of September 1938,
fully funded, armed with a governmental *ordre de mission* and
a sheaf of letters from French legations and embassies along
the projected route, he was ready to go.

THE SPRING and summer of 1938, as Claude prepared for
his journey, was a time of mounting unease in Europe. On
14 March, Adolf Hitler was driven through the streets of
Vienna as Austrians hollered their appreciation of their
country's enforced 'reunification' with Germany. Within a
week, though, the darker implications were already becoming
clear: the 'great spring-cleaning' of Jews began throughout
Austria. Jewish judges were dismissed and Jewish shops
were forced to post placards making plain their non-Aryan

SB/SR

Ministère
des
Affaires Étrangères

Direction
des
Affaires politiques
et commerciales

Service des Oeuvres
Françaises à l'Etranger.

Section des Oeuvres
Diverses.
====

RÉPUBLIQUE FRANÇAISE

Paris, le 17 SEPTEMBRE 193 8

Monsieur,

Pour répondre au désir que vous avez exprimé,
j'ai l'honneur de vous faire savoir que je viens de signaler vo-
tre mission à nos Ambassadeurs à Berlin, Varsovie et Ankara, à
nos Ministres à Prague, Belgrade, Sofia, Badgad , Téhéran et
Bangkok , à notre Haut-Commissaire en Syrie et à nos Consuls à
Calcutta et à Bombay./.

Agréez,Monsieur, les assurances de ma considé-
ration très distinguée.

Pour le Ministre Affaires Étrangères
et P
Chef du Service des Oeuvres Françaises à l'Étranger

Monsieur Claude PERI
65,Avenue de Neuilly
NEUILLY-SUR-SEINE

ownership. In the Spanish Civil War, General Francisco Franco was gaining territory along the eastern front. France's new premier, Édouard Daladier, convinced that war with Germany was inevitable, won sweeping powers to rearm.

Come April, Hitler's designs upon Czechoslovakia were no longer in doubt. The British parliament announced that all Britons would be measured for gas masks. At the end of the month, France and Britain promised to defend Czechoslovakia and, on 20 May, two weeks after Hitler and Benito Mussolini had publicly pledged lasting friendship to one another, the Prague government ordered four hundred thousand troops to the Austro-German border.

If June brought at least the fantasy of a transcendent good in triumph over the forces of darkness – in the shape of a new US comic-strip hero called Superman – it also carried fresh news of the coercion and repression that was fast characterizing Nazi Germany. In Berlin, a law was passed banning 'degenerate' art. Any Austrian wishing to marry was now required to 'prove' Aryan ancestry. Offices, workshops, factories and retail outlets were ordered to give Jewish employees fourteen days' notice. Only in the world of sport was there any reassurance that civilization might not be facing a rout. On 22 June in New York, world heavyweight champion Joe Louis took just two minutes and four seconds of the first round to demolish the only man ever to have beaten him, Germany's Max Schmeling.

WATCHING THE changing map of Europe, in telegram contact with Madeleine, Claude was becoming aware of the dangers that he would be sure to face on his journey. Political certainty was out of the question: would Japan, which throughout June had been bombing Canton, be in control of Indochina by the end of his trip? Would Spain crumble to Franco? At what point might Hitler draw a line under his territorial and ideological ambitions? Moments of diversion were rare, and mostly US-derived. At the beginning of July, Americans won all five titles at London's Wimbledon tennis championships; on the fifteenth, Howard Hughes was hailed a ticker-tape hero by two million New Yorkers for his record round-the-world flight, a three-day, nineteen-hour and seventeen-minute staggered hop via Paris, Moscow, Omsk and Yakutsk in Siberia, Fairbanks, Alaska, and Minneapolis.

As Claude approached his own start date – organizing an overhaul for the Ford, taking briefings from Salan in the Colonial Ministry, establishing contact with agents along the route – it seemed increasingly likely that tension over the future of Czechoslovakia might ignite war any day. The fourteenth of September brought martial law to the Czech Sudetenland, where the German minority, egged on by Hitler, had been agitating to become the latest addition to the expanding Third Reich empire. On the twenty-first, the Czech government bowed to the threat of military force and ceded the territory to Hitler; and in Munich, on the last day of the month, Mussolini was photographed shaking hands with British premier Neville Chamberlain, backed by a smiling Hitler and jowly, apple-cheeked Hermann Göring. After twelve hours of talks, the leaders of France, Germany, Britain and Italy had agreed that Germany would henceforth rule Czech Sudetenland. The Czechs, in return, were given a guarantee that the rest of their country would be protected against aggression.

That afternoon, on the eve of Claude's departure for Berlin, Chamberlain was cheered by a large crowd at Heston airfield in the south of England. Later, outside 10 Downing

Street, in front of a thicket of radio microphones, he held aloft a single sheet of paper: Hitler's signature, promising that the takeover of the Sudetenland marked the end to German expansion. 'I believe,' Chamberlain told reporters, '[that] it is peace in our time.'

CLAUDE ARRIVED in Berlin – '*voyage sans histoire*', according to his logbook entry – at a moment of vigorous Francophile posturing. Acquiescence to Germany's demands in Munich had triggered a spate of nationalistic printing and now, on Berlin's street corners, vendors were selling postcards picturing the four smiling heads of government. These images, it seemed, were everywhere. 'In shop windows and in public places,' Claude noted, 'there were immense portraits of Daladier, Chamberlain and Mussolini, bearing the legend "Saviours of the Peace".'

Claude paints a picture of Germany – the brute noise of building work, the grind of heavy machinery – as an assault on the senses. 'Construction of the autobahns is carried out feverishly night and day; in factories, the eight-hour law is unknown; in the fields, farmers do their utmost to ensure a maximum yield.' Arriving finally in the capital, some eight hundred miles later, he was 'lulled to sleep by the noise of cement mixers, interspersed with whistles from the foremen'.

He strode the streets of Berlin alone. He toured the 'Exhibition of Degenerate Art', newly arrived from Munich, which featured the work of Max Beckmann, Emil Nolde, Paul Gauguin and Vincent Van Gogh under lurid captions such as 'Thus did sick minds view nature!' and 'German peasants in the Yiddish manner'. A companion exhibition – 'Clean Living and Joyful Work' – appeared to Claude to be intended to 'guide Germans towards healthy eating' while pointing out the dangers of over-indulgence. He found it less easy to raise a sardonic eyebrow at what was by now a daily public spectacle, the 'distressing' pillaging of Jewish shops and apartments by 'teams who cruise the streets, smashing shopfronts and throwing furniture out of windows'.

Claude's masterstroke came a few days into his stay in Berlin. 'Carried along by the tide of exhibitors' at a hunting exhibition, he found himself – as he later somewhat disingenuously told a Saigon newspaper reporter – 'being presented' to Hermann Göring, Reich Minister without Portfolio, Reich Commissioner for Air, Prussian Prime Minister, Prussian Minister of the Interior, Commander-in-Chief of the Air Force, Plenipotentiary for the Implementation of the Four-Year Plan, Master of the German Hunt, Master of German Forests, creator of the first Nazi concentration camp at Oranienburg, and Hitler's number two. Göring and Claude discussed hunting, a subject of mutual passion, and several days later a French Embassy attaché arrived at Claude's hotel to tell him that the military and economic leader of the Third Reich was inviting him to spend a day at his country estate.

'At the appointed hour', a 'powerful Mercedes' pulled up, in the front of which sat two SS soldiers. They 'burned' northeast up the new Berlin-to-Stettin autobahn, immortalized in propaganda photographs of the time as a pristine asphalt runway, curving majestically through ancient forest, along the verge of which families spread out picnic rugs and lifted moist slices of ham and cheese from squares of greaseproof paper. Less than an hour, three checkpoints manned by 'unsmiling' militia and some forty-five miles later, Claude was being ushered through the vast oak doors of Carinhall, built four years earlier as a memorial to Göring's first wife, Carin.

Claude was both overwhelmed and bemused. The house

stood in the middle of the Schorfheide forest, centrepiece of a hundred-thousand-acre expanse of woods, lakes and moorland in which, by decree of the Führer, no other construction was allowed. It looked on to a small lake, the Wuchersee, surrounded by old oaks, juniper and gorse, at the end of which lay a gleaming mausoleum containing Carin's pewter coffin. The architecture struck Claude as 'faux rustic' – the gleaming thatched roof, the parade of green shutters, the stag statues that flanked the entrance. His overriding impression was of a surfeit of poor taste: the marble swimming pool, 'profusion' of statues, a collection of more than a thousand rifles and hunting trophies. 'One has the impression of finding oneself in a museum, and wanting to cry out, "It's all too much!" '

Those who met Göring at the height of his pomp and influence often found him somewhat comic in dress and manners. He had an undeniable charm, though, and his extrovert nature and ability to laugh at himself had by the late 1930s made him a popular public figure. Even his corpulence somehow suited him, giving maximum exposure to his extensive wardrobe. In June 1934, he celebrated the completion of Carinhall by hosting a reception. Among the guests were ambassadors from America, Italy and Britain. The latter, Sir Eric Phipps, described with aloof amusement Göring's arrival in a forest clearing, slewing to a halt in a racing car, hefting himself out of the cockpit clad in 'aviator's garments of indiarubber, with top boots and a large hunting knife stuck in his belt'. After lecturing the dignitaries on the flora and fauna, Göring sped away. When his guests arrived back at Carinhall, they found their host awaiting them in a change of costume: white drill trousers, tennis shoes, a white flannel shirt and green leather jacket, the hunting knife still wedged in his belt.

Claude's host Hermann Göring (in white jacket) and guests
at Carinhall, his country mansion

Göring received Claude in his office, 'more of a gothic
chapel than a war office', according to Claude, 'with immense
bay windows giving on to the lake and, further off, Schorfheide forest. The furnishings were of an unheard luxury; on
the walls hung magnificent tapestries; thick Persian carpets
covered the floor.' Claude, aware of the bizarre nature of the
meeting – conscious that he, an intelligence agent, should
never have been allowed to get this close to such a senior
German figure – absorbed every last detail. Except for a
'standard' telephone and bank of 'call buttons', Göring's desk
was bare. Claude was motioned over to a chair. Dazzled by a
desk light, it appeared to him that Göring was sitting in deep
shadow. An interpreter – 'a strapping lad, with bright eyes
behind gold-rimmed glasses' – stood at Göring's side.

Whether Göring suspected ulterior motives is unclear, but

it seems likely that he'd arranged the meeting simply because he wished to talk hunting. He asked Claude about his journey and about the different varieties of game one might encounter in back-country Vietnam. He confessed of his longing to take part in '*grandes chasses exotiques*', explaining that a friend – whom Claude had coincidentally taken out hunting some five years earlier – had told him 'about your marvellous country, a big-game-hunter's paradise'. He hoped to head out there before long, he said, adding without apparent irony, 'Now that long-term peace is assured, I'm looking forward to taking some hunting trips in far-off lands.' He got to his feet. 'It is always,' he boomed, 'a pleasure to meet a Frenchman.'

On home turf, at leisure, Göring could be a seductive presence, and Claude fell for the older man's '*bonhomie, gentillesse et douceur*'. This was understandable: Göring was no stereotypical Nazi leader, with little, say, of Heinrich Himmler's penchant for sadism or Paul Joseph Goebbels' fanatical intellectualism. He was a contradictory, complex character, at once a hunt-lover in whose office hung a sign saying '*Wer Tiere quält, verletz das deutsche Volksemptfinden*' (He who tortures animals wounds the feelings of the German people) and a man who did not permit his affection for children to stand in the way of the efficient operation of extermination camps. He banned vivisection; levied hefty penalties on anyone shooting beyond their allotted quota; forbade hunting from horseback or from cars, and using wire, steel traps or poison; and, with the same vigour, filled Carinhall and his Berlin palace with looted paintings by Rubens, Lucas Cranach and Gobelin.

Clapping a hand on Claude's shoulder, Göring guided his guest to a waiting car. Had he had more time, he would no doubt have shown off his six-hundred-yard-long model railway, even lined up his battalions of toy soldiers, tanks and artillery across the Persian carpets, but other business was pressing. Before Claude was chauffeured back to Berlin, however, Göring insisted they drive into the forest together to see his bison, imported from Sweden and Canada, and visit a 'work camp'. Claude, again – almost despite himself – was impressed. 'The fiercest animal, by the name of Ivan, came towards the fence. Only the Field Marshal is able to approach him, a fact of which he is very proud.' They drove on, Göring radiating pride. 'The whole reserve,' Claude assessed, 'has been created uniquely for Göring's pleasure.' At the forestry work camp, as the scrubbed nineteen-year-olds lined up beside their bunks, Göring 'seemed like a kid on his holidays, swinging a spade, joking with everyone'.

Claude saw Hermann Göring just one more time, back in Berlin the next day. General Karl Bodenschatz, Göring's adjutant, had invited Claude to an official lunch with senior Luftwaffe officers. Claude, itinerant spy, was treated like a visiting diplomat: French wine and 'exquisite meat' were laid on in his honour. 'After the meal, the conversation veered naturally towards politics.' When Claude – with characteristic directness – asked whether Germany was preparing for war, he was given the stock answer: 'No, we're guardians of the peace.' Leaving the building, hearing the now-familiar sound of breaking glass further up the street, he glanced across Prinz Albrecht Strasse at the Luftwaffe headquarters opposite. Göring was standing at the window, watching the desecration of Jewish property 'with an odious grin on his face . . . the proud blue eyes were now filled with hate. I was finally seeing Göring as he truly is.'

CLAUDE LEFT BERLIN on 1 December 1938 with two gifts from Göring's office: a certificate stating that he was now a member of the German Hunting Association and a book, *Hermann Göring: The Man and his Work*, a hagiography by chief of staff Erich Gritzbach. A letter from one of Göring's secretaries, enclosed with the package, gives some idea of the degree of flattery to which Claude had successfully subjected his Nazi hosts. 'In the book you will find a plate section containing the photographs you wish to publish. You are welcome, also, to extract passages from the book. I hope that you will be able to find someone to translate the text from German.'

Claude had pulled off an impressive deception. His true feelings, as later outlined in a speech to a group of senior British military figures in India, were far more realistic about the nature of the new Germany. *Mein Kampf*, he said, was 'a hymn of hate' and its author an 'astonishing' orator, not above manufacturing a hammy sob when listing the sufferings of, say, the Sudeten Germans. Hitler was the 'god of a new cult', an 'evangelist' for whom the Reich replaced the family as society's essential foundation, who was cultivating 'an atmosphere of fear and anxiety' among his people. Eighty million Germans, Claude stated, 'constitute a gigantic stomach which cannot be satisfied solely by home cooking'. War 'appears difficult to avoid', though sometimes, he judged, 'surgical intervention is necessary to prevent a tumour killing a patient ... Hitler must be dealt with using the only language he understands, that of force.'

Driving in thick fog through the newly annexed Czech Sudetenland to Prague and on south towards Hungary, he was continually buttonholed about the French 'betrayal' of Czechoslovakia at Munich. On one occasion, a Czech businessman told him, 'The Poles played the German card and they're still in one piece; we played the French card and we're a diminished country, under threat from a powerful neighbour, our defences stripped away.'

Entering Hungary, on improved roads, he had his first accident, careering off the asphalt into a ditch in the middle of the night. In drumming rain, he unloaded the car, stacking his cases under tarpaulin in the middle of the road, and hefted paving slabs in front of the wheels. He managed to drive it out, but the damage was obvious: skewed steering, broken brakes and, as repairs got underway in a Budapest garage, 'a bill that kept on growing'.

As well as political insight, Claude's journal offers an impression of the last months of peace in a Europe that would soon be forever changed. There is an innocence to his description of Hungarian peasant women strolling through their villages in their 'ample-busted, beautifully embroidered' Sunday best, of the 'garlands' of paprika hung up to dry on the walls of houses, of roads empty of even a single other car.

Approaching Sofia – the rain still coming down, the road at one moment red mud, the next 'a rocky field', with only 'miserable' straw-roofed huts and lumpen, glassy-eyed sheep to break the monotony – the Ford hit an accelerating incline. The brakes jammed; the car skidded and slewed, rattling over the rough ground. In the distance, through smeary glass, Claude could just make out the lights of an oncoming train. The slope bottomed out onto mud and then, finally, the wheels hit hardcore. Claude looked up. 'The "Simplon" passed right in front of my nose. The passengers were sitting down to dinner.'

CENTRAL EUROPE, DECEMBER 1938
TO FEBRUARY 1939

HE'D BEEN GONE a month, and winter was moving in. Driving east from Sofia, as November closed in on December, he recorded night-time temperatures of minus four degrees centigrade, then minus six. Yet his complaints at the hardship of the journey are brief, tersely comic – 'my teeth chattered', 'ice formed on my shoulders' – and balanced with observations that show an enthusiastic engagement with culture, archaeology, history and landscape. Halfway to Istanbul, he passed through villages 'with names that sing: Klissoura, Karlovo'. He took photographs constantly: of ruins, villagers, of his own car at moments of crisis, axle-deep in mud. Sometimes he'd ask a passer-by to take a shot of him poking a puny stick into clogged-solid mudguards, or standing beside his vehicle in mud-stiffened trousers, scratching his head theatrically. When the road got too bad, he took to the fields. Most nights he camped, woken, on good days, by the dawn sun exploding through the fabric of his tent. On 1 December 1938 he reached Istanbul, and two days later was already off again, waiting on the quayside for the Bosporus ferry.

East of the Bosporus, making for Ankara, progress was slower. At Eskisehir, a hundred miles west of his destination, Claude was detained by police, only to be rescued by a Frenchman who ran the local flying school. In the cinema, surrounded by weeping men and women, he watched newsreel footage of Mustafa Kemal Atatürk's funeral from November: 'their saviour'. When he left, it was again across fields, rather than along the impossible roads, his wheels girded with snow chains. In the high desert, at three thousand feet, three-quarters of the way to Ankara, the mercury hit minus ten. 'Nothing succeeded in warming me up. Finally, unable to think of anything else, and in danger of dying of cold, I set light to eighteen litres of precious gasoline.'

Solitude and physical discomfort were fast becoming the journey's defining themes. Moreover, under these conditions, the crucible that held whatever remained of the colonial dilettante in Claude was slowly being scorched away, leaving behind a tempered, warrior spirit. As he travelled, he was also developing political discernment, an ability to sniff out underlying tensions and their causes, his keenest senses trained, of political and professional necessity, to pick up on anything that might affect French interests overseas. A long report on Syria, Iraq and Iran – through which he passed during January 1939 – notes 'extremely rapid progress of the German colony . . . Germany is well placed'. At that time, though, he judged that France still had 'enormous influence. For a long time French has been a compulsory language. The only foreign-language Persian newspaper is in French. The culture is French.'

His logbook and letters home also show a simpler relish for the act of travel itself; in the hospitality of Bedouin camel drivers; in the rare pleasure of a hot bath; in the sight, in Ankara, of cats with eyes of contrasting colours. His sensuousness – the pleasure taken from honey, mohair, fruit, from striding alone in the desert above Damascus 'lost in thoughts that were beyond my ability to express' – is matched by a more cerebral, though no less passionate, engagement with the history of the regions through which he was passing.

Alone for such long periods, his first rendezvous with Madeleine still weeks away, Claude began to see his car almost as a human companion. 'Poor Ford,' he sympathized as the vehicle underwent yet another major overhaul, this time near Tarsus, on Turkey's south-east coast, near the Syrian border.

Desperate for company as he left Ankara in the days before Christmas, he bought a dog, only for it to escape when he pulled in at a fuel stop an hour later. A month on, halfway to Beirut, he spotted a train of donkeys laden with rocks, and his empathic description of them says much about the suffering he had endured over the last month: the mornings when he'd woken with eyelids frozen together; the nights spent wading through snowdrifts shouting for help; the time he'd left a village only to be warned by the mayor that he was heading for 'certain suicide'. 'There's something touching in the resigned way these poor beasts suffer. Pitiful donkey, the Orient's beast of burden, for what crime are you atoning?'

As he continued south, and the weather grew warmer, so his spirits lifted. At Tarsus, after a stretch in which he'd been towed from the mud almost daily by camel teams and tractors, he was asked an exorbitant sum to be pulled just two and a half miles. Caricaturing the tractor driver – *'Moi, zé souis français, z'aime la France mais ti comprends mon tracteur il aime benzine'* – he felt his old rage returning. 'I felt like killing him.'

In the desert, en route for Baghdad

Crossing the Syrian desert towards Baghdad, his zest and optimism – so often the counterpoint to his flashes of fury – came fizzing back. He drank sugary coffee in Bedouin tents and – near the Iraq border, traversing expanses of sand that seemed to him limitless as an ocean upon which his car was a lone vessel, with no navigation but the stars – he handed out cartons of cigarettes to a passing tribesman: 'His joy knew no bounds.' He leaned his rifle on the door sill and shot a gazelle, then a fox. Four airplanes circled low, faces pressed to cockpit glass. He reached Baghdad during the second week of January.

FROM HERE, some three thousand miles still lay between him and Madeleine, who was now ensconced as an agent in Calcutta. These eleven months had been by far the longest absence of their lives together. Claude's logbook contains no mention of Madeleine, nor of any other agent he met along the route. There are no clues to his feelings as he approached their first rendezvous since she'd waved him off on the quayside at Saigon.

Only one document has escaped this thorough self-censorship: a telegram sent to Madeleine at 69 Karaya Road, Calcutta by Claude from Prome, some forty miles north of Rangoon. How the original ended up in the possession of his family is not known, but Madeleine must have kept it, handing it back at some later date to Claude. Stamped 'Ballygunge, Calcutta, 15 May 1939', the text is classic truncated telegraphese, cryptic and – after some six decades – open to multiple misreadings. '*Joris gagnée telegraphie Rangoon accord 26 Bangkok Tendresses.*' I've reached 'Joris', Claude appears to be telling Madeleine: send a telegraph to Rangoon to say it's OK for the twenty-sixth in Bangkok. These were her instructions, and from Bangkok, if all went well, they would travel together to Saigon. No sender's name is given, but Madeleine had all the clues she needed. *Tendresses*. Caresses.

FOR THE MOMENT, though, as he left Baghdad, carrying the '*valise diplomatique*' for Tehran and Kabul, he was on his own. Crossing into Iran, he'd followed the advice of his superiors and sold his beloved Mauser rifle and Luger pistol, though had drawn the line at offloading his Leica camera which was now, as the border guards emerged from the heat haze, strapped to his thigh with insulating tape. Security through Iran was tight, with passport roadblocks on the edge of each town. Claude, 'having noticed the peculiarly Persian fondness for doctors', adopted a medical disguise. Only twice were his skills called upon. To a syphilitic policeman he prescribed 'several laxative pills'; confronted by a pregnant woman on the verge of delivery, he pleaded ignorance. 'I told her I specialized in male illnesses and knew nothing about women.'

With night-time temperatures regularly falling to twenty below, he bedded down in cramped dormitories attached to truck-drivers' cafes. The stench of cooking, unwashed bodies and opium made sleep difficult. Men lay nose to toe, several to a bench, across tabletops. 'There was a horrible smell of mould.'

Approaching Tehran – passing through an 'unreal' white mountainscape where camels with icicle-stalactite nostrils attempted to drink from frozen streams – he was attacked by a group of men who'd been watching him negotiate with a garage owner to buy new springs for his car. Claude fought them off single-handedly. 'What a terrible thing is a petrified

Persian!' He bundled the ringleader into the passenger seat
and, twelve miles further on, in the blue-grey desert, stopped
the car and made his prisoner shout, *'Vive la France!'* Then he
opened the door and pushed him out.

TEHRAN, MASHHAD in eastern Iran, then through the Afghan
mountains to Kabul and on into India: Lahore, Amritsar, then
Delhi, his speed building as he inched nearer Calcutta. The
pace of his journey at this point was beginning to affect his
health: descriptions of dinners with police chiefs and senior
magistrates are intercut with guttural references to fever and
'pitiless' mosquitoes. But at Agra, confronted by the bone-
white translucence of the Taj Mahal, something in him melted.
What he learned, and what he saw, resonated deeply.

'In truth,' he wrote, 'it is the most beautiful thing I know.'
The architecture, the expanses of white marble, the 'crystal-
clear' echo of the interior, the exquisite geometry, all this
roused him to emotion. He noted the arithmetic, numbers
now commonplace to any tourist: the twenty thousand
labourers who'd worked from 1631 to 1653 to construct a
fitting mausoleum for Emperor Shah Jahan's wife Mumtaz
Mahal. Yet what is most striking about Claude's description
is the degree to which he was moved by the poignant, by the
perseverance of that 'faithful love', by the thought that grief
could result in something so resplendent. 'United in death as
in life, the two lovers lie side by side in the splendour of the
Taj . . . this magnificent Temple to Fidelity.'

CALCUTTA, MARCH 1939

INSPIRED ANEW, he raced across India, towards Madeleine. *'Les kilomètres s'ajoutent aux kilomètres.'* He watched worshippers hurling themselves into the Ganges at Varanasi, and at Dehri, about to cross the Son River for the last three hundred miles to Calcutta, his car became mired in wet sand. 'Fifty coolies pulled, pushed . . . and eventually we reached a half-ruined bridge just wide enough for the Ford.'

Safely across, he pitched his tent for the night, but exhaustion and fever had soured his mood. 'Gripped by violent despair', and with the canvas pooling rain, he spent the following day holed up. Outside, villagers gathered in the downpour, squatting on their haunches around the sodden tent, watching in silence for Claude's next move. 'None of them thought to help me.' In the end he was rescued by a party of German tourists. They fed him, found a policeman to stand watch over the car, and put him on the overnight train to Calcutta.

Prostrate on his bed in the Great Eastern, Calcutta's Ritz, he wrote a rambling, semi-coherent letter to his mother. The car was 'dead', he lamented. 'I am so so tired . . . a thousand things to say . . . the car was bleeding oil like gouts of blood . . . enormous repairs . . . no point rambling foolishly like this . . . I'm going crazy . . . twenty-four rivers to cross before Rangoon.' Two days later, and running short of money, he chanced upon a friend he'd known from his years in the navy and begged a room.

CLAUDE SLEPT for two days, then sought out Madeleine. He spent a month in Calcutta, a hazy blur of heat-shimmer afternoons on the Maidan with Madeleine, longer hours at her rooms on Karaya Road while the Ford's innards lay spewed across the black-treacle floor of the cheapest garage he could find. These weeks in the city were remarkable not least for the fact that – compared with the hundreds of words devoted to the monuments and habits of every other city through which he'd passed – they merit such scant mention in his logbook and letters. Finally, there is a sense of immersion, of a blessed hiatus, a temporary suspension to his role as lone traveller and observer.

Calcutta in early 1939 – before the refugee chaos brought by Partition; before the city became a byword for overcrowding and poverty; a decade before Mother Teresa's Missionaries of Charity began rescuing abandoned children, lepers and the dying from the scabrous streets – was as British as Birmingham. To the exhausted traveller, there was much comfort to be had in looking up and seeking red brick, in walking streets with names that spoke of old Europe, of home – Waterloo, Lindsay, Newmarket. Not yet the 'nightmare experience' of India's first Prime Minister, Jawaharlal Nehru, Calcutta was a city that still had the power to seduce visitors with the sight of white-clad cricketers on the two-mile-square Maidan or horseback riders at dusk against the backdrop of Fort William and, beyond, the cafe-crème reaches of the Hooghly River.

In Ballygunge, the district that was Madeleine's temporary home, it was possible for the expatriate diplomat or businessman to lead as separate and unassimilated a life as had Claude's family in Hanoi, thirty years earlier. According to a 1908 Calcutta guide, Ballygunge centred on a 'fine' maidan, around which, 'and lining some of the adjoining roads, are many very fine European residences standing in extensive grounds, and presenting great attractions to those who are kept in business during the day in the hot and dusty town'. And it was within this milieu of cocktail and dinner parties on Robinson Street, Elgin Road and Circus Avenue that Claude and Madeleine spent their weeks together; here, too, that Claude addressed a group of senior British military figures about the state of Germany. Claude, recuperating, and weary of the rigours of solitary travel, sought out as much luxury as he could. With his bounty of travel anecdotes and ebullient nature, he made diverting company for his formal, British hosts. As a couple, he and Madeleine inspired curiosity, jealousy, even envy, for they possessed an aura of something exotic, rare and yet unmistakable: freedom.

INDIA TO THAILAND, MARCH TO JUNE 1939

CLAUDE BADE FAREWELL to Madeleine at dawn on 30 March and drove east, the scent of her still on him. Another two months of separation lay ahead of them, Claude estimated, after which they could return to Saigon together. The four weeks that he and Madeleine had spent together in Calcutta had seen war loom ever closer, and it was likely that, from Saigon, they'd be recalled to Europe, where they'd be needed most. On 15 March, German troops had invaded Czecho-slovakia, despite Hitler's promises at Munich. Objections from the French and British governments three days later were dismissed by Hitler, who refused to accept Chamberlain and Daladier's 'notes of protest'.

For the first time on his journey, Claude was not travel-ling alone: in the passenger seat sat Madeleine's terrier Totoche, an affectionate, ironic name that roughly translates as 'little fellow'. The *'chien écossais'* referred to in Claude's logbook quickly became the recipient of the feelings of love, admiration and protectiveness he normally reserved for its owner. Deep in the Burmese jungle, the diminutive Totoche assumed the role of guard dog, barking at the approach of tiger or elephant. Later, as they neared Rangoon, he and Claude chased crabs together by torchlight. 'With my wonderful, intelligent hound beside me,' Claude wrote happily, 'I could sleep without fear.'

In Calcutta he had made an acquisition: a Mauser rifle to replace the original, which he'd sold before crossing the border into Iran. Looking after the weapon and its ammunition proved a struggle, however: there were some twenty rivers to cross before Rangoon, and three times the car was lost underwater. Yet he managed somehow, and at the beginning of May at Teknaf – in modern-day Bangladesh, close to the Burmese border – he tracked down and shot a rogue elephant. The animal, he wrote, came smashing towards him out of the bamboo, but 'two bullets made him see sense. My return [to the village] was triumphant. The Burmese were delighted to be rid of their troublesome neighbour.' He handed his Leica to one of them and climbed on to the elephant's cranium to pose with his Mauser. In the photograph, the beast lies on its side, hide collapsed into pouches around its mouth, a single tusk pointing at the sky. Claude is squatting on his haunches in shorts, squinting against the sun, a swatch of Burmese cloth around his shoulders. His rifle butt rests against the elephant's neck, oil-shiny barrel over his knee.

The next six weeks were the toughest of Claude's journey. For much of the way there was no road: he drove along railway tracks, across fields and beaches, 'laughing like the madman I am'. From Calcutta he took the road north-east to Jessore, Jhenida, and cajoled his way on to a ferry at Kushtia which took him a hundred miles down the Ganges, depositing him finally on the eastern bank at Chandpur. From here the challenges mounted: crossing the Fenny just north of Chittagong, the Ford slipped from the pirogues onto which it had been lashed and had to be hauled from the river, water spewing from the engine casing. Though normally not prey to superstition, the sight of the car vanishing into the swirl triggered a sudden memory: the words of a Hanoi fortune-teller some twenty-five years earlier, when Claude

was six. According to 'Madame de Thèbes', Claude was
going to die a 'watery, fiery death . . . maybe that will be my
destiny'.

The hundred and fifty miles south from Chittagong to
Akyab took twenty days. Once more he lost the car underwater; when it was dragged to the bank and the bonnet
opened, Claude was confronted by 'nameless magma'. Most
nights he slept on the back seat, Totoche by his side. To his
relief, he encountered nothing but friendliness and hospitality from the Burmese. The sight of his car – an object most
villagers had never seen before – brought people out in their
most ornate costumes, singing and dancing.

Somewhere between Cox's Bazaar and Teknaf, as he was
hammering along the beach, the monsoon started. As a kind
of comfort, increasingly certain he'd soon lose the car for
good, he took to smoking the locally rolled cigars. Rescued
almost daily by the ever-patient Burmese, he decided on a
racial pecking order: the Burmese were 'sweet-natured and
subservient'; Bengalis were 'nosy, dishonest, humourless
and dirty'. Events conspired to confirm his theory: stuck in
wet sand in the face of a rising tide, he yelled for help from a
party of Bengali fishermen. When they ignored him, he ran
towards them, gesturing wildly in an attempt to convey true
emergency. They fled; he fired warning shots in their direction;
they slunk back to help.

Passing the halfway point – with Rangoon and Madeleine
now less than a month away – the bigger picture opened up
before him. No longer so obsessed by the obstacles and
perils, he found himself more able to absorb the beauty of
the moment: the phosphorescence of the night water, the
'jade' sea, 'mauve' cloud-shrouded hills and 'saffron' sunsets.
A cooler night – during which, for warmth, he covered

himself with sand – qualified as 'delicious'. He was even able to see the benefits of a diet shorn of bread, 'that beautiful substance': subsisting on rice and bamboo shoots, as well as the fish, mussels and crabs that he caught himself, was causing him to 'lose' his *'embonpoint'* and regain musculature. He ate mangoes from the tree, was welcomed and fed by one family after another and, out of motor oil, upended a gallon of olive oil into his engine. The faithful car now firing on just three cylinders – the triple-spark spelling out, to Claude's optimistic mind, *'con-fid-ence'* – he crawled into Prome and telegraphed Madeleine.

IN RANGOON, twelve thousand miles and seven months after leaving Paris, Claude was suddenly the object of intense journalistic interest. His confidence, at this point, was over-flowing: according to one reporter, he'd 'met Herr Hitler' in Munich and – more likely, this – was the first person to have driven solo from Chittagong to Rangoon. In the bar of the Strand Hotel, he opened a briefcase to reveal to the press 'literally hundreds' of photographs: political demonstrations in Czechoslovakia, Göring's country estate, the Ford sunk to the running boards in Anatolian mud.

From northern Burma – where for the first time he began to resemble the itinerant ethnographer he claimed to be, photographing and making notes on the *'beautés au long cou'*, Karen women whose necks appeared stretched by a tier of tight-fitting copper necklaces – he drove south to Bangkok. And now, after a scribbled note to his family – *'chers tous'* – he vanishes from view.

BANGKOK TO FRANCE, JUNE 1939
TO APRIL 1940

HE MADE BANGKOK ON 24 June, two days before he'd agreed to meet Madeleine. From now until November, when he returned to France, there is just a single item of documentation: an undated photograph. In it, Claude stands bare-chested, holding Totoche in his arms like a large baby. He is grinning; the wind is ruffling his hair and pressing Totoche's ears flat to his head. A small tent is just visible, flysheet flapping. It seems

Claude and Totoche, on holiday in the autumn of 1939,
photographed by Madeleine

like morning, the scrubbed newness of dawn, the start of a lover's day a long way from anywhere that could be called home. It is summer; there are rocks, sand, trees, a distant mountain range.

We do not know their itinerary, nor how long they took to return to Vietnam. By mid-October, though, they had reached Saigon, where Claude was once more contentedly submitting himself to the probings of a newspaper reporter, this time for a piece in *L'Impartial* headed '*Göring tel que j'ai vu*'. There is only conjecture as to their whereabouts before October. Yet, as Deuxième Bureau agents for the Colonial Ministry, they had continuing professional duties and commitments. From 1937 onwards, the ministry had been nervously watching the unfolding conflict between Japan and China, and its agents were detailed to chronicle any movement on the Indochinese border. Claude and Madeleine both had to file monthly reports for Raoul Salan in Paris, analysing the developments in the conflict to the north, the political situation in China, knock-on effects on Indochina, as well as whatever clues they picked up as to the organization of the Japanese secret services.

These monthly reports, filed by all Salan's field agents, provided crucial intelligence in the build-up to war, and their contents were discussed at Salan's daily noon meetings with Colonial Minister Georges Mandel. Security dictated that no agent ever signed off his or her report, and so the hand of Claude or Madeleine can only be guessed at. The reports themselves are masterpieces of concision, rich in detail: a bulletin from Japan, dated 21 November 1939, expends less than a hundred words describing a new airplane factory at Hashigawara, which had just been set up by Fiat with the aim of building one hundred and fifty-four bombers, fifty-four reconnaissance aircraft, a hundred and seventy 'engines' and six hundred and fifty tonnes of '*matériel divers*'. The result of all this endeavour, claims historian Martin Alexander, was impressive. 'The French defence authorities between the wars unquestionably knew their enemies.'

On 23 August 1939, a week before German tanks rolled into Poland, it was clear to Salan that war was imminent. An Anglo-French mission to Moscow, objecting to the movement of Soviet troops towards Poland's eastern border, had just been thrown out by Stalin: 'There was no longer any doubt,' Salan wrote. 'This was war.' Yet he was sure it would be unlike any other ever waged, and already he'd been working closely with agents from Britain's Secret Intelligence Service on techniques of sabotage, in particular the use of plastic explosive. And now, as war was declared, the names Claude Péri and Madeleine Bayard – who two years earlier had pulled off at least one successful detonation, of a Japanese supply camp in occupied China – leapt to mind. He telegraphed Hanoi, and ordered their immediate recall.

CLAUDE AND MADELEINE sailed from Saigon at the start of November. From the ship, on 3 November, Claude wrote a brief note to his mother, his slurred handwriting giving the impression – as so often in his letters – of thoughts running too fast for his pen. He'd done several newspaper interviews, he said, and one lecture: the reporters, he complained, had 'mutilated' his words. He hoped to be with his family around 10 December: 'it seems unbelievable!' After a fortnight's home rest – 'to put my affairs in order' – he planned to enlist. The life of an intelligence agent, which had suited him well enough until now, was not what he wished for come war. 'I hope you've made some approaches so that I'll be accepted [for active service] despite my discharge.' As with his other communications – and in line with Deuxième Bureau procedure – there was no mention of Madeleine.

They reached Paris in early December and reported to Salan at his offices on the Quai d'Orsay. Across the Seine from the palatial courtyards and ivory stucco expanses of the parliament buildings, Madeleine had a clear view of 86 Quai de l'Hôtel de la Ville, the top-floor apartment in which her mother had lived at the time of Madeleine's birth. A considerable distance had grown between Adèle and Madeleine since she had been away: where Claude was happy to lodge with his mother in Neuilly-sur-Seine, Madeleine made only the briefest contact with Adèle before taking a boxy two-room apartment at 19 Rue Béranger in the third arrondissement, a minute's walk from the Place de la République. This block remains intact today, and it is not hard to picture it as the perfect lovers' hideout: the dark granite central courtyard, too high and deep to ever see much sun; the endless stone stairways winding upwards in the cool; the scarlet and white of geraniums exploding from a hundred window boxes; the clatter and judder of wrought-steel elevators.

They found Salan in buoyant mood, full of the thrill of undercover work and in no mind to allow Claude to enlist as a regular combatant. Two weeks earlier he had returned from a three-month expedition through north Africa, posing as 'Raoul Hughes, special envoy for the *Temps Colonial* newspaper', detailing Italian movements as he journeyed through Alexandria, Cairo and Khartoum, and it was into this imperilled territory that he wanted to drop Claude and Madeleine. No longer would they be operating as ordinary spies, and to this end he enrolled them in a Deuxième Bureau sabotage course in the eastern suburbs of Paris.

Over the next three weeks, Claude was the very model of discretion with his family, explaining only that he was working 'in the offices' of Georges Mandel, which told them little they didn't already know. In truth, he and Madeleine were learning how to use the latest explosives, in particular '*le plastic*', a British invention that Salan had first studied under Commander 'Biffy' Dunderdale, SIS station chief in Paris. The British, Salan later wrote, had 'a greater understanding' of the use of explosives, and offered 'help and support'. At the end of August Salan had spent time in London at the SIS headquarters; and now, in Claude and Madeleine, he believed he'd found the perfect operatives, whose status as a couple conferred instant camouflage. They were striking, entertaining and urbane, well travelled and clearly in love. They were also fearless and patriotic.

Salan's plan was for Claude and Madeleine to operate at sea, and he organized training for Madeleine as a cipher officer. Claude, whose earlier discharge was of little concern to Salan, was already a qualified wireless operator. All that remained was for them to become adept with explosives, and Salan, assignments already in mind, requested a shipment of *plastic* from the British. Working with Claude and Madeleine, he devised a time-delay bomb which he described as 'an enormous, semi-elliptical metallic sucker, thirty centimetres in diameter and fifteen deep, plastered in TNT. For the detonator I chose a French navy watch . . . [which I] placed at the centre of the explosive, which is malleable. The flat part of the device is powerfully magnetic and can be easily fixed to a ship's hull.'

THOUGH THEIR NATION was now at war, the France through which Claude and Madeleine travelled northwards in the first days of December 1939 seemed disarmingly normal. From the train they could see no sign of conflict: no cratered farmland, no distant boom of artillery. On the roads, too, trucks and carts and bicycles moved at their habitual unhurried pace, through avenues of wintry, leafless poplars; and those to whom they spoke predicted a swift fight, confident that France had never been more impregnable, that the defensive Maginot Line of fortresses that now ran along the Western Front from the Swiss border near Basel, to Longwy, near Belgium's south-east corner, would mean that General Nivelle's forlorn cry of '*Ils ne passeront pas*' at the bloodbath that was Verdun in 1916 would now finally ring out as simple fact rather than wishful thinking.

Never mind that the northern frontier, near Belgium, lay unfortified: a second war, most French believed, was the last thing any world leader wanted. The Great War – '*la der des ders*', the last of the last – had made another European conflict unthinkable. Jean-Paul Sartre, mobilized in September 1939 along with hundreds of thousands of other reservists, was convinced that 'there will be no fighting, that it will be a modern war, without massacres as modern painting is without subject'. There was much about Sartre's duties as an artillery-section meteorologist, too, that spoke of a military with only one eye on the enemy: sending up balloons, watching them through his telescope as they shrank into the distance, he'd phone his officers with wind speed and direction. 'What they do with this information is their affair. The young ones make some use of the intelligence reports; the old school just shove them straight in the wastepaper basket.'

Sartre's diaries from these months of tense hiatus speak of a 'war machine running in neutral; the enemy is elusive and invisible; the men stand waiting at attention'. Often, disgust at those in command forces its way through the carefully applied layers of irony. 'Intent on exploiting the situation to the maximum, [the Germans] have displayed placards everywhere protesting their desire for peace. Besides, they didn't declare war on us; on the contrary, they were declaring peace as they invaded Poland – and we're the aggressors.' His fellow soldiers were 'timidly' hoping for peace, rather than preparing for battle. 'Many people are hoping for an "arrangement". Only yesterday a sergeant was telling me, with a gleam of inane hope in his eyes, "What I think is, it'll all be arranged. England will climb down." '

With newspapers dutifully relaying daily communiqués from the front that only occasionally veered from the predictability of 'Nothing to report' and 'A quiet day on the front' to such heights of military drama as 'West of the Vosges, an enemy raid was repulsed with losses', life in Paris, as Claude and Madeleine arrived in early December, charged ahead with characteristic insouciance. Christmas saw the opening of Twentieth Century Fox's *Stanley and Livingstone*, starring Spencer Tracy as Stanley. And for the week of 25 December itself, notwithstanding blackout restrictions, eighteen theatres, fifteen music halls and one circus were reopened to welcome the thousands of French troops and British Expeditionary Force soldiers spending their leave in the capital. 'Perhaps the biggest news,' thrilled the *International Herald Tribune*, '[is] the promised reopening of the Folies Bergères.'

But the stuttering progress of the war was never far from the front pages of the French newspapers, and along the corridors of the Colonial Ministry – through which Claude and Madeleine frequently passed – further conflagration was never in doubt. The actions of the Paris authorities spoke also of a deeper menace: through December, workmen stripped the Louvre of some three thousand paintings, including the *Mona Lisa*, several Rubens portraits, Millet's *The Gleaners* and Ingres' *La Source*, all of which, according to one reporter, were destined for a safe-deposit vault 'somewhere in France'. Along the Finnish front soldiers were struggling against the Russian advance in temperatures of minus twenty-three degrees centigrade, even while Soviet planes bombed Helsinki. And in Berlin, on New Year's Eve, Hitler gave warning, if one were needed, that worse was to come: 1940, he said, would be the most decisive year in German history, during which the Reich would face a battle for extinction or survival. 'We pray to the All Powerful that he should protect us in the New Year as he protected us in a tangible manner last year, and that he should strengthen us in the fulfilment of our duty.'

As 1939 became 1940, and the severity of the winter saw the Thames freeze over and the Seine turn piebald with ice floes the size of dinner tables, the French began to believe that the German advance was already in collapse. At the end of the first week of January, hundreds of people handed over two francs apiece to catch a glimpse of a Messerschmitt pursuit plane, brought down in a dogfight north of Nancy and placed on exhibition in the Champs-Elysées. Hitler was mocked by many of the entrants in an annual cartoonists' show in February, the posters for which carried the warning that 'people who don't laugh will be sent to a concentration camp'. By March, Allied propaganda was claiming that the German people were 'on the verge of physical and psychological collapse'. Exiled German nerve specialist Dr Martin Gumbert, interviewed in New York, was quoted as saying that his nation's health was being undermined by overwork, undernourishment and constant propaganda. 'Consumption of alcohol has trebled since

1932 and the suicide rate is the highest ever known. Before Hitler took power there were forty-eight thousand physicians in Germany. Now there is only one doctor for every three thousand civilians.'

Yet if the populace was being wooed into complacency by such talk – and while respected writers such as Louis-Ferdinand Céline, later a pillar of the Vichy establishment, predicted that war with Germany would result in 'the end of the breed', twenty-five million casualties and the linguistic survival of a solitary word, *'merde'* – the French secret services harboured no such illusions. What they did not know, however, and what their British counterparts appeared equally unable to provide, was any firm sense of Hitler's timetable. Asked to assess Germany's plans for the spring of 1940, the best that Britain's Joint Intelligence Committee could come up with in December 1939 was the vague conclusion that '[whichever] of these courses Germany will select will depend less upon logical deductions than upon the person and unpredictable decision of the Führer'.

Uncertainty as to the date of the next wave of the German advance was not going to prove a bar to Raoul Salan, though, and in early April 1940 he issued Claude and Madeleine with their first set of wartime orders. They were to travel to Marseilles, where a ship was waiting to meet them. They were to reveal their identity to no one but the captain. They would travel south by train as if they were man and wife, but instead of pressed shirts and lingerie, their suitcases would carry plastic explosive, fuse mechanisms and limpet-mine casings. They would, he indicated, be gone a while.

MARSEILLES, APRIL 1940

SS *Le Rhin* was a long-serving merchant vessel of the most sturdily unromantic and anonymous kind. She lay roped to the Marseilles quayside, a long crane-claw reaching deep into her belly for the last crates of coffee, a gaggle of longshoremen descending the gangplank. Built in Britain at the end of the Great War, and bought in 1923 by the Marseilles sea-freight operation Compagnie de Navigation Pacquet, she'd spent much of her life chugging sugar, cotton and coffee between the west coast of Africa and the south of France, her ageing coal furnaces seldom allowing much more than a stately six knots, black smoke hammering the sky. She was painted black, with a vertical bow and cutaway stern, single funnel at the centre, with hoisting arms at fishing-rod angles both fore and aft. Most days, the deck was crowded with sacks, containers and, when in dock, men who moved so slowly in the soupy spring heat they might have been wading through molasses.

It was 19 April 1940, and Marseilles was more frenetic than Claude or Madeleine had ever seen it. When they'd docked at the Vieux Port from Saigon at the end of November 1939 they'd been struck by the normality of it all, despite the outbreak of war, by the bustle of port life, the lines of fishmongers along the Quai des Belges, their stalls heaped with '*moules de Toulon*', oysters, sardines and tuna. And they'd whiled away a morning here, drinking absinthe in the Café de l'Univers, eyes closed in the late-autumn sun as their baggage was unloaded and the electric trams clattered back and forth over the cobbles.

Yet now, and contrary to expectation, the acceleration of the war in the first months of 1940 – U-boats muscling their way into the Mediterranean; the German invasion of Denmark and Norway on 9 April; the Anglo-French counter-attack less than a week later – had triggered not only a formidable rise in the numbers of liners and cargo ships using the port – up fifty per cent from 1938's seven thousand vessels, eight hundred and thirty thousand passengers and fourteen million tonnes of merchandise – but a chaotic congestion on the quayside. According to one observer, there was now enough unprocessed cargo – timber, coffee, wine, salt, sugar, concrete – lying mountainous along Quay de la Fraternité and Quai des Belges 'to fill Parc Chanot', a sizeable city park. As Claude and Madeleine fought their way through and over a heap of cotton sacks, and Totoche tumbled yelping after them, it must have seemed as if the anarchy of war – the looting and abandon, the lack of confidence in any kind of tolerable tomorrow – might begin at any moment.

THEY STRODE UP THE gangplank, each carrying two beaten-leather suitcases. Claude wore uniform, the brass-buttoned, double-breasted wool jacket of the Marine Marchande, with a white shirt and black tie; Madeleine had a calf-length navy skirt and pale chemise. The sun was brilliant on the water and the sentry posted at the top of Le Rhin's gangplank watched them as they approached, smiling at each other, their hands touching, Claude doing most of the talking, Madeleine shaking her head and laughing.

They set down their cases and Claude asked to see the captain. The sentry demanded identification. Claude repeated his request, taking a step closer, his voice a whispered growl. The sentry blinked, turned, leapt onto the deck and ducked into the wheelhouse. Inside they could hear him calling out, a tremor in his voice.

From the quayside came an anxious, high-pitched yapping. Madeleine looked around. '*Viens! Totoche!*' The terrier stood still, ears pricked, head darting from one side to the other. Madeleine whistled, raised a hand and the animal suddenly caught sight of her. She lifted him into her arms. He nuzzled her neck, licked her cheek.

An older man appeared on deck. His face was pinched, his hair centre-parted and brilliantined in a style that, on a younger man, might just have been fashionable. His mouth turned downwards at the corners, as if something unpalatable had just passed under his nose.

'Cannebotin,' he grunted. '*Capitaine. Et vous?*'

Claude handed him a single sheet of paper, and René Cannebotin read through it in silence. When he'd finished he glanced at Madeleine, then at their suitcases. He looked at Totoche with his head on one side. He tutted.

The choice of *Le Rhin*, under Cannebotin, had been carefully thought through: Cannebotin, who'd spent the last year of the Great War as a lieutenant in command of a naval explosives team, was no ordinary merchant journeyman. Through approachable, with an Edwardian-style courtesy – nicknamed '*Oncle*' by his crew – he was also a skilled sailor, with at least one successful Cape Horn crossing to his name.

The old generation, and the new. According to one source, Cannebotin, who had received no warning that he was about to gain two new crew, was swift to soften. He told Claude that he was less surprised than he might have imagined.

'I've been here before, you see. Any moment now we're

going to see a bunch of other folk turn up with enormous cases full of all your gear.'

Claude grinned. He put his arm around Madeleine's shoulder. 'Far from it. You're looking at the whole team. And as for explosives, there's more than enough in our suitcases.'

BY THE END OF the month they were in Casablanca and, with a couple of days in hand, Claude took Cannebotin, Madeleine and a small party of *Le Rhin*'s other senior crew on an expedition to hunt wild boar near Benahmed, some fifty miles inland. After the first day's hunting, they returned to their lodgings to find the landlady waiting excitedly at the door. She started speaking while they were still some way off. Claude and Cannebotin were unloading rifles and boots from the dust-caked taxi.

'Do you need a cabin boy?' She carried on talking without waiting for an answer. She knew of the best, she said, the very keenest, right there in town. Did they want her to fetch him? Still talking, she ran off down the street.

Gerard Poulin, describing that day, 30 April 1940, in a letter in the early 1950s to Claude's older brother Henri, recalled a typical Claude opener. Poulin, just fourteen years old and son of the local gendarme chief, had come running back with the landlady, a family friend in whom he'd long confided his 'dream of becoming a sailor'. Claude greeted him effusively. 'So here's the little cabin boy who wants to see the waves dance.' Claude spoke to Poulin's father that evening and the next day Poulin followed the crew through the bleached streets of Casablanca to the harbour, where his first billet lay at anchor.

GRAN CANARIA AND CASABLANCA,
MAY 1940

Though Cannebotin was still captain, it was soon apparent that it was Claude who wielded ultimate power. He commandeered well-appointed cabins – his adjoining that of Madeleine – and by the time they sailed south from Casablanca, destined for Agadir then Las Palmas, he was already referring to *Le Rhin* as 'my ship'.

They sighted the black headlands of Las Palmas, Gran Canaria, early in the first week of May. On board, surrounded by males, no longer alone with Claude, Madeleine had grown so quiet that some of the crew, still knowing nothing of her background, guessed she was suffering first-timer's nerves. What little she did say seemed directed at the young Poulin. She could be seen listening silently, nodding as he nervously explained himself. The rest of the time, as Claude stormed boisterously around the ship, she sat on the foredeck and read, or stood at the gunwale as Totoche scampered and skidded over the wet metal.

In these early days, she revealed next to nothing of herself, though her actions caused talk. On mornings when the sea was still, she'd emerge on deck with a pair of pearl-handled pistols, loft an empty tin can high overboard and then snipe at it, left barrel, right barrel, till the clips were empty and the can, holed as machine-gun casing, disappeared into the Atlantic blue.

Las Palmas in the spring of 1940 had little in common with the strip-lit, techno-pulsing Canaries capital of today, where the air is blue with scooter smoke and boys and girls with orangey tans stagger from bar to bar clutching bottles of vodka-cut lemonade. On the eve of the Second World War, the harbour was low-rise and whitewashed, climbing only briefly into the hills that are now checkerboarded with identical villas. Then, the tallest structures were the twin steeples of Catedral de Santa Ana; today, the cathedral lives in the shadow of timeshare apartment blocks.

It remains Spanish, however and, in 1940, it was also the object of German territorial ambition. Situated just off west Africa, the Canary Islands were a potential east-Atlantic staging post to Hitler. Despite Spanish neutrality, he began negotiations with General Francisco Franco, the leader of Spain, to build a naval base in Las Palmas. In return for his

SS *Le Rhin*, laden with explosives, about to drop anchor in
Las Palmas harbour, May 1940

cooperation, Franco would be rewarded with Gibraltar, British since its capture in 1704.

Le Rhin dropped anchor in Las Palmas harbour, an innocent French merchantman en route to Dakar. Claude and Madeleine took the launch to shore and, for a week, acted as regulars in the shorefront cafes along Avenida Maritima. Though Claude's German was poor, and Madeleine's barely stretched to a couple of words, they passed late nights drinking with the officers from the seventeen German cargo ships that were using Las Palmas as shelter from the prowling Allied navies. Most of the German sailors had been trapped in Las Palmas since before Christmas, and had long ceased to be circumspect.

They made friends easily. The German crews on shore had by now grown irritable with each other's company. They were pasty from too much beer and too little action and their faces, as they gazed blankly across the turquoise water at the skirts of seaweed sprouting from the hulls of their anchored vessels, seemed to Claude and Madeleine at times close to catatonic.

Though Claude and Madeleine's behaviour was unremarkable, the way they drank till all hours as any on-leave merchant sailor would have done, their every movement had been choreographed by Salan, working alongside British intelligence. They were to be unobtrusive, to make friends and gain trust. One night, they were seen singing in Plaza Fuente Luminosa, close to the harbourfront: a line of German sailors, arm in arm, Claude and Madeleine in the middle.

As subtly as they could, they sought out the officers of the *Corrientes*, a U-boat supply ship that, bigger than the other German vessels, was moored outside the harbour wall. Egged on by Madeleine, the captain finally consented to lay out his charts across a restaurant table, pushing aside the bottles of olive oil and a thicket of empty wine glasses. It had been eight months of hiatus, after all, with too few distractions, and with Claude at Madeleine's shoulder, raising a toast to the *Corrientes*, the captain stabbed a finger at his ship's position. We're all sailors here, he said: war, what war? And besides, he added, no one could torpedo us: we've ringfenced the ship with coal barges.

CLAUDE AND MADELEINE bade farewell to the captain and crew on the afternoon of 8 May, and the same evening *Le Rhin* left for the open sea. The weather was good, the swell gentle and soporific. Once out of sight of land, René Cannebotin set the engines idling.

Night passed, then another day. Claude and Madeleine unpacked the explosives, spreading the components across the floor of Madeleine's cabin. A third person was in the room, too: *Le Rhin*'s chief mechanic, whose name has not survived, recruited by Claude on the way from Agadir, and he listened acutely, in silence, his face pale. Madeleine kneeled and drew a map: *Corrientes*, the circle of barges, the line of approach.

At dusk on 9 May, *Le Rhin* turned about and began the approach to Las Palmas once more. Claude, Madeleine and the chief mechanic prepared the explosives. They'd be using two bombs, the parts assembled and checked in Paris by Raoul Salan: British-made explosive – a substance not yet known to the Germans – packed into two steel half-globes, painted carmine-red. The detonators were Salan's customized French navy watches, which Claude wedged into the centre of the putty, screwing the mines shut with a flat, circular piece of magnetized metal.

The outline of the Canaries was just visible in the moonlight, a smudge of pencil lead. Claude called to Cannebotin to cut the engines and navigation lights. The crew were all on deck. Claude and the chief mechanic stood beside the launch. Claude growled warnings of caution at the men who'd carried the explosives from his cabin. He stepped into the launch and Madeleine – dressed in black, her blonde hair masked by a bandanna – beckoned the porters forward. They passed the bombs to Claude, who stowed them in the bow and covered them with a tarpaulin.

The launch was hoisted to the water and its hull slapped the oily swell. Overhead passed the pale shadow of a night-time seagull. From the launch, Claude threw a last wave at Madeleine, holding his hand aloft as he started the inboard and gripped the tiller for the long ride across the sea.

Gerard Poulin later recalled that it was with considerable anxiety that the crew watched Claude go, following the fizzing 'V' of the launch's wake in the moonlight until clouds moved in and the small boat was lost to sight. When the water turned silvery again, a mercury sheen to the slow-belly swell, the sailors pointed in different directions before falling gradually silent. Madeleine lifted Totoche into her arms, lay her cheek against his ear.

Nearing Gran Canaria, Claude saw first the jagged silhou-ette of the central range. He held a westerly course, pulling into the lee of La Isleta, the bulbous northern peninsula. Some-where near Playa del Cobadal, several hundred yards short of the *Corrientes*, he let the anchor chain slip through his salt-warm hands into the black water. It was past mid-night; when he looked up he could see lights on the bridge and in the officers' quarters.

The two men slipped into the water, one limpet mine apiece, and kicked off. Claude would later tell how they'd 'pushed' the explosives out in front of them as they swam, suggesting that he had made buoyancy aids, perhaps using small rafts of cork, or lifejackets from *Le Rhin*. They swam silently, and some way apart; even at this distance they could hear each other's breathing and, as they drew slowly closer, the low hum of the ship.

When they reached the first of the coal barges they rested for a couple of minutes. They hung on to the low gunwale, their legs loose in the water, beginning to feel the cold. Then they felt their way to the stern, ducking under the rope that lashed the barge to its neighbour. They fanned apart, Claude heading amidships. *Corrientes* loomed above them, massive and architectural.

In open water, no longer in the lee of the coal barges, they swam underwater, coming up briefly for air, gulping swift deep breaths before diving again. They were close enough now to see faces at the bridge windows; on deck two men were smoking, gazing out towards the open sea. And then all Claude could see was the convex wall of grey steel, rising dully skyward.

Claude and the other man unwrapped the bombs. They trod water, their knees banging the hull. In deep shadow, no longer lit by moonlight, the smooth curve of the limpet mines seemed a rich blood-black. Claude set his detonator, gingerly let the mine pass below the surface of the water and swam downwards. He swam with the bomb under one arm, frog-kicking hard, his free hand tracing the rough steel downwards till he was almost out of breath. Still kicking, feeling the pressure in his temples, he guided the mine flat against the hull. It made contact with a flat clank and he pushed for the surface.

They had two hours' grace, but swam as if just minutes remained, breaking into a fast crawl once they'd passed the coal barges. They did not pause until they reached the launch, heaving themselves over the stern panting and shivering. They were colder still when they pulled alongside *Le Rhin* and the hoist ropes were lowered and Claude, looking up, saw Madeleine's pale face grinning down at him.

She gave them blankets, and Claude and the chief mechanic sat on the deck on upturned crates as the engines were fired up and *Le Rhin* turned northwards. They drank whisky and watched the clock and told the gathered crew of how they'd done it. After two hours they got to their feet and walked aft. Claude and Madeleine, arms round each other in the cool, saw a phosphorous firework flash on the horizon, too distant for sound.

'Champagne!' Claude shouted above the hollers of the crew. 'It's on me!'

As WIRELESS OPERATOR, Claude was first on board to hear the news. The night of 9 May, while he was attaching limpet mines to the hull of *Corrientes*, German troops were invading the Netherlands, Belgium and Luxembourg and, as *Le Rhin* steamed north, he intercepted the latest bulletins, passing them around the mess at mealtimes.

On 13 May, as the ship docked at Casablanca, the Germans breached the French defences at Sedan in north-east France and established their first three bridgeheads south and west of the River Meuse. The Germans hammered on, and on 15 May British and French troops in Belgium began to retreat. Early that morning, French Prime Minister Paul Reynaud cut into Winston Churchill's sleep with a panicked telephone call. 'He spoke in English, and evidently under stress,' Churchill later wrote. '. . . "We are beaten; we have lost the battle." I said: "Surely it can't have happened so soon?" But he replied: "The front is broken at Sedan; they are pouring through in great numbers with tanks and armoured cars." '

France and Britain had been at war with Germany for more than eight months, but for much of this time it had seemed an imaginary conflict, against a phantom enemy. Troop boredom along the front, the result of week after week of inactivity, was worsened by extreme hardship: the winter of 1939 to 1940 was the coldest since 1889, with temperatures in the east falling to minus twenty-four degrees centigrade. 'We are so numbed with apathy and cold,' wrote one frontline soldier, Captain Georges Sadoul, in his journal, 'that many of us do not bother to wash, or to shave, to put on our shoes or even to undress properly when going to bed.' When JU87 dive bombers – Göring's legendary Stukas – came howling out of the sky above Sedan on 13 May, their sirens at full wail, submitting French forces to an eight-hour bombardment, the scraps of remaining morale quickly disintegrated. General Ruby, Deputy Chief of Staff of the Second Army, witnessed his own men 'cowering in their trenches, dazed by the crash of bombs and the shriek of the dive bombers; they had not developed the instinctive reaction of running to their anti-aircraft guns and firing back. Their only concern was to keep their heads well down. Five hours of this nightmare was enough to shatter the nerves and they became incapable of reacting against the enemy infantry.'

In Casablanca, for a week while *Le Rhin* lay at the quay-side, Claude and Madeleine read every newspaper, listened to each radio bulletin and gleaned what they could from cafe gossip. Both were astonished at the speed of the German advance, but felt sure that the Allies would be quick to regroup and that the very fact of German troops on French soil would be enough to inspire retaliation. Yet both of them, just children during the Great War, had little concept of how their fellow countrymen had been changed by that conflict, by the loss of one million three hundred thousand compatriots, another million left sightless, without limbs or otherwise disfigured, by the sudden creation of six hundred thousand widows and seven hundred and fifty thousand orphans. By contrast, for many of the soldiers mobilized in September 1939, the Great War was painfully recent. Gazing from the window of the train that was taking him to his regiment on the Moselle, Private Gustave Folcher, a farmer from the Languedoc, glimpsed 'a huge cemetery with crosses laid out in lines, left over from the war of 1914, which doesn't do much to cheer us up'.

Their politics honed abroad, and with an understanding above all of France as an imposing but sensitive imperial presence engaged, in the Far East, in magisterial combat both with communist rebels and a predatory Japan, Claude and Madeleine were out of touch with the subtler undercurrents of domestic politics. Even Georges Mandel who, as Colonial Minister, was their closest link with high government, was atypical, and his cynicism and distrust of Germany – qualities he conveyed throughout his department – were views that, while hardly representative, were shared by many of his staff. Come mid-June, Mandel – a Jew, and now the newly appointed Interior Minister – would be the most important member of Paul Reynaud's government opposed to an armistice, a lonely figure indeed.

Far more common, even among the military, was a resigned form of pacifism, rooted – in the words of historian Julian Jackson – 'in exhaustion, in deep pessimism – or realism – about whether France could survive another bloodletting on the scale of the Great War'. The gas attack that almost blinded Jean Giono in the first war also crushed his patriotism. 'There is no glory in being French,' he wrote. 'There is only one glory: to be alive.' This defeated stance was widespread throughout the intellectual classes. For Léon Emery, writing in the newspaper published by the primary schoolteachers' union, anything was preferable to conflict: 'rather servitude than war'. And among the general population, too, there was neither the energy nor the taste for war, however manifest the evil: fifty-seven per cent of the population, according to France's first-ever opinion poll, endorsed the appeasement of Hitler made official by the Munich agreement of September 1938.

FRANCE, JUNE 1940

LE RHIN docked at Marseilles on 1 June, six days after British troops had begun their evacuation from Dunkirk. Before nightfall, Claude and Madeleine, under orders from Mandel, boarded the train for Paris. The news they gathered from the handful of other travellers heading north was far from good, though the outlook was not wholly bleak. Despite General Gamelin, then commander-in-chief of French forces, having told Reynaud as long ago as 1 May that he did not have the ability to defend Paris, the German advance appeared to have slowed somewhat. There had been counterattacks, two of the most notable – on 17 and 19 May, at Montcornet and Crécy – coming from Colonel Charles de Gaulle's Fourth Armoured Division. And on 24 May, for reasons that are still the subject of debate, Hitler – possibly nervous that the speed of German progress westward had left an over-exposed southern flank – gave orders for his troops to halt their advance along the coast of the English Channel. By the end of 31 May some hundred and twenty thousand British, French and Belgian troops had been evacuated.

Claude and Madeleine arrived, though, to a seemingly deserted Paris, from which a third of its five million inhabitants had already fled and where the lawns of the Quai d'Orsay that fronted the Foreign Ministry were now grey with ash from the bonfires begun on 16 May and on to which officials, terrified lest their papers should fall into German hands, had heaped the contents of their briefcases, filing cabinets and archive rooms.

Winston Churchill, meeting French leaders late that after-noon – noting the 'utter dejection [that] was written on every face' – was astonished to look down from the meeting room to witness 'clouds of smoke [rising] from large bonfires, and I saw from the window venerable officials pushing wheel-barrows of archives on to them'.

There is neither official record nor journal entry for Claude and Madeleine's days in Paris at this point, though later British government sources, trying to piece together their movements over the next few days, believed that, while in the city, Claude was summoned by Admiral Darlan, head of the French navy and future Vichy Prime Minister. Darlan, well aware of Claude's undercover skills, and suspicious of the political leanings of Vice-Admiral Émile Muselier – still in possession of both vigour and charisma, despite being well into his sixties – 'ordered . . . Péri to spy on Admiral Muselier just before the Fall of France and to obtain his plans for carrying on the war after that melancholy event'.

When Claude caught up with his mother and sister-in-law on Friday 7 June, though, he referred to none of this. Neither did he mention Madeleine, about whom he appears to have been determined his family should remain ignorant. He was still married, after all, even if Marguerite Paire and his infant son André were in Saigon. Instead, he focused on what they must have already feared, that within days Paris would be taken by German troops. Since the day Claude and Madeleine had docked at Marseilles, the Germans had moved south from Belgium with astonishing speed: on 6 June, they crossed the Somme west of Amiens; by 9 June, with Rouen now occupied, the sound of distant gunfire could be heard in central Paris. Claude told his family to 'leave quickly': sixty years on, his sister-in-law still recalls the urgency in his voice.

He and Madeleine, though, opted to stay and these last days, as all around them the city emptied, were cloudless, high-blue and flawless, almost dreamlike: 'strangely calm and beautiful', according to Alexander Werth, Paris correspondent for the *Manchester Guardian*. On 10 June, with Claude's family now having fled south to Bordeaux and then Marseilles, Premier Paul Reynaud announced that the administration too was to evacuate the capital; and Claude and Madeleine – brooding over orders that they had no intention of carrying out – sat together in cafés along the Left Bank while across the river one large black Citroën after another pulled up in front of the Foreign Ministry and ferried away government ministers.

It is unclear why they delayed, why they waited for one long day after another as the Germans drew closer, but maybe they stayed as long as they did at least in part out of sentiment, from a wish to be together in Paris as long as possible, aware that the opportunity might never come again. There was, too, something transcendent and otherworldly about the city in these last days. Though 3 June had seen heavy bombing in the westerly fifteenth and sixteenth arrondissements, home to the Renault and Citroën factories, and though three days later steel girders were laid across the Avenue des Champs-Élysées and the Place de la Concorde to prevent the landing of troop-carrying aircraft, the city, under continuous blue sky, seemed bizarrely at peace. André Maurois, having lunch in the garden court of the Ritz Hotel on the Place Vendôme on Sunday 9 June, found himself looking round at the full tables and smiling solicitous waiters and wondering whether perhaps there had not been some mistake, whether such normalcy could really be possible if the Germans were indeed only half an hour away by car, as the newspapers were claiming.

If the pavement cafes along the Champs-Élysées were full that hot weekend, there were, at the same time, indications of a spreading panic. Werth wrote in his diary that he'd heard of 'terrific dissatisfaction among the Paris working classes. They have been given the strictest orders to stay where they are; if they leave Paris they'll be treated like deserters.' Queues of cars a block long were starting to build at petrol pumps. His final cable to his editor in England described 'faint sweet scent of resin and burning trees stop it may be woods burning somewhere', a sensation over which he puzzled later. 'For a moment I even wondered if it wasn't some treacherously pleasant-smelling new gas, which in a few hours would burn the guts out of you. Isn't there some filthy gas which smells of geraniums or freshly mown hay? If so, why not trees?'

By Monday morning north–south arterials such as the Boulevard Saint-Michel were raucous and fluid with refugees: 'cars crammed with luggage', observed one resident, 'heavy trucks loaded with people and suitcases, people on bicycles, others pushing a small handcart, with a dog tied underneath on a lead, huge country carts going as fast as two or three plough horses can pull them, loaded with bales of hay on which sit old peasant women'. The pavements were impassable with suitcases; shops that just two days earlier had been trading were now shut. Simone de Beauvoir – who had spent Sunday afternoon at her local cinema before going on to write a letter to Sartre at the front over a glass of beer at Café Mahieu on Boulevard Saint-Michel – now packed her bags. 'I felt the German advance like a personal threat. There was only one idea in my head . . . not to be caught like a rat in occupied Paris.'

Those without cars, bicycles, trucks or horses headed for Gare Montparnasse. There were, estimated Latvian newspaper correspondent Arved Arenstam, 'about twenty thousand people in front of the station, most of them seated on their belongings. It is impossible to move, and the heat is unbearable. In its present state of nervous tension the crowd has lost all its charm, and has none of the friendly gaiety that usually characterizes the French en masse . . . I have now been standing in this seething mass for over three hours . . . Children are crying all round, and the many babies in arms look like being crushed to death.' By the end of the day, German troops had taken Fère-en-Tardenois, sixty-five miles east of the capital; and, a mere twenty miles to the north, had passed through L'Isle d'Adam.

The pace of the German invasion rendered it mythical. 'Reality was so strange,' recalled the novelist Jean Dutourd, 'that it became almost indistinguishable from fiction.' At midday on the morning of Tuesday 11 June, the surreal became manifest: clouds of such density and opacity covered the sun that, said Werth, 'one had to go through the smoke screen with a pocket-torch – one couldn't even see halfway across the Place de la Concorde. In the darkness the sun was a pale-green disc.' The air was mineral with soot: 'Apocalypse', reckoned museum curator Yvon Bizardel, contemplating burning oil depots, put to the torch in the face of the incoming army. And through the poisonous mist, like survivors from some Shakespearean battle, came bedraggled French troops, 'stragglers without rifles', according to an English eyewitness, 'ragged and dispirited – many of them wounded. A defeated rabble! Some are drunk and babble wild, incoherent tales of rout. There are shouts of *"À bas la guerre!"'* Down with war.

Somehow, and despite the citywide clamour for transport, Claude and Madeleine managed to get hold of a truck, and onto this, Claude later recounted, they loaded machine guns, small-arms ammunition and a 37mm anti-aircraft gun. It is unclear who provided these – whether the navy, under orders from Darlan, or the Colonial Ministry – but several sources vouch for their existence.

Come dawn on Wednesday 12 June, Claude and Madeleine were in no doubt as to the fate of Paris; yet still they stayed, electrified by strangeness, by the heat-blown, pre-storm stillness. Sometime that day, a Swiss journalist heard lowing in the deserted city centre and came upon a herd of abandoned cows, frightened and hungry. The surrounding streets echoed with their bellowing. Viewing the same ghostly quiet avenues, Supreme Allied Commander General Maxime Weygand issued a four-point declaration, an admittance that defence was pointless. '1. Paris is declared an open city; 2. There will be no defence on the outskirts, or on the city's rim, or inside the city; 3. There will be no destruction of bridges and no defence preparations within the city; 4. In the event of retreat, fighting troops must not cross the city.'

By Thursday, the Germans had entered Évreux – fifty miles west of Paris and well south of the Seine – and were closing in on the capital's western flank. Police *préfet* Roger Langeron watched the torrent of refugees. Aware more than most of the irresistible mathematics of it – since it would be police-department figures that, a week or so on, showed that, of a prewar inner-city population of more than two million eight hundred thousand, now just nine hundred thousand remained – he could hide neither his sorrow nor his shame. 'Will this exodus go on until the very last minute? No other sounds than those of cars, horses. No human being speaks. The atmosphere is heavy.'

It was this passivity that, as he watched, was fuelling in Claude rage and disgust. As he and Madeleine planned their

own escape during these last hours, figuring the best route
south along roads they already knew would be tunnels of dust
from the slow-hoof shuffle of refugee caravans, they sensed
defeat already in the air. 'More curious than anguished,' as
one Parisian put it, 'we awaited our imminent fate.' Later, too,
Claude in particular would speak with venom of the failure
and impotence of his compatriots – the way they dropped
arms without a whisper, leaving women, children, the elderly,
their very soil, undefended. For both of them, the shock of
these days struck deeper than anything they'd yet experienced,
and for the next weeks they talked of little else. It was on the
forge of these events that the shape of their future was cast.

AT DAWN ON Friday 14 June, columns of German infantry
were marching on the centre of Paris. There was but a single
recorded attempt at resistance: a machine-gun post, manned by
a handful of infantry, assembled at the Porte d'Orléans. Eventually a gendarme – dutifully following Weygand's instructions
– ordered it to be dismantled. As the sun rose, the asphalt
began to tremble at the approach of the German tanks, motorcyclists and armoured cars. '*L'affreuse chose s'est réalisée*,' wept
Langeron. 'An immense, an interminable defile of motorized
troops has begun to cross Paris. They are coming from Saint-
Denis and from the northern suburbs and in the direction of
Montrouge. First motorcyclists with sidecars, in their leather
overcoats. Then the weight of armour, of tanks. The streets are
virtually empty, and the majority of houses are shuttered.'

By mid-morning, German command cars were cruising
the Champs-Élysées and swastikas were flying over the Foreign Ministry on the Quai d'Orsay, the Chamber of Deputies,
Senate, Eiffel Tower and – 'most grotesque of all', according
to Associated Press correspondent William Shirer – the Arc de

German troops parade through central Paris, 14 June 1940

Triomphe. Shirer's Berlin colleague Louis Lochner, riding with the German forces, saw before him a ghost town. 'At the Place de la Concorde no ... merry-go-round of honking autos, screaming news vendors, gesticulating cops, gaily chattering pedestrians as usually characterizes this magnificent square. Instead, depressing silence broken only now and then by the purr of some German officer's motor as it made its way to the Hôtel Crillon, headquarters of the hastily set-up local German commandery. On the hotel's flagstaff, the swastika fluttered in the breeze where once the stars and stripes had been in the days of 1919 when Wilson received the cheers of French crowds from the balcony.'

Sixteen Parisians committed suicide that day, noted Langeron. The most eminent, Comte Thierry de Martel, chief surgeon at the American Hospital, had made it clear to US Ambassador William Bullitt that he could not live in a Paris overrun with Germans. At daybreak he shaved, tied a mortuary band around his neck and injected himself with Phenobarbital. When his cook found the body at 8.25 a.m. she discovered nearby a copy of Victor Hugo's *Hernani*. The book was open, and a phrase underlined. 'Since one must be grand to face death, I rise.'

Claude and Madeleine witnessed all this. They saw the two men who pulled to a halt outside the district hall in a field-green vehicle and announced in halting French that German troops had occupied Paris, that uprising would be punished by death, that arms must be turned in and that, for the next forty-eight hours, no one would be allowed out of doors; they heard the sporadic yelps of 'Bravo!', the scattered applause, of Parisians watching German soldiers march down the Boulevard Saint-Germain; they watched as General Kurt von Briesen, head of the German 30th Division, taking the salute towards midday at an impromptu victory march down the Champs-Élysées, shot up in his stirrups out of sheer excitement. Their hearts full of violence and grief, they turned, climbed into their truck and began the long drive south.

THEY DROVE without stopping, taking turns to sleep, seldom getting much above thirty miles an hour, trying to find roads that were not choked with refugees. Some eight to ten million people were on the move, few with any idea where they were headed. Private Gustave Folcher, retreating with his unit through Verdun, wrote in his diary of attempts 'to chat to the civilians ... The people are half mad, they don't even reply to what we ask them. There is only one word in their mouth: evacuation, evacuation.'

Everyone was heading south, grandmothers with rolled mattresses strapped to their backs, children carrying bundles

Refugees on the road, heading south

of clothes, men pushing bicycles loaded until their frames were lost to sight. 'Most pitiful', to Folcher, was to see 'entire families on the road . . . The wagon is driven by a woman, often in tears, but most of the time it's a kid of eight, ten or perhaps twelve years old who leads the horses. On the wagon, on which furniture, trunks, linen, the most precious things, or rather the most indispensable things, have been hastily piled up, the grandparents have also taken their place, holding in their arms a very young child, even a newborn baby.'

Desperation and hunger produced lawlessness among the refugees, transforming them into 'locusts', in the words of Captain Georges Sadoul. Arriving in abandoned villages, people broke locks and raided larders and wine cellars, stripped beds of sheets and blankets. Unmilked cows hobbled through fields, lowing in pain. Beside the roads wounded or

dehydrated horses were left to die, and refugee accounts tell of
the stench, the swollen bellies, the hooves in the air. And then
came air attack: Stukas drilled their machine-gun fire down
the straight hot roads where the only cover was heat-scorched
hedges. It was, observed Arthur Koestler, 'a peculiar irony that
the war had turned the most *petit-bourgeois*, fussy, stay-at-
home people in the world into a nation of tramps'.

It took Claude and Madeleine two days to reach Marseilles, their eyelashes scorched with dust, their vehicle spilling
over with refugees picked up en route. Like anyone who was
part of the *'Exode'*, they were struck by the sense that the spirit
of a people had been crushed and that, bleaker still, the French
themselves had stood passively by, observers to the fact. The
towns through which they passed early on were skeletal: esti-
mates show, for example, that the population of Lille fell from
two hundred thousand to twenty thousand, Chartres from
twenty-three thousand to just eight hundred, while towns in
the south saw an equally marked rise. Numbers in Pau grew
fivefold from thirty thousand to a hundred and fifty thousand;
Bordeaux doubled to six hundred thousand; and Brive, which
started out with thirty thousand residents, ended up with a
hundred thousand. To Claude and Madeleine, it seemed that
the entire society was disintegrating around them; and henceforth, when asked, Claude would say he was Corsican, never
French. 'La Corse' spoke to him of freedom, of a people who
prized and had long fought for their independence; when he
thought of France he now felt only anger, and a fierce shame.

The sight of dejected soldiers – staggering in twos and
threes, sometimes their only possession a single, shared frying
pan, 'walking like blind men', in the words of one witness, 'like
beggars who had even given up asking for alms' – intensified
Claude and Madeleine's shared sense of mortification, of

ignominy by association. They saw children without their
parents, old men weeping in the fields, chalked signs on village
doors – 'see you in Lyon'; 'keep going, Christophe' – grown
women fighting over groceries behind the counters of abandoned shops. By the end of their journey, they'd heard of
worse, too: of women basting themselves in mustard to deter
rapists, of men all too quick to desert their families at the
offer of a ride in a truck. Faced with such an extreme national
collapse, small wonder that, for some, sangfroid was the only
refuge. As the poet Claudine would drily recall from the calm
of old age, '*Nous n'étions pas des héros.*'

MARSEILLES HAD BEEN bombed in their absence and two
ships – the Italian cruiser *Capo Olmo* and the French warship
Chellah – now lay smoking, their superstructures ribboned
and gaping. *Le Rhin*, moored in the shelter of a grain silo, had
escaped damage.

Gerard Poulin, the fourteen-year-old cabin boy, later
recalled Claude asking him – 'he was truly paternal, always
looking after me' – if he'd been scared. 'Absolutely!' Poulin
replied, then noticed the anti-aircraft gun lying in the back of
the truck. 'I felt reassured by that.' Madeleine, though, was
starting to question the wisdom of having someone so young
on board: she'd grown to see Poulin as a little brother, and
moreover one that should be safely at home, not playing at
soldiers.

Claude told René Cannebotin of his new orders – officially, a new explosives job; unofficially, Darlan's plan for
him to spy on Muselier – and Cannebotin prepared the ship
for departure. As he did so, Claude strode through the vessel,
shouting for volunteers. He had a voice that commanded
attention, as capable of gentle confidence or whispered menace

as it was of startling aggression. By mid-afternoon, revolver shoved in his waistband, he'd gathered a small group of men and led the way ashore.

With memories of the seismic tremor of German tanks down Paris' boulevards still playing through his mind, Claude kicked into the nearest warehouse, pistol in the air. He was after anything he could sell on, he told his men, as well as weapons, ammunition and goods more directly useful in combat. This seemed less like piracy to him than legitimate war spoils: if he did not take it, then the Germans certainly would.

He worked his men all afternoon, confronting lack of compliance from dockyard hands with 'a revolver under the nose', in the words of one witness. By nightfall, using a commandeered forklift and the truck he and Madeleine had driven from Paris, he'd collected enough to fill *Le Rhin*'s hold, a dishevelled mound of goods stretching along the quayside the length of the ship. Later British documents, cataloguing the cargo, list a surreal haul: three tons of paper; eighteen bales of scrubbing brushes; thirty-eight bales of jute sacking; six thousand pairs of leather boots; two 'peanut machines'; a ton of pig iron; cement; refrigerators; one hundred and twenty-four car-tyre inner tubes; three tons of 'duckboards'; forty-eight cases of medical supplies; eleven tons of 'lime'; five tons of 'grinding machinery'; thirty-four cases of electrical supplies; and fifty cases of 'pearls, etc'. Also looted – though curiously absent from the British manifest – were ten thousand bottles of claret.

As he roamed the warehouses on the quayside, so Claude gathered not only cargo but also some dozen volunteers, any man who wanted, in his deliberately vague pitch, to 'continue the fight'. According to Patrick Whinney, then a British naval lieutenant, who later came to know Claude and Madeleine well, there were 'Frenchmen, Belgians, Algerians, blacks, whites, Chinese, all sorts'. They came not because they believed in the task before them, for Claude gave no such details, nor even through faith in *Le Rhin* as a potential warship, since she was clearly ageing and far from being the latest technology, but because they saw in Claude an animal fearlessness that seemed the only authentic response to the events of the past five weeks.

LE RHIN sailed that evening, no longer Cannebotin's ship but, unequivocally, under Claude's command. Once the cargo was stowed, it was he who gave orders to leave; and as the vessel joined the tail end of a merchant convoy bound for Oran in western Algeria it was he who stood at the bridge, charts of the western Mediterranean open before him. At some point during the night, though, it seems that Claude diverted from his original orders. According to Gerard Poulin, the ship split from the convoy and began to zigzag westward, a movement designed to confuse U-boats. While the rest of the convoy continued south towards North Africa, skirting east of the Balearic Islands, Claude ordered *Le Rhin* to chart a course that seemed, to those on board, to lack any coherent strategy. As dawn broke, the coast of eastern Spain became visible to starboard: the Costa Brava, Barcelona, Tarragona, into the Gulf of Valencia.

Claude spent much of the morning in the wireless room, emerging dark and volatile with each new piece of intelligence. The Germans, he relayed, had captured Orléans and Metz; Paul Reynaud had stood down as prime minister and now, in his place, stood Marshal Philippe Pétain, the revered hero of Verdun, with General Maxime Weygand, another Great War veteran, as his minister of defence. In the wardroom, a transistor was tuned to French radio and at noon Claude and Madeleine and the other senior ranks were sitting down to eat when the voice of the Maréchal came on the air. 'It is with a heavy heart,' Pétain announced, 'that I say to you today that it is necessary to cease fighting. I have this evening approached the enemy to ask if he is ready to try to find, between soldiers, with the struggle over and in honour, the means to put an end to the hostilities.'

Defying the orders issued him in Paris – and with significant quantities of plastic explosive no longer destined for their original target and now in Madeleine's safekeeping – Claude ordered Cannebotin to sail for Gibraltar. His mood was

Claude, en route for Gibraltar, 18–22 June 1940

sombre, and he kept mostly to himself. During these next four days, even Madeleine chose to stay out of his way. In the wardroom, Claude was a coil of tension and menace and the other men spoke carefully when they approached him. He resembled someone in the early stages of bereavement: choked up with denial, still unable to believe what had been lost, fighting grief with anger. There were snatched moments of tenderness – Madeleine's hand on his waist when she thought they were alone – but for much of the time Claude appeared as he was captured around this time by a crewman's camera: jaw in his hand, roughly shaven, hair GI-cropped, leaning on the gunwale watching the coast of Spain inch by. The swell was easy, and the sun bore down from a deep blue sky, but he wore full uniform despite the heat: buttoned jacket, tie, shoes polished till dazzling.

The journey to Gibraltar felt interminable, and when General de Gaulle broadcast on the BBC foreign service at dusk on 18 June, the sense on board *Le Rhin* was of a split, previously no more than rumour, which would, the moment the crew heard his speech, suddenly become manifest. De Gaulle, who'd been flown to London from Bordeaux early on Sunday 16 June in an airplane lent to him by Winston Churchill, was heard by the crew and officers of the ship declaring that 'the cause of France is not lost'. He pleaded against defeatism. 'But has the last word been said? Must we abandon all hope? Is our defeat final and irremediable? To those questions I answer: No!' Like France itself, *Le Rhin* responded with schism: on one side, those who supported Pétain and who feared the prospect of war; on the other those, like Claude and Madeleine, who could already see beyond Gibraltar, to London.

Somehow, for the next four days, the animosity on board

remained latent. Twice more they gathered to hear de Gaulle broadcast. 'I now speak for France,' he stated on 19 June. 'It is the bounden duty of all Frenchmen who still bear arms to continue the struggle.' Three days later, with *Le Rhin* finally within sight of the sheer east cliff of Gibraltar, de Gaulle's views on the armistice came over the air shorn of any pretence at diplomatic sweetness. 'It would . . . reduce the country to slavery.' Privately, like Claude and Madeleine – both of whom, along with de Gaulle, would shortly be sentenced to death in absentia by Pétain's government – de Gaulle was already seeing the regime as fatally sick, morally corrupted. As he wrote in his memoirs, in hyperbolic language uncannily close to that often employed by Claude, 'in reality this annihilation of the State was at the bottom of the national tragedy. By the light of the thunderbolt the regime was revealed, in its ghastly infirmity, as having no proportion and no relation to the defence, honour and independence of France.' A refusal to fight now – even if 'foreign arms' should eventually liberate the country – would mean that France's 'self-disgust and the disgust she would inspire in others would poison her soul and her life for many generations'.

De Gaulle, recalling his first broadcast, wrote of his intention 'to hoist the colours'. As *Le Rhin* neared Gibraltar's harbour wall on 22 June, Claude, for whom the literal always held more appeal than the figurative, gave orders that the white ensign – reserved solely for Royal Navy and Royal Yacht Squadron vessels – should be raised. Under cover of darkness, and lest the British should find his intentions open to misinterpretation, Claude handed a midshipman a hammer and told him to nail the flag to the mast.

GIBRALTAR, JUNE TO JULY 1940

Gibraltar, the night of 22 June 1940, was preparing for the imminent arrival of the British aircraft carrier HMS *Ark Royal* and battlecruiser HMS *Hood* – at forty-two thousand tons the biggest warship in the world. They were the first two ships of a seventeen-strong convoy that the British Admiralty hoped would regain control of the western Mediterranean. As yet, though, the squadron was quiet, understaffed, the docks mostly empty, and a mere eight anti-aircraft guns defending the Rock. The civilian population was dwindling weekly: evacuation of all but essential government workers and the military had started in May, and by the end of the year some fourteen thousand had left, billeted to Casablanca, Madeira, Jamaica, Northern Ireland and London.

At dawn on 23 June, Claude and Madeleine walked out on deck to their first view of the glory that is Gibraltar, the asphodel-sprinkled olive groves rising up the western escarpment, the pale early sun on the red-tiled roofs and shuttered white houses of the town. Later they walked the streets in the cool, passing the unmistakable marks of British imperialism: scarlet post boxes and telephone kiosks, brick-built Victorian police stations, street cops with dark-navy uniforms and high-domed helmets, pub signs hanging motionless in the still morning air, the first stallholders setting up their pitches. At nine, Claude walked Madeleine back to the docks and then turned on his heel and returned into town.

With no appointment, he rapped on the door of the French

naval mission. He arrived, as the log of the mission chief Capitaine de Frégate de Bryas tersely notes, carrying 'a true arsenal of weapons, with which he set up various melodramatic scenarios during the following tragic days'. To members of his crew these incidents swiftly became part of the legend, recounted, repeated and embellished. The common thread was Claude's determination to be in combat as soon as possible, and he used everything he could – even, on one occasion, an attaché case of plastic explosive, detonator set and ticking, left on the chair in de Bryas' office – to ensure that he would not be ignored.

At Claude's request, de Bryas put him in touch with the British Secret Intelligence Service, and for the next three days, leaving Madeleine on board, Claude shuttled between the French and British, trying to figure out in which direction his and Madeleine's futures lay. Early on, it seemed as if *Le Rhin* might be able to continue the war as part of the French navy which – under proposals from navy chief Admiral François Darlan, ratified on 22 June by Pétain's cabinet – looked likely to set up a base in French North Africa. Two days later, however, when the armistice was signed and capitulation became concrete, Darlan gave orders that, should the Germans ever threaten to capture French ships, the vessels should be scuttled.

Engaged in vigorous if unconventional diplomacy, Claude began courting the British. With his spoken English still little better than first-grade, he relied on his counterparts to speak French. As soon as news of the armistice broke, he 'reported to the British admiral', according to British intelligence documents, 'and informed him that he was prepared to fight for the British'. Claude gave orders for the medical supplies looted at Marseilles to be handed over, along with dry and perishable foodstuffs. When Italian fighter planes bombed the harbour,

Claude told his men to return fire. The British were impressed: 'Commander Péri was congratulated by the British authorities on the good firing of his guns and the discipline of his crew.'

CLAUDE WAS TREADING a precarious line, finding himself increasingly sickened by the very mention of France, and yet still with a crew of fifty-six Frenchmen under him, most of whom had made it clear that their loyalties lay with their own country. He was now also out of uniform, having jettisoned his French merchant-navy blazer on arrival in Gibraltar. Yet, to the French authorities, he was still their agent, and – sometime between 23 and 26 June – Claude was approached by the French consul, on the orders of Darlan, to blow up HMS *Hood*, newly arrived from Britain.

What Darlan had in mind was a *Corrientes*-style sabotage, a mission that had become all the more impressive when it was learned that the Germans now believed that the destruction had been caused by shelling. British secret-service papers, reporting subsequent conversations with Claude in Gibraltar, claim that the French consul 'handed [Claude] a piece of paper, which purported to be a message, received in code, from the French naval intelligence officer in Casablanca, instructing him to take advantage of the good relations with the British naval authorities to sink HMS *Hood*; this was to be done with the sabotage equipment which he had on board *Le Rhin*.' Claude's reaction was immediate, and characteristic: 'He took the document to the British authorities, and made a number of intemperate suggestions as to what they should do with the French. He complains that his advice was not followed and that the consul was allowed to return to France. He then sent a cable to the French authorities not only refusing the instructions but also telling them that he considered them traitors and that he would continue to fight France and Italy on the side of Great Britain.' Two days later, the response was cabled back: Claude was court-martialled and condemned to death. 'He also received orders instructing him to return immediately to Casablanca which he naturally refused to do.'

Keen to recruit men as disaffected with France as he was, Claude spent the evenings in the pubs and restaurants, Madeleine on his arm, talking up his ship. They were en route for Britain, he promised, where the vessel was to be converted into a 'Q' ship, an armed merchantman used either as a decoy or to destroy submarines. One such signing was twenty-year-old Jean Ayral, who'd escaped France with a boatload of Polish refugees at Bayonne near the Spanish border, on the Atlantic coast, and ended up in Gibraltar in the third week of June. Ayral, who'd just completed his first year of engineering studies, found that his flawless English earned him swift access to the drinking company of a party of British petty officers. The next thing he remembered was waking the following morning in a hammock on board *Le Rhin*. The holds, he noticed, 'were stuffed to bursting, and barrels jammed the deck'. As bodies began to move in the neighbouring hammocks, it was clear that the previous evening had witnessed extreme drama. 'Did you see how he hammered them?' one man asked another. 'Incredible,' came the reply. 'And what about her? Nerves of steel.'

A more intimate witness to events the previous evening was a Belgian doctor, Albert Guérisse. Guérisse, who had fled through France after the fall of Paris, had arrived in Gibraltar from Sète on a British collier, determined to continue the fight against the Germans. Having asked around on the quayside for a likely berth, he and another Belgian refugee had persuaded a fisherman to row them across the harbour to

Le Rhin. Claude greeted them, Guérisse later recalled, with outstretched arms: 'Welcome to my ship!'

Stepping aboard, Guérisse noticed 'a girl, blonde and sophisticated, tilted back in a cane armchair, her long slim legs stretching up to a rail of the bridge'. She caught his eye: a long, level gaze. Guérisse looked away. Inside, Claude ordered a sailor to show the two Belgians to the showers. Once they'd washed, he said, they were expected in the wardroom.

Guérisse's account has him arriving in the mess at six in the evening, as requested, and finding the table laid with white linen, wine and beer glasses, bottles of aperitifs, an ice box. He was feeling uneasy: whenever he passed members of the crew they fell silent at his approach, only beginning their conversations again once he was well out of earshot. The ship also perplexed him: with its twin anti-aircraft guns it was clearly no ordinary merchantman, an impression reinforced when, taking a wrong turn, he opened a door into one of the holds and glimpsed a spaghetti jangle of bicycles and several barrels of wine.

Claude introduced Guérisse to the officers, among them Cannebotin; Claude's *Corrientes* partner, *Le Rhin*'s chief mechanic; and Madeleine, 'who does us the honour', he grinned, 'of living aboard'. Claude dominated proceedings, sitting at the head of the table, with Cannebotin on his left and Madeleine on his right; he toasted Belgium, then France; dinner began. Claude ordered bottle after bottle of claret, pressing the Belgians on their escape from northern Europe, the route, the transport they'd found. As the sunset blazed across the sea outside, and the meal became more riotous – Cannebotin chain-smoking cheroots, chortling at Claude's stories – only one remained silent. Since her first nod of greeting, Madeleine had not said a word. Now, as the evening wore on, she seemed to Guérisse to be becoming increasingly agitated, her eyes darting between the mess door and the line of internal portholes that gave on to the passageway outside.

As the plates were being cleared, Claude raised a hand. In the mock-formal delivery he favoured on such occasions, he began with an elaborate apology. Despite past successes, he said – reaching behind him to rap a knuckle against a small brass plaque on which was engraved '10 Mai 1940 – Las Palmas' – he was now facing 'mutiny'. He wanted the ship to 'continue the struggle' with the British; yet, despite an offer of dual nationality secured from authorities at Gibraltar, it looked as if most of his crew planned to sail for Casablanca and await orders from Darlan. Surrounded now by silent officers – and watched from the portholes by a dozen pairs of eyes – Claude was shouting. His eyes were rimmed with red. Madeleine, Guérisse noticed, had started smoking hard.

Faces appeared at the windows; it seemed to Guérisse as if there was something almost choreographed about the build-up, as if Claude was the puppet master, as if all this had long been planned. Those who didn't want to follow him and fight for Britain, he yelled, were *'lâches'*, cowards.

The chief mechanic got to his feet. 'Cowards?' he shouted back. He brought his beer glass down on the edge of the table and held up the splintered base. Claude vaulted across the tabletop, but before he could land a blow the mechanic had lunged forward, glass in hand.

The mess door was open now, and crew were pouring in. Claude's face was running with blood from lacerations over one eye, and at that moment there was a sudden, slow-motion silence as Claude reached out to steady himself. Madeleine kicked back her chair. She reached inside her jacket, pulled out a revolver.

'You,' she muttered, levelling the barrel at the mechanic. 'Have you no shame? You, of all people.'

No response. Blood was pooling at Claude's feet. He put a hand to his forehead. His shirt was spattered scarlet, fast losing its original white. In the hush a low, far-off hum was just audible.

'Put him in irons,' Claude muttered.

As with much else in the lives of Claude and Madeleine, the battle for control of *Le Rhin*, which took place on the long night of 26 June 1940, swiftly became its own myth. Crew members, depending on their loyalties, told different stories. One had Claude and the mechanic in a ring-fight, during the course of which Claude – despite believing that he'd lost the sight of one eye – succeeded in crushing his opponent's ankle.

All agree, though, that this was a pivotal moment, before which the most likely outcome was that sheer arithmetic – the determination of most crewmen to not desert France – meant that Claude and Madeleine would have had to find another vessel. Yet, by the end of the night, all but six of an original crew of fifty-six had agreed to disembark.

A composite narrative would have Claude, Madeleine at his side, standing on the bridge around midnight, the faces of his men turned up towards him, pale in the moonlight, as he presents his case. At points he has to hammer on the handrail with the heel of his pistol to command attention; his fight with the chief mechanic in the early evening has left him with a bandaged head, damaged eye obscured, and he finds it hard to focus: the features of the men below appear to be floating, disembodied. Guérisse has told him that the eye is unharmed, but even now the wounds are cleaned – a gash in the lower eyelid, two more above his cheekbone – he can see only blurred shapes. He'd lain on his bunk as Guérisse had attended to him, Madeleine stroking his blood-matted hair, and had been unable, at that moment, to picture the future.

The chief mechanic, his ankle strapped by Guérisse, is now lying in his hammock and, despite Claude's display of superior aggression, other ringleaders have emerged. They are all nationalities, many of them men Claude recruited in Marseilles: Arab, African, Chinese, French, Polish. Insults begin to fly, a babble of obscenity in a score of different languages. Claude touches a hand to his bandage, now sodden with blood.

Suddenly, one of the stokers starts to climb the steps to the bridge, a ten-inch spanner in his hand. Others are behind him, all chanting, 'France! France! France!' He orders them to retreat, but they keep coming and in an instant they are on the bridge. Aided by a couple of men, Claude launches into them; Madeleine, no more than an observer now, is pressed flat against the bridgehouse, eyes closed.

Claude wrenches the spanner from the stoker's hand and throws it overboard, a high looping throw into nothingness, the noise of it hitting water lost amid the chaos of screams, the echo of bodies against plate metal.

Doors are banged open as Claude takes the fight inside, into corridors so narrow only one-to-one combat is possible. Madeleine runs to her cabin, locks the door, buries her head in her knees.

Sometime before dawn, the shoreward straggle begins: fifty men, in three shifts, piled into the lifeboat. At sunup, only Claude, Madeleine, René Cannebotin, Albert Guérisse and six crewmen remain on board.

BY MIDDAY ON 27 June, a new command structure was in place. Claude made himself captain, demoting Cannebotin to navigator; Guérisse was now his second-in-command, and Madeleine cipher officer. The rest of the day was spent in familiar style: Claude and Madeleine canvassing for fresh volunteers, taking the launch alongside the other French ships now anchored in Gibraltar harbour, arguing for an alliance with the British among men who had already heard much of the previous night's combat on board *Le Rhin* and who needed little persuasion to hear Claude plead his case. It says much for Claude's magnetism that even now – sleepless, with his head bandaged and focus blurry – he had little trouble recruiting volunteers. A line of sailors queued up on board the merchantman *Château Latour*, to be joined by two French pilots, a young military doctor, another Belgian officer and a group of university students, whose knowledge of the sea was limited to holiday fishing trips, spear-diving in the striated azure of the western Mediterranean.

The focus on youth – on the on-deck parade that evening of faces that had scarcely even seen a razor – brought Madeleine's thoughts back to Gerard Poulin, the fourteen-year-old cabin boy. Where Claude had seen no reason to discourage Poulin from staying with the ship, Madeleine felt differently, and she sought him out.

Poulin, recalling the moment in a letter to Claude's family some thirteen years later, spoke of Madeleine's unswerving resolve. 'She insisted I was too young to remain on board.' Cannebotin, called by Madeleine as backup, took a gentler approach, giving the boy the choice. Madeleine, though, would not be dissuaded, and there is something about her decisiveness here – as the three of them tussle, the boy starting to cry – that makes one wonder how much of her own lost youth she had unwittingly identified in Poulin. Her childhood had been taken from her, her teenage years spent dreaming of escape, her twenties violated and now, in front of her eyes, here was a boy who seemed to be wishing death upon himself. When she remonstrated with him, unmovable and yet soft as a worried mother, she might have been addressing her own, younger self.

'An instant later,' Poulin remembered, 'up came Commander Péri. He asked me what I was going to do, and I recounted the conversation I'd just had with Commander Cannebotin and [Madeleine Bayard].' Claude listened to the boy's version of events, to his description of how Cannebotin had implied that the decision was his, then how Madeleine had stepped in, not to be crossed.

'*Eh bien, mousse*, my cabin boy,' Claude smiled. 'It looks like you're leaving tomorrow.'

POULIN – 'my eyes full of tears' – was allowed to delay his departure for twenty-four hours, time enough for him to witness the reception on board of Admiral Émile Muselier, who was in Gibraltar to win over Claude as part of his campaign to recruit ships and men for his embryonic Forces Navales Françaises Libres. Two photographs survive of Muselier's visit to *Le Rhin*. The first, taken by Madeleine – and reproduced just once, in a wartime issue of the *London News Chronicle*, with Claude's face blacked out and, in the text, all identities obscured – is a close-up of both men. Despite the hand-inked 'X' across his features, it is clear that Claude is grinning. Muselier, taller by a good four inches, stands straighter, more formal, with a fresh-lit cigarette nudged under a sparse, foxy moustache. Afternoon light casts their features into half-shadow. Claude appears more at ease than Muselier. There is something protruding from his jacket hip pocket, possibly the heel of a gun.

The other is a group shot and in this, like the first, Claude is already wearing a lighter dressing over his wound. It hangs lower over his right, injured eye, but his mood appears unaffected, and there is no indication of fatigue. Cannebotin, Claude, Muselier and Madeleine stand in a sun-soaked line, formally posed, with another rank of men behind. With the exception of Cannebotin, who wears a sour-fruit grimace, all are smiling at the camera. There is a sense of lightness, almost euphoria, a holiday feel: gone is the tension of the preceding days, when nothing felt certain. Most striking is the expression on Madeleine's face. Standing in the second row, her head appears between the shoulder of Muselier and that of another, unnamed uniformed officer. Until now, and certainly in company, she'd been taciturn, even grave, fully conscious – as in her warnings to Poulin – of the dangers ahead. Now, though,

Admiral Emile Muselier, head of the Free French Navy,
flanked by Claude and Madeleine, Gibraltar, 28 June 1940

it is as if a weight has been lifted; she seems effortlessly beautiful, her hair tied loosely back, a rollered wave of hair across the top of her head, in the early-forties fashion.

MUSELIER HAD ARRIVED in Gibraltar the previous evening, 27 June, with hopes – as he wrote in his memoirs – of finding 'a significant number of French warships'. He was disappointed: all he could see was the *Président Houduce*, a trawler, 'several merchant ships', and *Le Rhin*. Undaunted, he spent the morning of 28 June with Claude, touting for volunteers for his Free French Navy. The two men toured each vessel in turn and it would be easy, if one relied only on Muselier's version of events, to believe that Claude had made a sudden about-face, deciding after all to fight with his compatriots.

That, certainly, is what Muselier wanted, and on 29 June – no doubt in an attempt to prevent him defecting to the British – he appointed Claude commander of the Free French naval base in Gibraltar. Claude, whose wished-for status as a British commander had yet to be ratified, accepted, and that evening Muselier – confidently assuming that his power base in Gibraltar was secure – left by flying boat for London, where Charles de Gaulle and Winston Churchill were awaiting him.

As his plane banked west, Muselier looked out of his window at the harbour below. The dawn sun was just coming over the Rock, turning the roofs of the town from dull terracotta to paintbox shades of carmine, poppy, brick and umber, slanting downhill through the west-facing olive groves and sparking sudden brilliant reflections from the metal of the moored ships' scrubbed decks. The French ships – six in total – lay in line, snug as slugs, and he was close enough, as the plane began its slow climb northwards towards Portugal, to see the figures on board, even discern captain and crew. He could see waving arms, faces raised to watch him go, mouths open as if in wild cheering.

On the deck of *Le Rhin*, though, the men watched him in silence. Claude, with his white bandage, and Madeleine, hair blowing gold in the sunlight, stood close together. They glanced up at Muselier's plane, then exchanged a look, turned and went inside.

ON 30 JUNE, the day after Admiral Muselier flew north, the British cruiser HMS *Arethusa* sailed into Gibraltar harbour. On board was Vice Admiral Sir James Somerville, under orders from Churchill to take control of the fighting ships that were gathering in the western Mediterranean. This was an appointment of strategic importance, and Claude moved quickly to make himself known to Somerville.

'Force H', for which Somerville had responsibility, was a substantial fleet, comprising seventeen vessels, including the aircraft carrier *Ark Royal*, battleships *Valiant* and *Resolution*, battlecruiser *Hood* and cruiser *Arethusa*. Somerville carried orders that showed more than anything the depth of mistrust between the British and French and which, in turn, helped finally decide Claude and Madeleine's own path.

On 29 June, as *Arethusa* was turning east to enter the Mediterranean, the British Admiralty cabled Somerville with instructions about his approach to the French fleet in north Africa. Leaving Britain, he'd been told 'to secure the transfer, surrender or destruction of the French warships at Oran and Mers-el-Kébir, so as to ensure that these ships should not fall into German or Italian hands'. Now, however, the details were spelled out. He was to offer the French commanders four options: join forces with the Royal Navy; sail to a British port and surrender the ships; sail to a French port in the West Indies

Claude's champion, Sir James Somerville

where the ships would be demilitarized or entrusted to a neutral power; or be sunk by gunfire. Somerville arrived in Gibraltar quiet and anxious, fearful how such stark alternatives would be greeted.

For Claude, by contrast, the prospect of the imminent destruction of French warships was a piece of joyous news, and he lobbied hard to sail south with Somerville. To the French consul, observing Claude's manoeuvrings during these days – and as yet unaware of Claude's wish to take part in the demolition of his own nation's fleet – Claude and his crew were already men to be treated with caution. 'Left to themselves, these individuals are considerably more dangerous than useful . . . their energies need to be channelled.'

Somerville sailed for Mers-el-Kébir on 2 July, and Claude – to his frustration and anger – was powerless to do anything but watch the fleet go. A day on, he and Madeleine were picking up yet more tantalizing news: Force H, moored just off the North African coast, had delivered its ultimatum. In response, Admiral Marcel Gensoul, commander of the French squadron, said that he would disarm his ships. Somerville, hoping that the French would see sense, gave them more time, and at half past four in the afternoon his go-between signalled back from Mers-el-Kébir that Gensoul – in the event of enemy threat – would be prepared to take his ships to Martinique or America. Once again, Somerville reiterated the British demands and, just before six that evening, with no further word from Gensoul, he ordered the British warships to open fire. One French battleship was sunk, two were crippled, and nearly one thousand three hundred men were killed.

BY THE END OF the first week of July, still no decision had been made about *Le Rhin*'s future, and the atmosphere on board was tense. While Madeleine lay in her deckchair reading and sunbathing, an unshaven Claude sat down with his dictionary. The letters he wrote to the British authorities – his English leaden and formal – carried an unmistakable subtext: take me seriously, they urged; I am here to fight. 'On board *Le Rhin*,' the first begins, 'are three agricultural machines on rubber wheels and easily movable, which could constitute a good anti-tank defence . . . 790 metric tonnes of cement could be put at the disposal of the military authorities . . . some officers on board are specialised in anti-tank defence and would be able to give lectures.' A second letter was yet more specific, listing the goods which had to be unloaded if *Le Rhin* was to be used 'in special missions'. Secrecy was vital: 'Should the Admiralty put a tugboat or a barge at my disposal, my crew would unload the ship, because it's not convenient for Spanish dockers to come on board and see her special dispositions.'

The letters were successful only in part: according to British documents, 'a portion of the cargo was offloaded'. Claude, who received a 'token payment' of £46, insisted that his crew should also benefit, 'and in addition a quantity of wine and cigarettes to the value of £33–10d was placed on board for distribution among the crew'.

Though briefly mollified by alcohol, Claude's men were growing restive. Boredom had heightened their feelings of sexual frustration, which must have been exacerbated by the daily sight of Madeleine, in blouse and culottes, lying on deck with her legs bared to the sun. Realizing that the time had come to force Somerville's hand, Claude shaved, packed his briefcase, and strode across town to the British Admiralty headquarters.

According to Guérisse, to whom Claude recounted the story, Claude sat down in relaxed fashion, briefcase on his knees, in the office of one of Somerville's subordinates. He had brought a parcel, he said, for each of the three naval officers with whom he'd recently had dealings, all of whom had acted as envoys from Somerville to pass on the news that no decision on *Le Rhin* had yet been made. He then sprang the locks, and gingerly lifted out three brown-paper parcels. They were ticking. Claude turned and left the office.

TWENTY-FOUR HOURS later, an Admiralty messenger arrived on board *Le Rhin* with a letter from Admiral Somerville, who'd spent the intervening period in communication with the British Secret Intelligence Service in London. He'd been told that Claude and Madeleine were agents of Raoul Salan, that they'd spent years in the Far East, and – more recently

– had become skilled with plastic explosive, a substantial quantity of which they still had on board *Le Rhin*. In short, they could be relied upon. Somerville told Claude that *Le Rhin* was booked on the next convoy for Britain.

THE EVENTUAL willingness of the British to take on *Le Rhin* said everything about the professional reputation of Claude and Madeleine, for not only was the crew inexperienced, but the ship herself was in need of a comprehensive overhaul. Built in 1920 in the northern-British port of Hartlepool, measuring two hundred and seventy feet by forty-one, she'd originally been capable of more than nine knots; twenty years on, with her triple-expansion Mackie and Baxter engine surviving on a diet of poor wartime coal, her top speed was little more than six. First impressions were not favourable: according to Lieutenant Patrick Whinney – who had fled France in July as a founder member of the British Naval Mission at Admiral Darlan's headquarters at the Château de Maintenon – *Le Rhin* was 'old, slow and out-of-date, her condition poor'. Whinney would oversee the ship's first refit, though he wondered initially whether this was wasted energy: 'In the normal course of events,' he later wrote, 'her final voyage to the scrap yard could not have been long delayed.'

On board, conditions were cramped and, as they sailed west in convoy on 21 July, quickly became claustrophobic. Fitted to carry twenty passengers in seven cabins, *Le Rhin* was now home to three times that number. Only Claude, Madeleine, Cannebotin and Guérisse had cabins to themselves, quarters that sat one storey above the deck, directly below the bridge and wireless room. What had previously been Cannebotin's spacious captain's suite was now split between him and Claude, whose door adjoined that of Madeleine.

Down a flight of waxed wooden steps, at deck level, were the officers' and engineers' messes, the galley and the pantry. This was the heart of the ship, directly above the engine room; and here, amidships, in a cramped space next to the coal furnace, Claude had put a set of leg irons that had already had their first occupant, the chief engineer, who had been offloaded in Gibraltar.

Claude and Madeleine kept to themselves during these early days. Despite Somerville's backing, they had no idea how they would be received once they reached Britain or even, to begin with, for which port they were bound. Cut off from France, having sacrificed all contact with their previous colleagues, they were suddenly isolated.

Moreover, the news they'd gleaned during the last days in Gibraltar was far from good. On 11 July, Marshal Pétain had assumed supreme power in France, replacing 'Liberty, Equality, Fraternity' with 'Work, Family and Fatherland'. A week earlier, the Germans had landed in the Channel Islands and assumed power without a fight. By the middle of the month, Göring's Luftwaffe was accelerating its attacks on shipping in the English Channel, a tactic designed to lure Royal Air Force fighters into dogfights that Göring felt sure his Messerschmitts would win. Churchill's renaming of the Local Defence Volunteers as the Home Guard may have come two days after *Le Rhin*'s departure, but would nevertheless have been unlikely to soothe Claude and Madeleine's fears: early Home Guard platoons paraded with weaponry as diverse and eccentric as cutlasses, shotguns, petrol-bomb catapults and six-foot spears, and were formed by ageing farmers, retired soldiers, even bishops.

As July became August, they drew ever closer to a country tensed for invasion – whose prime minister had already cleared with Cabinet the use of poison gas against incoming German troops; where the failure of the British Expeditionary Force to rescue much of its heavy armament and transport from France had created an anxious shortage that factories were now struggling to fill; and where beaches were being hurriedly mined and bridges readied for demolition. German intelligence agents, reporting back to Hitler, had contributed to a bullish mood among the Führer's lieutenants, with Göring, commander-in-chief of the air force, now giving his pilots a mere five weeks to realize victory.

How much of this news filtered through to the crew is not known, but as the ship entered the northern half of the Bay of Biscay, within sight of Cape Finistère on a soup-calm midsummer night, three sailors approached Guérisse on the bridge.

The tallest and burliest of the three, acting as spokesman, told Guérisse that they had changed their minds, and no longer wanted to go to Britain. Guérisse warned them that if they didn't return to their hammocks he'd wake Claude.

'Just give us a lifeboat,' came the reply, later recalled by Guérisse. 'We'll fend for ourselves.'

Guérisse refused, once again demanding that the men back down. When they made no move he picked up the communication tube and called for Claude.

There was a moment's silence, then Guérisse heard hurried footfalls in the stairwell below him.

Claude kicked open the door to the chart room, dressed only in a pair of trousers and a jacket; no shirt, no shoes. He pushed Guérisse aside, advanced on the mutineer and struck him in the face.

Through the bridge windows, as Claude vented his rage, Guérisse saw moonlight on the gently shifting ocean, broken abruptly by the shoreline, barely two miles to starboard. When Claude stopped shouting, and had ordered the deserters below decks to be clamped in chains, there was quiet. Guérisse could feel the grind of the engines coming up through the soles of his feet.

ALL THE WAY to England, as the ship passed the Scilly Isles and entered the Bristol Channel, Claude and Madeleine talked tactics. Guérisse and the other officers now seldom saw them, often not even at mealtimes, for they'd often order food to be brought to their cabins while they considered the best approach, how to play the hand that would guarantee them the swiftest return to the battle zone.

There was, they knew, a great deal in their favour: a workable ship, men, two 90mm cannon, a 20mm and a 37mm anti-aircraft gun, fourteen machine guns and an arsenal of other small arms, including a prototype Soviet rifle that Claude, as with most of the weapons, had stolen in Marseilles. Still more persuasive was their experience and skill, factors bolstered by the sizeable quantity of plastic explosive they possessed, which Claude had passed to Madeleine for safe-keeping.

As they contemplated the makeup of the ship, it occurred to Claude that her most effective use would be undercover, that he should press for a refit that would convert her from a lightly armed merchantman into a Q-ship. These vessels owed their conception to the instructions of Winston Churchill to Sir Hedworth Meux, Commander-in-Chief, Portsmouth, in November 1914 'to take up . . . a small or moderate-sized steamer . . . to trap the German submarine which sinks vessels by gunfire off Havre'. Throughout the First World

War, Q-ships designed as U-boat hunters masqueraded as regular cargo vessels, their twelve-pounders, Maxim guns, torpedo tubes and depth charges concealed behind dummy lifeboats or fold-down gunwales.

The life of a Q-ship commander was more than ordinarily stressful: according to Vice Admiral Gordon Campbell, whose various undercover vessels had sunk three submarines during the war, most collapsed with health troubles within twelve months. It was a perilous, borderline existence, with the survival of the crew contingent upon the ship's credibility as a decoy. General orders stated that, in the event of a submarine sighting, 'every effort is to be made to escape, and if the submarine opens fire, engines are to be stopped, and the ship's company (except the necessary engine-room staff and the guns' crews, who must be carefully out of sight behind the bulwarks alongside their guns) commence to abandon ship'. The U-boat commander, witnessing a seemingly innocent merchantman being abandoned, would then pull closer. 'The submarine should be allowed to come as close as possible to decoy, and fire then opened by order of the whistle or steam siren, colours [White Ensign] being hoisted at the same time.' The smallest oversight could prove fatal – to quote the orders' more positive gloss, 'it is the strictest attention to small details that ensures success'.

Because of the hazards of their work, not least the fact that they were likely to be shot if captured, the volunteers who joined the regular merchant personnel of Q-ships earned notably more than the regular naval recruit. Officially, they were classed as Special Service personnel, though – with their weeks-old stubble and oil-smeared Guernseys – they more resembled dishevelled long-haul trawlermen. To Claude and Madeleine, such subterfuge was not only close to second nature, but also a thrill, a source of life. As with the work they'd done so far, existence on a Q-ship was a double life, twice the vital charge, where the mundane had no place. Posing as merchant sailors, the crew were trained marksmen, skilled in the use of depth charges, grenades, rifles and pistols. Night sailing was done with lights extinguished, and it was often under cover of darkness that the ship would undergo its transformation: one Q-ship, the British cargo steamer *Farnborough*, could become a Danish vessel overnight, complete with national colours running down both flanks, a new name on the bow, a raised foredeck with awning stanchions and jackstaff, dummy ventilator and extra funnel, and an awning on top of the bridge.

To pitch *Le Rhin* as a Q-ship also solved a central problem, and one that had dominated Claude and Madeleine's time together ever since they'd fled south from Paris six weeks earlier. Determined that nothing should part them, and aware that, in Britain, women were not permitted to serve on fighting ships in wartime, they decided to put themselves forward as an indissoluble team. The presence of Madeleine on board, they figured, could be the greatest asset of *Le Rhin* as Q-ship: the visible female presence would be their most effective disguise.

THEY ROUNDED Land's End still in convoy, the ships charting a zigzag course intended to confuse U-boats, as they headed east past St Ives, Newquay, Boscastle and round Hartland Point. At this point in their journey, crossing the open water of the Bristol Channel, approaching the coast of Wales, there was still a danger from German submarines operating out of newly established bases in Brittany, and Claude ordered a constant watch.

'A filthy ship': *Le Rhin* becomes *Fidelity*

The further east they travelled, the more exaggerated were
the tides and the greater the risk of grounding on shifting
sandbanks; on the final approach to Barry, they were guided
by a pilot, then finally towed in by tug. This was no luxury:
the rise and fall of spring tides at Avonmouth, just twenty
miles east up the Severn estuary, can exceed forty-two feet.
Five cables off the Barry lighthouse, in high-water depths of
just thirteen and twenty feet, lay two separate wrecks, both
of which could protrude menacingly above the water at low
tide.

BARRY DOCKS, WALES, AUGUST 1940

Le Rhin BERTHED in Barry docks on 5 August 1940, in the middle of a heatwave. Claude and Madeleine watched from the bridge, and as the tug towed them past the lighthouse into the outer harbour, then eased them through the first set of locks, it was almost as if they'd been spirited to a neutral country, where war was no more than a distant rumour. Candy-coloured windbreaks lined the pale-ivory sand of Whitemore Bay; when they listened hard, they could hear the seagull cries of children, aloft on the warm breeze.

Yet even before the ship's hawsers had been thrown to shore, Claude was starting to feel edgy. Why had *Le Rhin* been sent to this somnolent backwater rather than to a vigorous naval base such as Liverpool or Portsmouth? There was the air of a stage set about the place: the ranks of impeccable red-brick semis that overlooked them as they sat in a rising dock, waiting to enter the docks proper; the far-off line of cranes, awaiting their cue.

The impression of unreality was understandable. Bustling Barry – which just a half-century earlier had barely been a hamlet, with less than fifty inhabitants – was a recent creation. The development of the docks in 1898 to help Cardiff deal with expanding coal exports led to the town becoming Wales' biggest coal port by the eve of the first war. Trade brought tourism, and for the hordes from Cardiff and the valleys, arriving by train, brake and charabanc, a trip to Barry Island had become a jaunt enjoyed by thousands every summer weekend through the 1920s and 1930s: a 'day by the sea' for 'the kids', as one local poet put it, 'And sherbet and bars and paper hats, / And a rattling ride on the Figure Eight; / We'll have tea on the sands and rides on the donkeys, / . . . And we'll all sing together in the Cardiff train / Down to the holiday sea.'

As the ship was towed towards its dock, Claude and Madeleine, standing on deck with Guérisse and Cannebotin, saw a group of uniformed British officers, small as toy soldiers, scrutinizing their approach, hands peaked over their eyes against the glare of the sun across the water.

The moment the gangway touched the quayside, the officers strode aboard. Claude, watching them come, gave a cry of recognition: he knew one of the men, a British intelligence officer he and Madeleine had met in Paris six months earlier. The officer nodded, gripped Claude's hand.

'The explosives?'

Guérisse, recalling the exchange some years later, said that Claude 'let Madeleine answer': a nod in her direction, the hint of a smile.

'They're safe,' she said.

'You've got them?' the officer asked her.

She lowered her head. 'In my cabin, yes.'

A longer silence. 'Your cabin,' the officer repeated thoughtfully, the English accent making his French suddenly wooden, staccato.

Madeleine looked straight at him, eyes alight. 'Under my bunk.'

Claude snorted with laughter. '*C'est vrai*. Madeleine's been sleeping on it.'

FIRST IMPRESSIONS, in the words of one of the English naval officers on that first boarding party, were of 'a filthy ship, no one speaking English, a smell of coal and oil and damp sacking, the deck crowded with all sorts of stuff, barrels and packing cases, a French name on the bow, flying not only the white but also the blue ensign. A beautiful woman, a man with her who was unshaven, jumpy with energy. And the crew: pirates.' Later in the day, a junior officer walked up the gang-plank with orders from his boss, the naval officer in charge of Barry docks: Claude must take down both flags. Claude, speaking as slowly as he could, lest any ambiguity remain, explained that this was impossible: the ensigns were gifts from Admiral Somerville, and were anyway nailed to the mast. If the base commander insisted, he'd have to climb the mast himself and remove them personally. *Le Rhin*, he finished, was now a British ship, with a British crew.

He called his men on deck. From now on, he told them – though he was yet to have any such official confirmation – they were British sailors, and they would need new identities. All of them had been sentenced to death by the French government and it was for their protection that they would no longer be allowed to keep their old names. So, he said, what would you like to be called? 'Nelson,' one man called out. 'Wellington!' shouted another.

Claude named himself Jack Langlais – literally, Jack the Englishman. Madeleine stayed Madeleine, but changed Bayard to Barclay, a choice crewmen attributed to the visible high-street presence of the local bank where Madeleine, consolidating her new nationality, was said to have opened an account. Albert Guérisse chose to become Irish, rather than English: Patrick O'Leary, before long shortened to 'Pat'. 'Wellington' and 'Nelson' were, in the end, vetoed by the British, and in their place came Rogers, Archibald, Ferguson, Lever, Norton, Pearson, Patterson, Thorne, Stone: a roll-call

of sturdy Anglo-Saxons, broken only by 'Doudet', the choice
of Cannebotin, the shared pet name of the ousted captain and
his beloved wife, back home in their spotless apartment on the
Marseilles waterfront.

News of *Le Rhin*'s dishevelled arrival in Barry was
immediately transmitted to London, and Lieutenant Patrick
Whinney was sent by the Admiralty as liaison officer. His
first task was to file an assessment. 'Our initial question,' he
remembered, 'was whether the ship was pro-Nazi. She was
pretty suspect, certainly, and had acquired a reputation in
Gibraltar for being out of control. In those days we didn't take
things for granted, and so I went down to Barry and reported
to the naval officer in charge.'

A French-speaker, Whinney introduced himself to
Claude. 'I was astonished by him. He was full of bombast,
as if he planned to win the war all by himself. His first words
to me were, "I'm very glad to meet you, I'm going to join the
Royal Navy." I remember thinking that this was never going
to happen. He had ideas way above his station.'

Claude had drawn up sketches of how he believed *Le Rhin*
should be converted into a Q-ship, and these he showed to
Whinney, who relayed them to the Admiralty. As Whinney
explored the recesses of the ship, he was struck by the challenges that awaited the mechanics who would carry out the
refit. 'The ship was rapidly going to seed when she arrived.
I'd never seen such a dirty ship: it was like going into a house
in which no repairs had been done for years. *Nothing* was
maintained.'

With Whinney and Barry's other naval officers, Claude
was straightforward. Contemporary notes by the Director
of Naval Intelligence record Claude asking 'that his ship's
company . . . be taken into the Royal Navy, and that *Le Rhin*

be taken over by the Admiralty in order that they should continue the services for which she was destined.' He was, though, often some way short of factual, stressing not only his putative Corsican ancestry but also – to quote secret-service minutes – the persuasive if erroneous detail that 'his father and his grandfather were sailors before him . . . He carries on the traditions of the sea, the tradition of loyalty and courage.' For added gravitas, he gave his year of birth as 1903, making him thirty-seven rather than thirty-two; Madeleine, in her turn, said that she was born in July 1912, not February 1911, and so was now just twenty-eight instead of going on thirty.

Before *Le Rhin* could be cleared for use in the Royal Navy, diplomacy dictated that Admiral Muselier be approached. The Frenchman, now based in London as head of the Free French Navy and fully aware of Claude's anti-French feelings, agreed on one condition. Should he require *Le Rhin*, and provided the Admiralty was kept informed, '*ce navire pourra être mis à ma disposition pour certaines operations*'. This the Admiralty granted, though with the stipulation that the ship 'not pass from Admiralty control'.

CLAUDE AND MADELEINE rented a house on Redbrink Crescent, a long horseshoe of bow-fronted Victorian semis on Barry Island – the biggest of which, atop red sandstone cliffs with a view clear to the Exmoor hills, were home to the dock pilots and their housemaids – and asked O'Leary, Claude's favourite officer and his second-in-command, if he'd like a room. He accepted.

Le Rhin – rechristened HMS *Fidelity* by Claude – was towed into number-one dry dock and the riggers and boiler-men and platelayers of C. H. Bailey (Tyne Engine and Ship Repairing Works) set to work. From their top windows three hundred feet above, Claude and Madeleine could look down on their ship, and beyond that the expanse of the whole crowded dock system: the rows of pylon-giant coal-delivery hoists; the wedge of merchantmen that snugged side by side across nearly the whole expanse of the main dock; the vast central clock tower of the four-storey dock-office building; the light-sabre anti-aircraft spotlights roaming the night sky. Most evenings they heard the sirens: even when the battery was silent, *Fidelity*'s guns spat fire at the distant bombers.

At the tail-end of summer, as dockers began emptying *Fidelity*'s holds into storehouses on the quayside, and Claude opened negotiations to sell his looted sugar, cement, refrigerators and car tyres, the last of the holidaymakers left Whitemore Bay. Away from work on the ship, and the industry of the dock basin, Claude and Madeleine found themselves wondering how to fill their time. Barry Island, their new home, was half a holiday resort, half a sleepy suburban community. They could take the causeway to Barry town, but the attractions of the Barry Dock Hotel – first destination for most disembarking sailors, with its table after table of bored prostitutes – exerted little pull.

As soon as they could get away, they went to London. Over the next four months, there would be many such trips – some on the Cardiff-to-Paddington express, others chauffeured by Whinney in his Riley sports car. Months of lone automobile travel across Eastern Europe and Asia had taught Claude some unusual emergency-maintenance techniques. Heading east one day – Whinney driving, Claude as usual in the passenger seat, Madeleine in the back – they drove into a rainstorm. Whinney tried the wipers. No response. Rain, unhindered, smeared ragged across the windscreen. Claude told Whinney to pull over. 'It's all right,' Whinney remembers Claude promising. 'We are saved.'

Water pouring off his nose, his navy uniform soaked to black, Claude sprang on to the bonnet of the car and unbuttoned his fly. Whinney looked up, astonished, as Claude emptied his bladder across the glass: broad, methodical sweeps that left no section urine-free. Madeleine watched expressionless. When Claude climbed back in, shedding water like a wet Alsatian, still she made no sound.

'But you know what?' Whinney recalled, smiling slowly. 'It worked.'

LONDON AND BARRY DOCKS,
SEPTEMBER TO DECEMBER 1940

AND SO A PATTERN developed: Whinney would drive along the Embankment, past Parliament, and drop Claude and Madeleine at the Admiralty headquarters on Whitehall. Claude, in Whinney's words, 'was very powerfully represented in London: he had entry to a number of places to which I'd never have been able to gain access.' It is uncertain how far his influence extended; unclear, certainly, whether Claude's straight-faced and frequent 'I must go and see Monsieur Churchill' can be read as fact; but from the start there is documentary proof that Claude – his route eased by the intervention of Admiral Somerville – was in continual, personal contact with the head of naval intelligence, his deputy, Captain Frank Slocum, and other senior naval figures.

Claude and Madeleine took rooms at the Piccadilly Hotel, on the corner of Regent Street and Piccadilly, a five-minute walk from the Royal Academy to the west, and the Lyric, Apollo, Globe and the other theatres of Shaftesbury Avenue to the east. The Norman Shaw-designed Piccadilly – one of the 'most aristocratic and expensive hostelries in London', according to Baedeker, 'convenient for those who wish to be near Mayfair, the parks, and the most fashionable shops' – was only marginally less costly than the Ritz, with suites costing upwards of sixty-three shillings. Like the handful of others in its class – the Carlton, Claridge's, the Berkeley and Grosvenor

The oriental-themed Piccadilly Hotel, Claude and Madeleine's
favoured London base

House – it was also a favourite dancing spot, boasting its own
orchestra and nightly cabaret.

They ate often in Soho, particularly at L'Escargot, then the
unofficial London rendezvous for French resistance fighters.
Here, over one long evening, Claude consented to have his
portrait painted, and the picture survives today in his sister-in-
law's *voile*-darkened Dijon apartment: a rough oil, on a square
of plyboard the size of a large hardback, showing Claude in
the uniform of a Royal Navy commander, head cocked back,
his face rounder and more boyish than in reality, brass buttons
agleam.

Other nights were not so peaceful; as often as Madeleine
had the company of a garrulous, charismatic Claude – buying

round after round, physically affectionate, a generous racon-
teur – so she had to suffer the constant possibility of eruption.
One such night, they took a table in a French restaurant –
on the face of it a strange choice, given their hostility to
France. Dinner, though, began quietly. They ordered, began
their starters, and then the *patron*, on being told the identity
of his two new customers, hurried over to introduce himself.

'You're French, yes?' Claude said, standing. 'FRENCH?'

On surrounding tables, all conversation ceased. The *patron*
nodded, and went on to explain, his voice quavering, that
he'd sold his restaurant in Paris in the early spring and transferred his capital to London.

Claude leapt at him. He grabbed him by the lapels of his
jacket. 'Traitor!' Then he unleashed a hammer punch of such
ferocity that the man was knocked off his feet. Claude followed his fall, and amid screaming waiters – and oblivious to
Madeleine's cries for calm – the two men wrestled and clawed
at each other until O'Leary, nervous for their collective future,
managed to pull Claude clear and force him – still screaming
obscenities – into the street.

MOST NIGHTS these same streets were an eerie mix of silent
blackness – just the occasional purr-past of a Humber or
Bentley, their headlights obscured by Dymlite shields – and an
emergency carnival of yowling-wolf sirens and firemen hosing
bomb blazes from the top of fifty-foot revolving ladders.
There were eight-foot sandbag walls in the windows of the
Dorchester on Park Lane, and accordion concerts to Blitz
refugees on the platform of Aldwych Underground station.

On 24 August, four days after Churchill spoke of the
fortitude and service of Britain's fighter pilots – 'Never in
the field of human conflict was so much owed by so many to

so few' – London received its first daytime bombing raid. The end of the first week of September brought the Blitz in earnest: the demolition of much of Thamesside; three hundred killed and four times that number injured. On 17 September, a week after Buckingham Palace was hit, Churchill announced that British air-raid casualties in the first half of September had been two thousand dead and eight thousand injured, four-fifths of them in the capital.

In London, witnessing the destruction wrought by German bombing – the trio of pinafored nurses standing at an open first-storey hospital doorway, at their feet gaping space where once an emergency ward had stood with all its beds and transfusion machines – Claude and Madeleine became increasingly impatient to enter active combat. Yet they did not let the sight of German bombers reduce them to impotence. 'After some of the worst bombing,' a wife of one of Claude's crewmen later recollected, Claude and Madeleine 'went down to the East End of London, and gave away blankets and food from a lorry he had taken down there. [Claude] was a brigand perhaps, but with a lot of good points.'

At the Admiralty, their diligence was paying off. Whinney saw Claude's 'frequent expeditions to the Admiralty in London' as a means to satisfy a 'voracious appetite for more and more armament'. This ambition, Whinney later recalled, had to be kept carefully in check. 'Only shortly was it borne in on him that, unlike land fortifications, a ship was of a certain unexpandable size and that the maximum size of a gun was strictly limited by what the hull and superstructure, heavily reinforced though they were, would stand.'

Ironic distance notwithstanding, Whinney was growing fond of both Claude – whose 'volatile fire and glowering jealousy' seemed entirely in keeping with the Corsican ancestry of which Claude had boasted – and Madeleine, who struck him as 'very feminine, a natural blonde, of slight but strong build, large blue eyes, and a nose slightly crooked . . . [who was] every bit as tough as [Claude]'. What impressed him most of all, though, were Claude's powers of persuasion. 'He succeeded in getting an incredible amount of favours; his level of success was extraordinary.'

At such moments, striding down the steps of the Admiralty, Claude would shout out in first-grade, verb-confused English, 'I am one/two/three machineguns!' And, one unforgettable afternoon, 'I am Royal Navee!' Finally, he'd become the full Englishman: Jack Langlais, Lieutenant Commander RN.

FOCUSED ON his own career development, on high-level negotiations over *Fidelity*'s equipment and on spending long nights of jazz at the Café Royal with Madeleine, Claude had begun neglecting the day-to-day management of his ship. Returning from London to Barry mid-autumn, he was confronted by despondent men: ever since he and Madeleine had left two weeks before, there had been continual pilfering from the holds. Though this was common practice in Barry – it's not hard to find former dockhands even today who remember how they used to shake Lucky Strikes from their multipack boxes and stow the cartons under their shirts, or recall the dock policeman who mercilessly searched every docker who passed his post, confiscated the contraband and whose lodgings were subsequently raided to reveal hundreds of pounds' worth of sugar, whisky and tobacco – it also threatened to derail Claude's campaign to rebuild and arm *Fidelity*, for the promises of weapons he'd secured from the Admiralty were contingent, in part, upon the sale of the ship's cargo.

Claude instructed his men to be vigilant and then – in a characteristically unpredictable gesture – handed every one of the ship's refitters a bicycle; to the foremen he gave motorbikes. Madeleine, following his cue, went through the cargo and discovered cases of lingerie, which she distributed among the married workers: 'For your wives,' she told them in English, softening each man with a smile, then a kiss on the cheek.

Whinney, looking back on this sudden flurry of generosity, said that Claude went on to present him with 'bolts of grey flannel cloth with which my wife made clothes for our children, as well as some six or eight Arabic sugar cones'. To the 'parents of Barry', Claude gave 'hundreds of pairs of children's shoes so badly needed and in such short supply at that time. Admittedly he had not paid for them in the first place but he could have made more display had he wished by a more public presentation to, say, the Lord Mayor of Cardiff. He chose the more direct approach.'

Driving Claude's spontaneous largesse was the belief that, as he would later put it in a letter to the Admiralty, 'the captured goods belong to me personally and I therefore consider that I may dispose of them as I see fit'. Thefts from *Fidelity* – 'his' ship – were a personal matter: to observers such as Whinney, the way he pursued the culprits, and the nature and severity of the punishments he imposed, showed how intimately aggrieved Claude felt.

On his return from London, Claude focused his attention on the dry-dock foreman, under whose watch the stealing was carrying on. The two men, Whinney recalled, 'were soon at loggerheads, with a resulting slow-down in work on board as the foreman turned an obvious blind eye to the increasing depredation of the cargo, until the point was reached when

[Claude] gave formal notification that the next dockyard matey found stealing on board would be prosecuted in the civil courts'. Claude ordered a permanent watch at the head of the gangway: a sentry, with fixed bayonet and instructions to arrest anyone suspicious. For a few days, the cargo was left alone, and attention turned back to the work underway: the construction of the depth-charge platform, the floatplane hoists and fore and aft gun emplacements, the sunken bath that Claude had ordered for his cabin.

Within a week, though, the inevitable had come to pass: one of the older riggers, hunched over and shuffling, was stopped by the sentry. Inside his jacket were two five-pound

Claude Péri becomes Jack Langlais,
Lieutenant Commander RN

cones of sugar. Claude called the police; the dockhand was charged, then released on bail. When the foreman tried to remonstrate on his man's behalf, Claude cut him short: 'I gave warning,' he snapped, 'let justice be done.'

The day before the court hearing, though, the accused man appeared on the dockside asking to see 'the captain'. Claude agreed, but rather than hear him out in private, he conducted the interview on deck. He was giving a performance, his audience a group of platelayers and riggers, Whinney, a few crew-members and Madeleine. The thief began to plead for clemency; Claude watched him 'silent and scornful', according to Whinney. When the man started weeping, Claude spoke. He talked quietly – 'always a danger signal', in Whinney's assessment – and with logic and menace, his voice a low growl, began a systematic demolition of the thief's character, the morals of his parents, the sexual availability of his wife and children. He finished, stood with hands on hips. On board, normally a ruckus of shouting and the boomy echo of below-decks activity, the only sound was the soft fizz of drizzle on the deck and the choked sobs of the guilty man. Claude let the silence rest a while longer then – aware that the men, who'd earlier been exchanging accounts of his recent fight in Soho, would now be anticipating a physical assault – gave the warning most likely to be heeded. Next time anyone was caught thieving, he growled, they'd be sent first to him. Only when he was done would the police be called. When he turned for his cabin, his metal heelcaps sounded loud as rivet hammers on the new steel deck-plates.

THAT EVENING, Claude and Madeleine picked up the foreman in a taxi at the end of the working day and took him into the blacked-out centre of town. In the Barry Dock Hotel they bought him beer after beer, and Claude – in a final attempt to secure acquiescence from the dockhands – told the foreman the whole story. He explained who they were, what they'd done and the events that had brought them to Britain. He gave no names, but conceded just enough to assure him of the seniority of his Admiralty connections. He went on to detail his plans for the cargo. It was, he told the by now docile but attentive foreman, his 'present to the Empire', and he hoped it would provide enough money to pay for two new Spitfires.

British-government documents detailing Claude's nego-tiations with the Admiralty survive, and provide evidence of the finesse with which he exercised leverage over different departments of the War Office. Touring Whitehall with an interpreter at the beginning of October 1940, Claude secured an interview with Marshal Sir John Salmond RAF, and told him of his plans. Salmond heard him out and passed him on to one of his deputies. During this meeting, Claude made three stipulations: 'that in no circumstances shall any of the money go to General de Gaulle; that the proceeds, less £1,000, should be devoted to the purchase of Spitfires; and that the £1,000 should be distributed among his crew of forty Frenchmen who, like himself, appear to have recently acquired British nationality and who, for many weeks, [have] received no payment at all.'

By the end of the month, the Admiralty had declared *Fidelity*'s cargo to be 'prize' – legitimate war spoils, to be dealt with as it wished – and began the sell-off. The proceeds, in line with Claude's request, would pay for the production of one, possibly two Spitfires; £1,000 would go to Claude. Reaching this decision had been far from straightforward. Government documents show that Claude's cargo – described as having been 'collected' in Marseilles – was the source of temptation as well as conflict. In no doubt as to the desirability of the goods, those officials present at a late October meeting in the Procurator-General's office were in disagreement as to the best way to secure their possession. Three courses were suggested: '1. To treat them as a free gift; 2. To seize them in prize; 3. To requisition them.' The first was rejected: 'it appeared desirable to give the transaction some legal colour'. The choice of number two was an opportunistic gamble: the Procurator-General 'stated he thought it was very unlikely the goods would be condemned if they were placed in prize. Furthermore, the Judge might require evidence to be produced as to where the goods came from, etc. and it would be undesirable to have to produce such evidence.'

Trucks began arriving at the Barry quayside within the week and Claude and Madeleine watched as three hundred tons of sugar, two hundred and thirty tons of rice, ten tons of coffee and the same weight of haricot beans were driven away in Ministry of Food wagons. The rest – cement, paper, hospital stores, 'art silk', duckboards, inner tubes, clips for rubber hoses, socks, pig iron, linen, curtains, six thousand pairs of brown and black military boots, jute sacking and scrubbing brushes – was transferred into warehouses on the dockside and disappeared more gradually, whenever the Admiralty found buyers. By Christmas the bulk was gone, leaving behind an eccentric miscellany: toy irons, automobile springs, five cases of Sirop de Dr Marceau laxative, four hundred and eighty-five walking sticks, electric stoves and seventeen bales of corks.

Sales so far had realized more than £8,700; on Christmas Eve, Claude and Madeleine stood in the bar of the Piccadilly Hotel, a bottle of Dom Perignon open on the counter, delightedly reading and re-reading a rectangular piece of embossed paper, its copperplate swirl promising to pay 'Lieutenant Commander J Langlais the sum of one thousand pounds only'.

FOUR MONTHS into their time in Britain, their English was improving rapidly: no longer were Claude and Madeleine reliant upon French-speakers to act as translators. They were English – Jack Langlais and Madeleine Barclay – and any Frenchman who dared to suggest otherwise was briskly dismissed. Félix Gonneville, a Free French naval officer stationed in Cardiff, recalled an initial reception on board *Fidelity* that was 'more than cold! Péri believed that his ship was British, that every single Frenchman was responsible for the defeat, that those in London *"n'étaient que de beaux parleurs"*': smooth talkers. Yet by the end of the meeting, Claude's early anger had burned away to reveal embers of softness, geniality, hospitality: 'He finished by offering us aperitifs!'

Englishness, for Claude – if not for Madeleine, who had not only preserved her first name but also much of her wardrobe – was developing into a matter of obsessional concern, and sometime before Christmas, according to a story that circulated among the crew, he attempted bodily to erase his nationality. He found a doctor in Cardiff who agreed to perform a blood transfusion: the full eight pints, turning Claude into a full-blooded Englishman.

GREENWICH, JANUARY 1941

IN THE NEW YEAR OF 1941, for the first time in many months, Madeleine was separated from Claude and cast adrift in London. She found something reassuring about the pale domes and colonnades of the Royal Naval College, Greenwich – here was the baroque of the east facade of the Louvre, a stability and symmetry that spoke to her of a wider Europe, and of her home. She arrived at Greenwich alone, a scarf tight around her neck, heavy overcoat, flat-soled shoes. It was the second week of January, and snow lay on the ground. In Greenwich Park, the pond was frozen over, the trees black against the sky.

Madeleine's arrival among Christopher Wren's crystal-grassed courtyards was the result of several weeks of troubled Admiralty thinking. Royal Navy regulations stipulated that women – whatever their social status or professional background – were not permitted to serve on fighting ships in wartime, but Claude had made his position unequivocal: without Madeleine, neither he nor his ship would fight for Britain. The fact that the British treated this demand so seriously indicates just how significant an asset they felt *Fidelity* would be to the fleet, as secret-service documents show: 'If the ship had not become part of the Royal Navy, she would have been lost altogether to the Allied cause.'

For Madeleine to become crew, however, she needed a workable cover, and so it was that she was ordered to Greenwich, in South London, to enrol on the officers' training course for the Women's Royal Naval Service. Should *Fidelity* be captured, she would, as a Wren, end up as a prisoner of war; in plain clothes, however, she would be taken for a suspected spy, which would mean facing execution. Her inclusion on the course was sanctioned at the highest level – 'on instructions from the First Sea Lord', according to Sybil, Lady Cholmondeley, who had founded the WRNS in 1916 and now, in early 1941, was its superintendent and daily adviser to director Vera Laughton Mathews.

Billeted on to a compressed month-long version of the usual eight-week course, Madeleine proved herself easily to be Claude's equal as self-mythologizer. Beryl Blackaby, WRNS wartime appointments officer, was given access to Madeleine's Wren file for the service's Roll of Honour. 'The records,' she recalled, 'show the following: Madeleine Barclay lived with her husband in northern France until the German invasion. There is no record in her file of what happened to her husband, but she took their very large yacht with a crew of six and sailed across the Channel to either Portsmouth or Weymouth . . . where she handed over the yacht to the Royal Navy. Her only condition was that she should be captain . . . The yacht was then used to ferry agents to France. On one voyage an E-boat (the German equivalent of our motor torpedo-boats) caught and torpedoed her. According to Admiralty records it is believed that all hands were lost. Her file ends, "It is hoped that she drowned, otherwise she was handed over to the Gestapo." '

This account, though fictional, was a credible-enough confection, and may well have been devised with approval from the Secret Intelligence Service, to which Claude and Madeleine had now been assigned. Her real identity – former French agent, explosives expert, markswoman – had to remain a secret; and so to tutors and fellow trainees at Greenwich she posed as the heroic widow – a homely, almost conventional figure, and one with whom the largely domestic intake of officer trainees – many of whom, as Mathews would write in her memoirs, 'had never done anything worth speaking about in their entire lives before' – could easily identify.

Madeleine merits no mention in Mathews' memoirs, but *Blue Tapestry* was published in 1948, when any hint of undercover work would never have passed the censors. Her presence at Greenwich, however, was a break with the rules. Conditions of Entry leaflets – 'Join the WRENS and free a man to join the FLEET' – insisted that a woman could only apply if she was 'a British subject and the daughter of British subjects, or of parents who were naturalised British subjects at the time of their birth'; any exceptions needed 'special approval from the Admiralty'. Wren officers had to meet a host of other criteria and would never, stated Mathews in an internal memo, have included women who were 'totally inexperienced in naval work and customs who had not been under any observation for suitability'.

Before being accepted on to the training course, candidates were assessed on four fronts: General Conduct ('of temperate habit YES or NO (delete as requisite)'); Character ('power of command or leadership, zeal and energy, judgment, reliability, initiative'); Social Qualities ('speech, appearance, manners, facility in games and sports'); and Physical Qualities ('General remarks on physique, health, bearing, etc., to give indication of whether likely to be suitable for strain of responsibility').

Had she been assessed by these standards, Madeleine would never have made the grade. Among the crew, there was the impression – never denied by Madeleine – that she was 'consumptive', or suffered from a 'fatal lung condition'. How much this was part of retrospective mythmaking is unclear but, approaching the Wren selection board as an ordinary candidate, it is likely that she would not have scored highly on Physical Qualities. Among the intake of January 1941, she was, from the start, markedly different. Mathews, who personally approved the selection of every trainee officer, later assessed that there were two categories of women who failed to make the grade: 'intellectual' women 'who lacked ordinary common sense', and 'motherly' types 'without any of the brains necessary to compete with what was really a technical and complicated job'.

Neither ordinary, motherly nor even particularly technical – and, moreover, a lone French woman, secretive and rootless and pining for her lover – Madeleine gave little indication that she was willing to be approached, or that she was open to friendship. At lectures she sat apart; during rest periods she walked the grounds or strode the Thames, the river alive with the shouts of pilots on the sailing barges, cargo planes coming into land, and the grind of tugs working out of the munitions factories on the northern shore.

There was much about everyday life at Greenwich that Madeleine found foreign. Never previously a churchgoer, she was now required to attend a daily morning service in the college chapel: a single prayer, a reading, a hymn sung to the accompaniment of the eighteenth-century organ. Breakfast, lunch and supper were taken in what one trainee described as 'the breathtaking beauty of [the] shadowy grandeur' of the Painted Hall, with its floodlit ceiling frescoes of cherubs cavorting in a heavenly cloudscape and rows of straight-backed leather-covered chairs and table candles under pale-vellum lampshades. 'Many a one,' wrote Mathews, 'has held her breath at the sight of those vast and perfect proportions

Wren officers dining in the Painted Hall, Royal Naval College,
Greenwich

... The beauty was awe-inspiring and one watched in whispers, but with head held high for here was the very essence of England.'

Anglocentricity, too, was at the core of the curriculum, whether it was Maritime Museum director Sir Geoffrey Callender's lectures on naval history, Captain John Grant's series on the Admiralty, or Admiral Sir William Goodenough's teachings on leadership. Lunch offered a break from the classroom, after which came forty-five minutes of squad drill, a skill for which Madeleine had never previously had much call and which she was unlikely to pursue ever again. Yet interspersed with the near-religious adherence to naval minutiae was a broader view of England, and one that awoke something vital in Madeleine, reigniting her sense of fun and humour. Lectures on the history of art spoke to a buried sense of aesthetics and form; access to the gramophone library allowed her, for the first time in years, to lose herself in Mozart, Chopin, Debussy, Fauré. She learned Scottish dancing and was even persuaded – her initial froideur now long gone – to partner up for squash and table tennis. Bedding down at night on mattresses in the cellar while overhead came the muffled boom of the city's defences and the mourning keen of the air-raid sirens, she found herself relaxing into the pleasures of female companionship; she allowed herself to be vulnerable, to trust a little more.

BARRY DOCKS, JANUARY 1941

BACK IN BARRY, Claude was busy recruiting. *Fidelity*, nearing the end of its refit, was now an SOE vessel, under the overall control of Captain Frank Slocum, Deputy Director Operations Division (Intelligence), and plans for its future were nearing completion. For this, the right crew was essential, and Claude had spent the early weeks of the New Year winnowing out those men who were not prepared to face perilous undercover work. The original complement, in Whinney's words, lacked a defining drive: 'Some had volunteered from impulse, perhaps to escape the Germans, some certainly to escape imprisonment by their own authorities, whilst others sought some kind of adventure, they knew not what; on the other hand there were those who had a genuine desire to continue the fight. By the time [Claude] had sifted through the lot the ones who survived his questioning knew they were there to kill Germans.'

The 'sifting' process, though, had left *Fidelity* short of hands, and so Claude told Slocum to put the word out for suitable mavericks. Slocum – keen as Claude to get *Fidelity* under sail – responded swiftly. Unlike the Secret Intelligence Service, the SOE – still in embryonic form at the start of 1941 – had no aircraft at its disposal: as late as March 1941, Brigadier Colin Gubbins, SOE Director of Operations and Training, was bemoaning the fact that agents then in training 'may well have to be landed by sea as no other means exist'. *Fidelity* – earmarked for Mediterranean spy drops and the rescue of escaped prisoners of war – was to be part of this fleet.

The first batch of SOE-vetted volunteers arrived in Barry on 17 January, among them Auguste Roulland, a twenty-three-year-old able seaman whose original posting, a French warship, had been holed up in Portsmouth since the outbreak of war. Given the choice of a British posting or returning to France, Roulland – shortish, muscular, quick as a fox – opted for the Royal Navy. 'They gave us twenty minutes to think about it,' he remembered. 'I like adventure; it didn't take me that long to decide.'

In the cauldron of rumour that was Portsmouth at the time, Roulland heard whisper of SOE's plans to land spies on the coast of France. Again, he put his name forward, this time to the naval-barracks commander. Two days later, he was blindfolded, bundled into a jeep and, forty minutes later, found himself in a staff room, surrounded by British officers. Not long afterwards – having been informed that he had been earmarked for 'dangerous missions' – he was shouldering his kitbag down the platform at Barry station.

Claude, he recalled, was waiting by the ship, and spoke to the new recruits in French. He issued his now-familiar warning: 'We are heading into certain danger, and there will be some of us who will not come back alive. If any of you wish to leave, now is your chance.'

LONDON TO LIVERPOOL,
FEBRUARY TO MARCH 1941

MADELEINE, HER Wren training over, was reunited with Claude in the Piccadilly Hotel at the beginning of February and together they disappeared from view for a few days. There was an urgency to their hours together, which was accentuated by Claude's penchant for sonorous, fatalistic talk. To Madeleine, and among his officers, he'd begun predicting a violent collective end, a prophecy often delivered with a euphoric gleam. Madeleine's response was to retreat into contemplation, often books: novels, mostly, and SOE sabotage handbooks.

Their wish for seclusion was only partly successful. On one occasion, with Madeleine elsewhere, Claude answered a rap on the door of their hotel room to find a British naval officer in the corridor outside. At his side were two briefcases.

Commander John Langley later recalled that Claude 'regarded me suspiciously'. Langley, who worked for the Secret Intelligence Service, had arrived with 'a small stock of our sabotage weapons together with fifty pounds of plastic explosive'.

'*Entrez, mon Capitaine, vous avez quelquechose pour moi?*' Claude asked him.

Langley, again in French, explained that he'd been sent by Slocum. Claude 'carefully closed the door and locked it . . . Within a quarter of an hour we were the best of friends; within another half-hour we had both made serious inroads into the bottle of wine he produced.'

At this point, Langley still had no idea of Claude's identity: all he'd been given was a room number, and a description: crewcut, beard, less-than-average height, broad shoulders, a handshake to turn knuckles to dust. Now, though, Claude turned to him with a grin.

'You said your name was Commander John Langley?'

'*Oui, mon Capitaine.*'

'Well then, I've been intending for a while now to change my name. Would it be all right with you if I called myself Jean Langlois [sic]?'

'I would be honoured,' Langley replied, 'to have a colleague whose name so closely resembled mine.'

HANDLED WITH CARE, as if they themselves were packages of explosives, Claude and Madeleine had finally been passed from the French secret service into the heart of British intelligence. It was the early spring of 1941, and – while still nominally under the wing of the Admiralty – they were now working for Section D of the Secret Intelligence Service.

Section D – for 'destruction' – was the first specialist dirty-tricks department of the British secret service, founded in March 1938 with the aim 'of attacking potential enemies by means other than the operations of military force'. Its London staff numbered Guy Burgess and, a few weeks after Claude and Madeleine had joined, Kim Philby. From the start, and from the top down, it was a mysterious and glamorous organization, prone to devising over-optimistic schemes: destroying the entire Romanian oilfield system; blocking the Danube by blowing up the narrow Iron Gates gorge; sabotaging Swedish iron-ore exports to Germany.

At its head was Major Laurence Grand, a totemic figure who not only wore the requisite black moustache but also carried an ever-present scarlet carnation in his buttonhole. 'Tall and thin,' wrote Philby, 'he looked startlingly like the dream-figure who should have approached me in Germany [where Philby had worked as a correspondent for *The Times*]. The difference was that his mind was certainly not clipped. It ranged free and handsome over the whole field of his awesome responsibilities, never shrinking from an idea, however big or wild.'

Expanding fast, Section D had moved in late 1939 into offices over St Ermine's Hotel, next to Caxton Hall in Westminster. This became the hub of the organization, from where officers such as Bickham Sweet-Escott – whose interviewer had warned him darkly that, 'for security reasons I can't tell you what sort of job it would be. All I can say is that if you join us, you mustn't be afraid of forgery, and you mustn't be afraid of murder' – oversaw the training of agents, the supply of their sabotage gear and planning and execution of operations. The fourth floor of the building housed a storeroom full of explosives which were dispatched by courier to agents overseas.

Central to the sabotage work that Section D carried out was plastic explosive, an invention of the Royal Arsenal at Woolwich. It was a device that – as Claude had already demonstrated with his destruction of the *Corrientes*, and Madeleine with her seemingly cavalier transportation methods – possessed one irresistible advantage over traditional explosives such as dynamite or gelignite: it could be cut, shaped, stored and moved about without any fear of sudden disaster. Effective use, however, required reliable and portable fuses and detonators, and it was in the development of these that Claude's new drinking companion John Langley had been employed for the past twelve months.

With the help of a professor of chemistry from the University of London, Langley 'evolved a little time fuse about the size of a pencil. It could set off incendiary bombs or high explosives. For its time delay it depended upon a corrosive solution eating through a fine steel wire.' Its action was simple; when the agent pressed a ridge on the pencil, acid was released that ate through a wire attached to a detonator at a rate that could be carefully preset, thus allowing the agent time to reach cover; it would prove so reliable that, by the end of the war, twelve million had been produced. The pencil fuse was also cheap, Langley chirruped: 'All you needed, except for a little ampoule of corrosive liquid, could be bought at the local ironmongers or hardware store. Any chemist capable of doing a little glass-blowing could produce the ampoule.'

IT WAS NOT UNTIL early spring, with *Fidelity* finally ready to leave dry dock, that Langley first met Madeleine. She and Pat O'Leary had been sent by SIS to Brickendonbury Hall, near Hertford, to study sabotage. Once again, Madeleine found herself in an almost all-male preserve.

Brickendonbury Hall was an ivy-clad Victorian mansion and the inspiration of Guy Burgess. Philby, who was commissioned by Burgess to lay out the first template, recalled that Burgess' original proposal had been for 'the establishment of a school for training agents in the techniques of underground work. It was an astonishing proposal, not because it was made, but because it had not been made before . . . He suggested that such a college should be named the "Guy Fawkes College" to commemorate an unsuccessful conspirator "who had been foiled by the vigilance of the Elizabethan SIS". It was a neat touch.'

In the end, though, a less poetic euphemism was chosen –

the Inter-Service Experimental Department – and, almost as soon as its first intake of students had arrived, with Philby lined up to teach basic espionage tradecraft and Langley to instruct on the techniques required to derail a train with a plum-sized gobbet of plastic explosive, Section D of SIS was absorbed by the new Special Operations Executive; and, once again, Claude and Madeleine found themselves in the hands of new employers.

The syllabus at Brickendonbury Hall, however, remained unchanged, and Madeleine and O'Leary learned unarmed combat, industrial sabotage and explosives concealment. It was highly specialized training – instruction, as one SOE agent later put it, in 'the use of very small quantities of explosive to destroy very important parts of machines, the kind of parts of machines which were irreplaceable' – but was not without its lighter moments. Another recruit remembered reporting 'first thing in the morning . . . There was a sergeant standing on a great big mattress there and he said, "I want you to run at me and knock me over", and we thought this a bit funny. He said, "Come on. Don't hang about." So I went at him and the next moment I was flying over his head.' Sweet-Escott's view was almost cartoonish: 'Among its instructors were Captains Fairbairn and Sykes, two ex-officers of the Shanghai Police, whose subject was Silent Killing. Sykes had many methods to impart. They were all long, complicated and hard to remember, but each of them ended with the phrase: "and then kick him in the testicles".'

The number of agents who underwent training at Brickendonbury during its first year was 'few', according to Philby: 'two small groups of Belgians and Norwegians, and a somewhat larger group of Spaniards', none of whom he mentions by name. Madeleine relished her time here, and the handbooks with which she was issued were seldom far from her side: at quiet moments on board *Fidelity* she was often spotted reading through instructions for devices that now seem almost comically James Bond-ish: incendiary cigarettes, exploding coal, edible paper, explosives hidden inside logs, time bombs secreted in bottles of Chianti.

The tutors, too, were an outlandish miscellany: Philby's subordinates included 'jolly George Hill [a former British agent in Russia after the 1917 revolution] . . . one of the few living Englishmen who had actually put sand in axle-boxes. Immensely paunchy, he looked rather like Soglow's king with a bald pate instead of a crown . . . Then there was an explosives expert named Clark, with a rumbustious sense of humour. Asked to arrange a demonstration for the Czech Director of Military Intelligence and his staff, he planted booby-traps in a copse through which they had to walk to his training ground. He had assumed that they would go through the wood in Indian file like ducks. Instead, they walked abreast, and the officers at each end of the line suffered nasty shocks. It was a fluke that no one was hurt.' As a security measure, all Philby's tutors were known by aliases notable for their easy poetry: 'Hill', thus, became 'Dale'.

From Brickendonbury, Madeleine and O'Leary – with Claude impatient to leave on *Fidelity*'s first mission – were posted a few miles north to Aston House, on the outskirts of Stevenage, for their final section of sabotage training. All they'd been told so far was that they'd probably be operating inside occupied France, that their work would involve the 'disruption' of German lines of communication: there were no specifics, no dates.

Aston House was, like Brickendonbury, a striking English country house. Since November 1939, it had also been home

'Station XII' – Aston House, near Stevenage, England – where
Madeleine and Pat O'Leary trained in sabotage

to Langley's research-and-development arm of Section D of
the Secret Intelligence Service and, true to form, was given a
laboured and unmemorable cover-name, Signals Development
Branch Depot No. 4, War Office. When SOE swallowed Section D, Aston House gained a further appellation – Station XII
– by which time it was also home to Langley, seven officers,
two laboratory technicians and a small posse of explosives
experts.

After the more theoretical, classroom-based instruction
at Brickendonbury – and the concentration on different sabotage techniques – the training that Madeleine and O'Leary
received at Aston House focused on the use of specific explosives, in particular PE3, or plastic explosive. As officers, they
were billeted in the mansion, unlike many of the staff, who had
been assigned rooms in the village. The house itself – bearded

with ivy, Nissen-hut laboratories protruding like ungainly limbs – sat amid a full forty-six acres of land. Though reduced to bare functionality, stripped of its paintings and books, it was clear that this had been a Queen Anne house of distinction, with an octagonal library at the heart of the ground floor and a big shuttered bay window looking out over lawns that had once been smooth as moss but were now speckled with wiry daisies. To the west of the house were the 'pleasure grounds': storage huts for the explosives and a disused chalk quarry, where much of the testing was carried out.

Madeleine's arrival at Station XII was an occasion of note: 'so few women' were sent there for training, Langley later wrote, that she was scrutinized and gossiped over by all the men. Meeting her on board *Fidelity* a year later, he recognized her immediately. Langley did not record how long she and O'Leary stayed but, with *Fidelity* waiting, it was unlikely to have been longer than a week or two.

Madeleine's training focused on the use of plastic explosive – referred to by Langley as 'cyclonite', by others as 'PE'. Most days were spent in the quarry in plain clothes, rigging charges under rail tracks and blowing the rear axles off decommissioned armoured cars. Writing later, Langley drew a picture of an endless succession of dangerous, pleasingly Boy-Scoutish experiments: 'We soon knew exactly how much was needed to derail a train, to blow a sizeable hole in the side of a ship, to detonate an ammunition dump, to destroy a large electrical sub-station, to shatter the tracks of a tank, in brief to do a great deal of damage behind the enemy lines with not much more than what looked like half a pound of butter and a tiny pencil time-fuse.'

Weapons developed at Aston House were trucked to Brickendonbury for testing. Of the two establishments, Aston

House was the more secretive – visitors were only allowed to see the quarry, never the workshops, and on such occasions, Langley recalled, 'those of us who had to be present went in old civilian clothes, always wore sunglasses and were introduced by fictitious names'. Even a trip to the village pub in Aston was an opportunity for Langley's men to further disguise their true identity. 'The local villagers were naturally more than curious about what was going on in the old aristocratic home. To satisfy this we would arrange for one of our men to drift occasionally into the ... pub where, after everyone had had a few pints of mild and bitter, he would let out – very confidentially, of course – that we were experimenting with special aircraft flares, special rockets for the Navy and special starshell fillings for the Army. "But don't whisper a word about it to anybody ... We don't want any German bombs dropped round here, [and] nor do you ... " '

The pioneering nature of the work at Station XII meant that Langley and his men were often visited by senior figures in the government – Alfred Duff Cooper, the Minister of Information; Clement Attlee, the Deputy Prime Minister – and they endeavoured to impress. One autumn, an unnamed cabinet minister – 'small', in Langley's assessment, with 'a pinched look and a bad cold' – called by for a demonstration. Langley led the minister into the quarry. It was a low grey morning, with light drizzle: 'in the humid half-light the old abandoned quarry took on a sinister appearance'. A length of railway track was visible, wet steel glistening. In other spots at the bottom of the quarry were a group of forty-gallon oil drums, a heap of lumber, a decommissioned military truck. 'The minister looked far from cheerful as he shook raindrops from the brim of his hat. "Go ahead," he growled. My Chief blew a short blast on a whistle.'

A man leading a dog walked down into the quarry. Passing the oil drums, the animal lifted its leg, forcing the man to wait. An 'untidy-looking' woman followed, carrying an umbrella and a shopping bag. When she reached the logs, she stopped, cupped her hands and lit a cigarette, before tossing away the empty packet and – like the first man – walking on. Finally, a man dressed in farm worker's overalls cycled into the quarry. As he neared the far side, potatoes spilled from his basket. He got off his bike, collected the potatoes and rode on.

A second later, 'there was a slight hissing sound and the pile of lumber burst into flames; next a slight report accompanied by a spurt of flame and streams of burning oil began running from an oil drum.' Langley's 'Chief' checked his watch: 'A minute to go.' They stood in silence, waiting until – like the finale of a firework display – there was a white-lightning flash and a crack of startling volume as half a pound of plastic explosive tore a two-foot section in one of the rail tracks. The spectators were silent.

Langley's 'Chief' turned to the minister. 'Military vehicles are also easy targets.' He pointed to the truck. 'Would you care to see us deal with this one, sir?'

The minister gave a small shiver. 'I have seen quite enough, thank you.'

Waiting for Madeleine and O'Leary to return, Claude's temper worsened. Arriving one day to inspect work on his new bathroom – which included, according to one of the dockyard workers, 'a fully tiled sunken bath' – his eye was drawn to the rimless mirror, hung in a position he found disagreeable. He picked up a hammer, smashed the mirror and strode out.

Most days, he sat alone in his cabin, where he'd now hung

a portrait of the young Napoleon, a man to whom, according to Claude's boss Captain Frank Slocum, Claude 'bore a striking facial resemblance'. The ship was ready, and *Fidelity's* liaison officer Lieutenant Patrick Whinney was preparing to sail with the crew to Milford Haven, where he had orders to hand over to Lieutenant Commander Jasper Milner-Gibson, who like Whinney was a fluent French speaker. 'Work on the ship was now finished,' Whinney recalled. 'The twenty-pounders were shipped and fitted, the big steel concealing flaps could be made to fall away with a resounding clang in two seconds, the machine guns and depth charges were well-disguised, and now came the moment for the ship to sail north to begin working-up exercises.' The impression was of a vessel wholly changed: as another crew member put it, 'She'd been transformed into a *bâteau piège* – a trap ship – equipped with two-hundred-millimetre cannons placed symmetrically on the foredeck, as well as skilfully camouflaged flap-down panels, and a large number of externally invisible anti-aircraft guns. There were also huge panels of differing sizes, on runners or swivels, which encircled the superstructure and could be used at will to alter the appearance.'

A great deal of money had been spent on *Fidelity's* transformation, and expectations were high. Documentation detailing discussions about her first voyage dates from January 1941, and it is clear that SOE bosses were lining her up for a crucial role – the rescue of escaping prisoners of war and the landing of undercover agents. Central to these operations in the Mediterranean was effective deception, and when Madeleine returned to Barry in the first week of March she and Claude ordered three of the younger, fresher-faced crew to report to Claude in his cabin. They entered one at a time, with no idea why they'd been summoned. Whinney, a witness, recalled Madeleine entering the cabin carrying three big cardboard boxes.

Claude opened the first box. He pushed the flaps wide and reached a hand in. Inside was a bundle of material: floral-patterned gingham, candy-coloured stripes, lacy flounces. He lifted out 'a rather cheap woman's day dress', walked over to the nearest sailor and, like an attentive fashion-shop assistant, held it up against the young man's chest. There was silence in the cabin. Straight-faced, almost dour, Claude and Madeleine stood back and scrutinized the sailor, who was now holding the dress himself, his face pale. Madeleine stroked her chin. 'Another?' she said.

Claude bent down, rummaged in the box and extracted a second dress, a diaphanous high-summer creation, with cinched waist and a plunging neck. Madeleine started laughing behind her hand. She winked at the sailor, then turned to Claude. 'Legs a bit hairy? And what about the chest?'

The sailor threw the dress to the ground. 'What's going on?' He was shaking; his breathing was rough, audible.

'For once,' Whinney remembered, 'the indiscretion was allowed to pass. Perhaps [Claude] had been waiting and hoping for such a reaction for he smiled amiably at the sea-man and leaning forward, in soft conspiratorial tones, replied: "I am going to turn you all into pretty young girls." '

At this, all three recruits raised their voices in 'horrified protest'; in response, Claude and Madeleine only laughed harder.

Claude held up a hand, and the room fell quiet. The boxes of women's clothes, he explained, were as much part of their armament as the twenty-pounders, the torpedo tubes and depth charges. Without betraying operational confidences, he added that there would shortly come a time when a well-fitting dress would confer anything but effeminacy: it would be central to their survival.

By the end of Claude's speech, the men were grinning. They tore open all three boxes and – garrulous now, joking and nudging each other – rifled through the clothes. They pulled out scarlet pinafores, pleated skirts, bonnets and shawls and then, goading one another, pulled the clothes over their work boots and oil-darkened overalls. Whinney watched amused, aware he'd never see the like again on a Royal Navy vessel. 'They minced around [Claude's] cabin striking bizarre feminine postures, egging each other on to what developed inevitably into the obscene.' And Claude, conscious that his men – like children with more serious work ahead of them – needed permission to play, let the game run until it was exhausted; and he and Madeleine, like benevolent parents, watched without comment. Outside, in the sudden cold of an early March morning, the last of the stores swung by crane from the quay towards the gaping dark of *Fidelity*'s hold.

WESTERN MEDITERRANEAN, APRIL 1941

FIDELITY SAILED to Liverpool on 22 March, stopping at Milford Haven for Whinney to change places with Milner-Gibson. It was night when they headed west from Barry, and blowing a gale. In Milford Haven, in the guttering dawn, Claude and Madeleine bade farewell to Whinney, their friend, advocate, sometime chauffeur and much else besides. When Claude and he shook hands for the last time, Claude pressed an object into Whinney's hand: a silver cigarette case, inscribed *'En souvenir du mauvais charactère de Jack Langlais.'* 'In memory of': as if Claude knew the future.

In convoy from Liverpool on 6 April, heading for the Mediterranean, the atmosphere on board was guarded – 'very 'oosh-'oosh', in the words of one of *Fidelity*'s most recent French recruits, Charles Osset, who during wartime sacrificed Osset for Thompson. Osset – a former electrician with the French navy, now steward in *Fidelity*'s wardroom – was initially inquisitive as to the ship's goal. He was told to stop asking questions, that 'there are a lot of spies on board, and within two minutes the captain will know everything you've been saying'.

This sense of precariousness – that a few careless words might sabotage their cover – was understandable. SOE had decided that *Fidelity*'s first mission would be to land two separate groups of agents on the south coast of France, and pick up three parties of escapers. She was also carrying some officers from SOE's Spanish section, who would be dropped off in Gibraltar under cover of darkness. She was 'to keep wireless silence whilst at sea, except for urgent matters'.

As second-in-command, Pat O'Leary had been given the job of piloting a small fishing boat, secreted on board, from which he'd drop off two agents – 'Angelica' and 'Aromatic' – as well as rescue twelve officers from the Polish air force currently being hidden by the French Resistance. The pick-up, as O'Leary's SOE Order of Operation made plain, was likely to be the more unpredictable of the two undertakings. The Order – which O'Leary had been instructed to commit to memory – laid out a precise sequence of events, scheduled to start at dawn on 25 April. The pick-up was to take place on the stone breakwater in Collioure bay, just over the border from Spain and some fifteen miles south-east of Perpignan.

'The leader of the group of fugitives,' ran O'Leary's instructions, 'will wear a Basque beret and a red scarf around his neck and if nothing suspicious is observed a member of [O'Leary's] crew will ask the person or persons in French who are there "How far is this from Perpignan?" The reply should be, "I am sorry, but I am a stranger to this district." '

At all costs, *Fidelity*'s cover must not be compromised: she was SOE's 'only ship of any size or armour', in the words of an internal memo, and 'if there is anything to arouse the slightest suspicion', then O'Leary should 'give up the operation and return' to *Fidelity*. Should it come to this, 'no clues shall be left behind. It must be continually borne in mind that the least incident might not only wreck all subsequent operations, but might give rise to diplomatic complications likely to cause considerable repercussions in future.' In the event of capture by the Germans, nothing less than heroism was expected. 'Each member of the crew will be supplied with a special tabloid. Nobody must be captured alive.'

Steaming south from England, anticipating action once again, Claude was ebullient. To Madeleine, *Fidelity*'s cipher officer – whose responsibility it was to send and receive coded messages – he dictated a telegram to SOE headquarters. '*Sommes en route pour operations. Tout bien. Temps splendide. Bon moral. Cherchons du Boche. Heil Churchill.*'

WESTERN MEDITERRANEAN,
APRIL TO MAY 1941

FIDELITY DOCKED in Gibraltar harbour at 8 a.m. on 20 April. Arriving in daylight was risky, and it is unclear why Claude was happy to let this happen: ship movements in and out of the port could easily be observed from mainland Spain, and British intelligence believed that in the daily influx of some four thousand Spanish workers there was at least a handful of Axis spies. Because of this, SOE wanted Claude to arrive and depart Gibraltar at night: whatever exchange of passengers and final camouflage there remained to do should be completed before sunup, during the course of a single night.

Fidelity spent three whole days in Gibraltar, not leaving until ten in the evening of 22 April, and while she was there she was anything but invisible. 'Everywhere was commotion,' recalled crewman Jean Ayral, seeing Gibraltar for the first time since Claude had welcomed him on board the previous June. 'Passengers disembarked, others were taken on. We stowed bicycles and a little fishing boat which we baptized the *berceau du marin*, our "sea cradle". The last of these amusing preparations was the camouflage. Everyone on board dressed in civilian clothes and a "women's crew" was assembled, with several young sailors whose job it was to hoodwink the enemy by parading on the bridge in women's clothing.'

Work on *Fidelity*'s disguise – as liaison officer Lieutenant Commander Jasper Milner-Gibson admitted in his report – was running way behind schedule: 'A great deal remained to be done.' To speed up the process, dockhands were transferred from Force-H destroyers: *Fidelity*, he said, was given 'every possible assistance'.

Madeleine and Claude, meanwhile, left O'Leary and Milner-Gibson overseeing the refuel and headed into town. They were conspicuous, a splash of colour in a world of starched white cuffs and lint-free naval braid. 'The Commanding Officer himself,' wrote Admiral Somerville's deputy in a disgusted memo, 'was conspicuously wearing three gold chains when he presented himself in Tropical rig to report the arrival of the ship. Although, admittedly, nobody could have possibly taken him for such despite the extremely queer figures which today are to be seen in British uniforms, it is clearly a matter for regret that such a mountebank was authoritatively wearing the uniform of a British officer.' The sight of Madeleine, intent on enjoying a brief holiday in the sun, moved him to equally caustic prose. 'A woman is maintained on board this ship who appears in some unorthodox manner to be part of the complement . . . the woman in question was heavily bedecked with jewellery.'

In the last hours before they embarked, Claude rushed around the ship while Madeleine waited on deck. This was not merely a chance to enjoy the spring sun, for Madeleine had been assigned the task of overseeing the ersatz females, and the deckchairs she now arranged on the foredeck would be where 'her' small squadron would base itself, once out of Gibraltar. She was in high spirits, and allowed herself to show signs of affection to the men. Charles Osset, then twenty-year-old officer-steward Thompson, remembered her tenderness, the humorous big-sisterly way she used to greet him whenever she was passing the wardroom. 'It was always very nice dealing with her. She used to come into the pantry, put her arm

Madeleine and Totoche, on the quayside
at Gibraltar, April 1941

around me and say, "So, my little Thompson, what have we
got for supper today?" ' More than sixty years on, little details
remained vivid. 'She was ill one day, and I had to go and serve
her in her cabin. I still remember that. She was very nice.'

Her *douceur*, however, did not mean that appropriate
respect was suspended. Milner-Gibson, recalling this first
cruise some months later, reassured a meeting at the Admiralty
– which by this time had heard rumours to the contrary – that
Madeleine was a 'quiet and unassuming woman . . . [who] was
at that time treated in a similar manner to any other officer and
[whose] behaviour had been in every way correct and proper,
as also had that of all members of the ship's company towards

her.' There was more than a little sleight of hand here: O'Leary later painted an almost domestic miniature in an interview otherwise about his later career, published in 1956 in London's *Daily Mail*. 'Her dainty cabin under the bridge, and just across the wardroom from Péri's, had a bathroom added. There she washed and dried his clothes and her own. I would glimpse her sometimes, in that feminine-fussed cabin, sewing buttons on Péri's uniforms, pressing her impeccably tailored WRNS suit.'

The night of 22 April, sailing east into the Mediterranean, was spent painting the ship yellow. In a gentle swell, on a warm night, this was arduous though not dangerous work: platforms were rope-slung from the gunwales and the men worked in shifts, starting at sea level and working up. The funnel was painted black, 'SS *Setubal*' was stencilled on port and starboard bows, and the Portuguese flag was hoisted. Boards were erected around the bow and stern guns, painted yellow and 'portholes' added. Viewed from any distance, the camouflage would have been effective enough, but closer inspection revealed the original grey still visible in faint streaks through the yellow. Scrutinizing the coverage in the tangerine dawn, Claude determined to keep *Fidelity* as far away as he could from other passing vessels.

By ten the next morning, 23 April, they had passed Cabo Sacratif, midway between Málaga, to the west, and Almería, to the east, keeping a safe distance nineteen miles offshore. *Fidelity* was making good time, though the stokers were suffering from heat exhaustion: he gave orders that the officers should serve two-hour shifts in the stokehole. Around midnight, under a clear moon, they were twelve miles off Cartagena, about to head north up the Costa Blanca, towards the French border.

The closer they got to France, the more the fishing traffic increased. 'Met numerous fishing vessels,' Milner-Gibson wrote in his log at 2 a.m. on 24 April. At dawn, conscious they were far from home, and an object of curiosity, Claude ordered the 'women' on deck. Madeleine took to her deck-chair, waited on by Charles Osset: 'I put a little table out for her, and her deckchair. She lay there, and I had to serve her all her drinks, to make sure she [looked like] a passenger on board a normal cargo ship.' O'Leary, interviewed in 1947 about his wartime career after receiving the George Cross at Buckingham Palace, saw a scene straight from Christmas pantomime: 'The guns had vanished behind canvas-built cabins, and outside the cabins, lolling in deck-chairs, were bevies of "girls" in scanty frocks, but in reality gunners at action stations.'

With the charade being played out in the sunshine below him, Claude kept to the bridge, 'only too anxious', in O'Leary's words, 'to pose as a bearded Portuguese master for the first German aircraft'. Among the crew, there was the sense that Claude was relishing the theatre of it; that his engagement in the make-believe, as much as the task in hand, was now driving him. It was along this stretch of ocean – the swell soft as evening silk – that he ordered the stokers to take a rest and, as the ship slowed to motionless, he lowered a lifeboat, rowed into the blue, and took photographs.

Unlike the photographs of his car journey across Asia, or from his hunting expeditions in Vietnam and Cambodia, these images have not survived, but Auguste Roulland, who'd been drafted to *Fidelity* in January, described a brief carnival, a holiday mood descending on the crew for a couple of hours as Claude 'put the little boat in the water and rowed around his ship taking photographs; some other men did a bit of fishing'.

Madeleine leaned on the rail, watching Claude across the sun-stippled surface, the slow dip of his oars, the knock-knock as he shipped them and raised his Leica for another shot: Madeleine smiling, her hand raised in a wave, the sound of Totoche yapping around her feet carrying clear across the stillness. Then one of his men called out – 'a fish!' – and Claude, laughing, rowed over, sweat in his eyes, and took another photograph. That night they feasted on the catch, a huge red snapper, in the wardroom, accompanied by bottle after bottle of Chablis so chill their glasses sweated in their hands.

By eleven in the evening, her crew feeling the sting of the day's sunburn, *Fidelity* passed Cabo de San Antonio, due west of Formentera. Ten minutes later, a Spanish cargo vessel crossed their bows, heading south. Through the night, as if the herald of something more ominous, the wind freshened and changed direction, the barometer dropping. At a quarter past five in the morning of 25 April – the date set for the start of the operation – the wind was gusting north-easterly, force four. Dawn came slowly, through low cloud, and in the galley the cooks secured crockery cupboards, locked drawers, stowed pots and pans. At 10 a.m., a Vichy-French war-transport vessel passed within sight.

In the wardroom, Claude, Madeleine, O'Leary, Milner-Gibson and Cannebotin bent over a chart of the Franco-Spanish Mediterranean border. With them were the two agents who were to be dropped from the fishing boat piloted by O'Leary. 'Angelica', formerly the Polish Consul in Toulouse, whose real name was Bitner, and Egbert Rizzo, an elderly Maltese civil engineer, codenamed 'Aromatic', reputedly for reasons of personal hygiene, handed Claude their forged identity papers for a final check. They were under orders from SOE to inveigle themselves behind enemy lines. Bitner, working also for the Polish government, was being sent to investigate whether the large Polish populations in the Nord and Pas-de-Calais *départements* could be drawn into active resistance; Rizzo's mission was to establish a two-way escape-and-infiltration link across the Pyrenees.

THEY WERE INTERRUPTED by the noise of shouting from outside. Claude ordered his officers to remain in the ward-room and ran to the bridge. At first he heard only a low growl; when he rested his hand against the window he felt vibration. He scanned the sky ahead: nothing, just a scatter of gulls hanging, apparently motionless, over the bow. Then, through the rear window, he saw it: a four-engined Junkers 90 trans-port plane, closing in on *Fidelity*'s stern. It was bat-black against the sun, and so low he wondered if it wouldn't clip their aerial mast on its way over. As he watched it, shielding the glare from his eyes, time seemed to stop: the plane, its shadow on the sea a giant plus-sign, the grind of its engines, all seemed to pause, momentarily hanging in midair. And then, roaring, it hammered overhead, the downdraft from its propellers lifting the dresses of the sailors on the foredeck. Claude saw black-and-white German crosses, then French commercial markings. Two hundred feet up, he estimated, no more. Even from where he stood, the shadows of day-old beards were clearly visible on the faces of his men, in their floral-print frocks and pinafores.

Crewman Jean Ayral, smelling burned gasoline as the Junkers passed over northwards, described his fellow sailors as 'champing at the bit: the plane was such easy prey. It was necessary to intervene to prevent *le groupe féminin* from lunging for their weapons.'

All day the weather worsened. At noon, Milner-Gibson noted with understatement, the wind was 'freshening'; by four in the afternoon, it had reached gale force, driving from the north-west. Other dangers were intensifying, too: at 1.30 p.m., a Vichy transport ship passed *Fidelity*, keeping two and a half miles to port, heading south. Claude, unsure whether their disguise still held, decided that he, and not O'Leary, should pilot the fishing boat for the drop-off of the two agents and rescue of the Polish airmen. O'Leary later recalled Claude's orders: 'a hiss'. As night approached it was cold on the bridge; Claude was wearing his duffel coat. The boat was pitching and yawing, its bodywork creaking. Madeleine, scarf around her neck, stood beside Claude.

'Understand this, Pat,' Claude muttered. 'If I don't come back, then you're in command.'

O'Leary was 'horrified: if Péri was lost on this trip there would be no more [trips]'. He turned, addressing Madeleine as much as his captain. 'Ridiculous. *Fidelity* can't exist without you. I'll go.'

Madeleine spoke: 'soft, Parisienne', but resolute. 'Pat *a raison*, Claude. Your job is to stay with the ship.'

As *FIDELITY* neared the French border, the impression among the crew was of impending threat, that they might at any moment find an enemy warship alongside them and be forced to attempt a conversation in Portuguese or Spanish. Osset remembered a 'Spanish gunship' approaching around this time. 'They had a good look at us, but luckily didn't ask any questions as no one on the bridge spoke Spanish.' The presence of at least one genuine female – 'our ladyship, sitting outside smoking' – offered persuasive additional evidence of the innocence of the '*Setubal*'.

Claude's close friend and trusted 'number one',
Albert Guérisse, alias Pat O'Leary

At eleven that evening, a mile and a half off Le Barcarès, a small village about ten miles east of Perpignan, Claude ordered *Fidelity* to a stop. The mistral had eased, and he gave final instructions to O'Leary and his crew – four men, plus the two agents. The fishing boat was lowered leeside of *Fidelity* and O'Leary, sitting down, gave orders for the off.

It had been an emotional farewell. Claude – conscious he might never see the men again – kissed each goodbye, grabbing them by the shoulders, grazing their cheeks with his beard. Now he and Madeleine and Milner-Gibson watched from the side as, in the swell, O'Leary's crew attempted to start the outboard.

The engine turned over, coughed dryly. For one hour, according to Osset – with Claude's worry turning to violent language, to threats that he would 'strangle the mechanic' – they tried to get it started. 'I tell you,' Osset shook his head, 'the language was *bleu*. I think if it had not been for Pat O'Leary, I actually think he would have killed the fellow.' It was well after midnight – petrol rainbow-leaching the sea – when they finally got going and O'Leary, holding a hand aloft, disappeared shoreward with his crew.

Morning came. Rendezvous was at 6 a.m., five miles north-east of Collioure, and *Fidelity* was there early. 'Nobody at appointed place,' Milner-Gibson recorded in his log. For the next six hours – Claude pacing the bridge, Madeleine nervously anticipating the next eruption – the ship circled the area. 'No sign was seen of the *berceau du marin*,' wrote Milner-Gibson, 'although visibility was excellent and a very good lookout was kept.' He began worrying over O'Leary's instructions, and he seemed to be attempting to comfort himself as much as his bosses at SOE when he wrote to them rehearsing the operational orders: '[they] were clearly understood'. He ran through the drop-off details, then those for the rescue of the Poles at Collioure, then the exchange of passwords. Making no mention of the lethal 'tabloid' with which O'Leary and his men had each been issued, Milner-Gibson, starting to sound perplexed as well as afraid, reassured his superiors that 'it was also clearly understood that, suspicious circumstances arising, the boat should retire and that any form of clash was to be avoided at all costs'.

AT 2 P.M., eight hours after the agreed rendezvous time, Claude sent a brief, panicky telegram to London. 'Nobody has come back. We foresee disaster. Our position delicate. Frequent meetings with inquisitive French boats. En route for the operation. Bad weather. *Mistral.* True name of Fergusson [one of O'Leary's crew] is Fourcade. His family is at Le Barcarès. Warn your agents in that region. Advise English consul in Spain.'

Claude had good reason to feel edgy: shortly after lunch, *Fidelity* had had her closest brush with the enemy yet: a Vichy cargo steamer, approaching at high speed, close enough for her name to be legible: SS *Sahel.* Claude veered wide, and hoisted two black balls, indicating that, for mechanical reasons, his ship was out of control. Roulland, recalling the delicacy of this moment – *Fidelity,* alias SS *Setubal,* poised between exposure and safe anonymity – watched a flashing light on the bridge of the *Sahel,* then saw it answered in kind by Claude. Making good speed, *Fidelity* then began to veer from port to starboard – 'to give [the] impression', in Milner-Gibson's words, 'of damage to helm'. The text of *Fidelity*'s messages do not survive, but to the crew the meaning was clear. '"Keep away from me", the captain was saying,' was Roulland's assessment. '"I'm not in control of my ship."'

ASHORE MEANWHILE, the first part of O'Leary's mission had been completed. Though they were running late, and had first made the mistake of beaching the fishing boat on a sandbank some way off the shore itself, O'Leary had landed agents Aromatic and Angelica without being spotted. It was dark, with no moon, and he had carried the aged Aromatic, plus radio set, to safety on his back. Time was against them: a falling tide meant that they had to unload all their gear – lead ballast, spare sails, outboard, rucksacks – and heave the boat back to floating.

They approached Collioure an hour late, the sky already

growing light. O'Leary was still hopeful: 'A handful of quiet fishing vessels, a sleeping deserted street and a few nets spread along the sea wall gave at first no sign of life,' wrote his biographer Vincent Brome. 'Then they picked out the small figure wearing the understood red scarf, sitting at the edge of the jetty.'

O'Leary called out the password. 'How far is this from Perpignan?' The expected answer came back. 'I'm sorry, but I'm a stranger to this district.'

Softer now, his engine idling, O'Leary asked where the others were, the twelve Polish airmen he was expecting to rescue.

'We thought you were coming last night. They're still asleep in the hotel.'

O'Leary agreed to wait ten minutes. The wind was rising again and O'Leary, despite misgivings, took to the shelter of the harbour. His men let out fishing lines. With four minutes to go, a uniformed French customs officer ran down the jetty. He yelled at them to show their papers.

O'Leary stalled. 'Don't be difficult,' he called back. 'You'll spoil the fishing.' The customs officer waited another two minutes, then turned and ran back towards the village.

O'Leary nodded at his crew and the helmsman started the engine and headed out through the harbour wall into a building wind, and violent waves. 'Soon no one could stand up or sit down,' wrote Brome. 'They lay down and clung to the thwarts. The boat heaved and tossed, shipping water.'

Fifteen minutes in, the engine cut. The fuel feed had broken, and petrol was hosing into the bottom of the boat. O'Leary repaired the line with a handkerchief tourniquet and set off again. Five minutes later, knee-deep in water, the men glimpsed a French cutter smashing through the waves towards them. They dropped their machine guns and hand grenades over the side, and waited.

They were towed to Port Vendres, interrogated, split into two groups and taken to jail. O'Leary made one attempt to break away from his gendarme escort but was re-arrested and incarcerated in Toulon naval prison.

AWARE OF NONE of this, Claude spent the night of 26 April awake, stalking the bridge as *Fidelity* mapped out a search arc through the waters in which O'Leary should by now have been sailing. Milner-Gibson, running on adrenaline, combed the shifting horizon through binoculars, alert for the pale-blade triangle of fishing-smack sails.

'Operation C' – the interception of a sailboat-load of Polish military evacuees – was scheduled for these hours, and there was a mounting sense of desperation as the night wore on. By the morning of 27 April, according to crewman Jean Ayral, Claude was close to abandoning the search for O'Leary's boat and – '*la mort dans l'âme*', with something dying in his soul – had ordered full steam for the waters off Narbonne, some twenty miles north of Le Barcarès, where the pickup of the Poles was due to take place.

Hours passed. Night fell. *Fidelity*'s coal furnaces had been running non-stop for five-and-a-half days. 'The engines were showing signs of strain,' worried Ayral. 'The boat couldn't even hold ten knots.' Through the long night, while Madeleine slept, Claude again remained awake. By dawn, he was hallucinating from lack of sleep, constantly on the edge of violence. The loss of O'Leary – his closest ally, fellow maverick – had knocked his equilibrium. 'Things were not the same after that,' Osset recalled. 'Sometimes, you only had to look at the captain the wrong way and he'd hit you.'

By the end of the night – idling through the seas off Narbonne, *Fidelity* wallowing in the heavy swell – Claude decided that it was time to withdraw, to head for Gibraltar and a change of disguise. The non-appearance of the Poles was baffling: 'Not one light on the water; not the slightest indication,' puzzled Ayral.

Shortly before dawn on 28 April, Milner-Gibson, on watch, spotted a merchant ship bearing down on them. Its actions were telling: 'On sighting us [she] took avoiding action and nipped into territorial waters, passing about four to five miles away from us.' Suspicions that their cover was blown were confirmed just before ten o'clock that morning. 'A French naval flying boat flew over and round us at low altitude with the observer leaning out and taking photographs,' he wrote in his log. 'Having done this, they turned round and returned to the northward. They had been quite obviously sent out specially for the purpose.'

Claude left the bridge and walked through to the cipher room, where Madeleine was sitting, headphones on, transcribing another message from 'C', Captain Frank Slocum, the deputy head of naval intelligence in London. The message Claude dictated in response was staccato, bleak. '*Aucune nouvelle operations. Dix heures sommes survolés très bas par hydro France. Certitude photo. Hydro venu specialement. Abandonnons operations. Essayons rentrer Gib.*'

IN LONDON, as news of the loss of O'Leary and the only partial success of *Fidelity*'s other two operations began to sink in, there was anxiety that future SOE sorties might now be jeopardized. Radioing Claude, however, Slocum counselled calm: 'If the *mistral* continues do not linger too long . . . do not worry too much over the fate of the *berceau du marin* and her crew. There are plenty of sympathetic friends in the neighbourhood, and they will probably find their way into Spain, where our Representative has been warned.'

Within SOE, the sense of urgency was more marked. Internal memos were reduced to series of questions, delivered without drawing breath: 'What happened when [O'Leary's] boat came to the shore? Did a member of the crew land? Is there confirmation of anyone's arrest? In what direction did the boat and ship leave? At what time?'

Ignorant of all this, Claude and Madeleine were sailing south once again for Gibraltar. Madeleine had spent most of the previous days on deck; now, though, she took to her cabin to rest. When the French seaplane had passed low over-head she'd been outside, her dress and scarf clammy with salt, and she'd raised her head and looked straight up at the photographer and waved, shouting at the other 'women' – hairy calves and workboots under wind-flapped hems – to do the same. As the plane banked for one final pass, she'd been close enough to see the pilot's eyes, the wild hair of the pho-tographer. Milner-Gibson, watching from the safety of the bridge, guessed the plane was as close as a hundred feet – 'very low altitude' – and as Madeleine lay her head on the pillow now, her ears were still singing from the blast of the engines.

THE NIGHT OF 30 April – the crew exhausted, with Claude's distress at having lost O'Leary sparking frequent arguments between 'Le Capitaine' and 'Madame' – was as wakeful as the previous ones had been. All men were on duty, this time with tubs of slate-grey paint, where before they'd had yellow, and foot-wide brushes. They dismantled the camouflage boards, packed away dresses and, at 5 a.m. on 1 May, ran up the white ensign and left Spanish waters. At noon, flanked by a corvette and destroyer, they re-entered Gibraltar harbour.

A debrief, then back to Britain. On the return voyage, Claude's mood was darker than ever. Milner-Gibson, completing his operational report just before *Fidelity* left the Mediterranean, believed the expedition had been 'compromised', and blamed Gibraltar: 'It was unfortunate that so much work had to be done [there], as security is almost impossible, owing to proximity of Spain and the fact that many dockyard workmen are coming in and going out to Spain daily.' *Fidelity*'s disguise, he went on, had been far from persuasive. 'Our camouflage, although reasonably good when seen from a surface craft distant more than half a mile, would certainly not fool an aircraft flying over at low altitude.' Like Claude and Madeleine – for whom this first sortie had been a mere preamble to the real fighting to which they believed they'd been called – Milner-Gibson was anxious lest SOE should now assign them a less front-line role. 'The officers and ship's company are now an efficient and intensely keen fighting unit. Their morale is extremely high and it would be a tragedy if this ship was allowed to moulder in harbour.'

He need not have worried. Within days of *Fidelity* docking at Liverpool, where the engines were to be overhauled and the superstructure altered again, SOE was debating whether to send her back to the Mediterranean or to East Africa. Here, operating out of Durban, *Fidelity* could be 'most useful' as part of an anti-Madagascar force. 'We have big developments in mind for this "Vichy" colony'; *Fidelity* could help with 'raiding parties, dropping agents and arms, interfering with local shipping, giving confidence to our friends'. Her brief thereafter would be peripatetic, never spending long enough in one place for her identity to be revealed. From Madagascar, then, 'she could proceed to the East or Persian Gulf where she will be able to prove her usefulness most effectively ... She will be more useful in these waters than in the Mediterranean where she may perform one exploit but will thereafter be "blown" or sunk.'

IN LIVERPOOL, out of the combat zone, Claude and Madeleine unlocked their wine cellar. The proceeds from the sale of *Fidelity*'s looted cargo had bought a Spitfire, which was now running sorties over the English Channel and into occupied France, with '*Fidelity*' painted under the cockpit glass, and a silver donor's plaque inside the cabin. The Ministry of Aviation had sent them a photograph of it, pristine on the asphalt at Eastleigh, which Claude had hung on the wall of his cabin, next to the portrait of Napoleon, and now they toasted both plane and pilot.

Liverpool, at the end of May 1941, was a city still adjusting to the shock of a week-long bombing raid at the beginning of the month. In Bootle, nine-tenths of all housing had been hit; throughout Merseyside, in the space of eight days, one thousand seven hundred people were killed and another eleven hundred seriously injured; a total of ninety thousand houses, some forty per cent of Merseyside's total, were destroyed. The homeless bedded down on school floors, and by the end of that week white flags could be seen fluttering from high windows. 'There is no doubt in my mind,' one eyewitness later told an interviewer, 'that had the raids gone on much longer in their intensity the people themselves would have pressurized the government to surrender.'

The dock area, through which Claude and Madeleine walked on their way to report to naval headquarters, had been badly hit. In Huskisson Dock, two miles west of the city centre, the ammunition ship *Malakand* had exploded in the middle of a raid, the blast tearing through the surrounding workshops and the timber-storage ground behind. From post-explosion photographs, there is little to mark the scene out even as a dock – roofs are shredded, concrete walls stripped of all but their steel rib structures, the dock basin reduced to an obstacle course of half-submerged chunks of charred and distorted metal. May and June had also been a time of determined Allied bombing of enemy cities. Hamburg, Bremen, Cologne, Mannheim and Brest were all attacked. The RAF bombed Germany's north-west for three consecutive nights, focusing on the Ruhr and the Rhineland.

The sight of the Cammell Laird shipbuilding yard in Birkenhead, across the River Mersey from the centre of Liverpool, was a relief to many of the crew, who were looking forward to a period of shore leave and a respite from Claude's punitive discipline regime. Charles Osset remembered Claude 'hitting everybody left, right and centre. His method of keeping everyone in line was to say, "When you do something wrong, I deal with it, and it goes no further. That way your record stays clean." ' Slocum, by now aware of Claude's approach to maintaining order, chose not to intervene. As he wrote in a placatory memo later in the year to those in the Admiralty who'd been expressing concern, 'I feel convinced of the commanding officer's sincerity to the British cause. There is a heavy price on his head in France, and so long as he remains in command of *Fidelity*, she will never disgrace her status as an HM ship.'

WHILE CAMMELL LAIRD'S engineers set about transforming *Fidelity* once more – replacing her square bridge with a more rounded profile; building a second, dummy funnel; erecting 'cabins' to hide a floatplane and a false forecastle to cover new four-inch guns – Claude and Madeleine travelled to London for their own holiday, basing themselves, as before, at the Piccadilly Hotel. Since the loss of O'Leary, Madeleine had been conscious of a shift in Claude: his volatility was more easily roused; he was edgier, quicker to see offence in the mildest remarks. The crew were suffering: one word out of place, or a late dinner, was enough to land a crewman in leg irons.

Among his officers, as with Madeleine, he'd started speaking in grandiose terms about their destiny: the Mediterranean sorties – of which there would shortly be another – were only the prelude to a more intrepid and influential tour in the Far East. Japan, he believed, was on the verge of invading Indochina. When that happened, he would be the perfect man to lead a counter force. *Fidelity* would serve as an offshore headquarters; and he and Madeleine, former Indochina agents, would head the operation.

In a spotless-chintz London drawing room, a bearded Claude and deep-tanned, Bardot-blonde Madeleine sat down to tea and fruitcake with Sir James Somerville and Lady Sybil Cholmondeley. Though none were strangers – Lady Cholmondeley later acknowledged that Claude was 'of course . . . a good friend', and that she knew Madeleine 'well' – they had never met as a foursome before. The meeting was Cholmondeley's doing, though probably at Claude's request, and the satin chaises longues, the bone-china saucers on their knees, the view across the rooftops of Georgian Chelsea, were her own.

Somerville, still in command of Force H, was one of Claude's best-placed contacts, and to him – as to friends in the

Ministry of Aviation – he listed his operational needs. He wanted a floatplane, first off, preferably a reconfigured Tiger Moth, and – in the words of a Ministry of Aviation memo – he needed 'four Vickers machine guns of the type used in aircraft'. He was prepared to barter: 'In regard to the Vickers guns, he has ten modern Browning 7.5mm guns, which are his own property, [and] for which he cannot get mountings. If we would give him the Vickers guns he would turn [the Brownings] over to us, although they are his own property.'

Cholmondeley, who would later recall having 'had a great deal to do with all the *Fidelity* people', was as fond of Claude and Madeleine as was Somerville, and on occasions was an influential advocate in their favour. Dame Vera Laughton Mathews, wartime WRNS director, wrote in her memoir that Cholmondeley, WRNS staff officer, had a 'champagne personality . . . She has the most silver tongue of anyone I have met. She can talk to anyone and of anything, and whether driving through falling bombs or skidding sideways through the world's worst traffic . . . she is so entertaining and witty and sympathetic.'

Like Cholmondeley – and in common with both Claude and Madeleine – Somerville possessed 'a calculated lack of formality and ostentation', according to his biographer Donald Macintyre. Despite their power and influences, neither Somerville nor Cholmondeley were conventional establishment figures. And so they sipped Earl Grey and laughed together, and when Claude and Madeleine stood on the marble doorstep and he took a bow and touched his lips to the back of Cholmondeley's hand, and Madeleine swept a curtsey, they believed they were one step closer to returning east, to lands that, for all their foreignness, were nearer home than any place had ever been, and where a kind of profounder heroism – '*de finir en beauté*', to use Claude's words – was a possible dream.

THEY RETURNED to unrest in Liverpool. Like others, Charles Osset was 'not very happy' with Claude's approach to discipline, nor was he put at ease to hear Claude speak frequently of 'how we would never leave the ship alive'. Though in some awe of Claude – 'everything he wanted done, he got done; the Admiralty gave him so much leeway' – he began to plot his escape.

Shortly after Claude and Madeleine's arrival from London, *Fidelity*'s officers hosted dinner on board for the commanders of two frigates that had recently docked. They arrived with their wives; for Osset, as officer-steward, it proved a long shift. 'We got the table ready, with flowers and everything, prepared the wardroom. It looked lovely. We got the drinks. Finally, at about half past eleven, my assistant turned to me and said, "Charles, you've been up since six o'clock this morning. It's time you turned in." There were only about three officers left, so I checked with him again and went to bed. I thought no more about it.'

Five minutes later, Osset was in his cabin, about to undress, when there was a rap on the door. It was his assistant, breathless. Claude wanted to see Osset, he said. Returning to the wardroom again, Osset stood to attention as Claude, his teeth stained with claret, stepped up close and, murmuring low, asked Osset where he'd been.

'I was going to turn in, sir,' Osset told him.

'When I want a drink,' Claude replied, 'I expect my steward to serve me.'

Osset paused. Claude's personal steward, as they both knew, was off duty, asleep in his hammock. But Osset apologized anyway. 'I'm sorry, sir. Nobody wanted any more drinks.'

Claude, louder now, repeated himself. 'I wanted my steward to serve me.' He hit Osset in the face.

'There was blood everywhere,' Osset remembered, his voice shaking. 'Next morning I was given a fortnight under arrest. The first day I was put in the hold, my legs in chains. After that I was allowed to walk around.'

Right next to the engine room, the steel floor of Osset's prison was 'very hot'. He was given no bedding, and so lay on the scalding metal to sleep. His rations were supplemented by French loaves, passed through a speaking tube from the pantry above.

After two weeks, he was summoned by Claude.

'So,' Claude smiled, 'it's forgiven and forgotten, is it?'

Osset nodded and, that afternoon, with permission from Claude to leave the ship and papers signed by a sympathetic officer that would enable him to gain access to the naval barracks, he packed a small kitbag and quit the ship. Repeatedly, and to officers of escalating rank, he reiterated his decision. 'I've been in the navy since I was sixteen years old, and until now none of my officers has ever hit me. If I was punished, I was punished appropriately. Unless I can hit back, I will not tolerate an officer hitting me. I'm not going back on board, sir.'

Claude, hearing of Osset's resolve, promoted him. But Osset was immovable. Three weeks later, without returning to *Fidelity*, he was posted to another ship.

CLAUDE'S COURTING OF Jean Ayral, now a junior officer, was more effective. He'd had his eye on Ayral ever since *Fidelity* had been attacked by bombers on the approach to Liverpool and Ayral, who was manning one of the 37mm anti-aircraft guns, had shot with calm accuracy. Ayral's professionalism – his 'remarkable sense of authority', in the words of another – had impressed Claude, who sensed that he would be a valuable crewman to have on his side. Early in June he asked Ayral if he'd like to join him and Madeleine on a trip to London: a reward, he explained, for his 'brilliance and bravery' during the German attack.

Later, Ayral recalled that Claude – aware that Ayral 'disapproved' of his methods of discipline, but nonetheless wished to remain on board for the chance to take part in 'brilliant' action – had treated him as a confidant, explaining the 'great things that he had planned'. At dinner in the Piccadilly Hotel, Madeleine quiet at his side, Claude told Ayral that he was planning 'an operation similar to that carried out by the British on the Lofoten Isles', a reference to the March 1941 Commando raids against German forces on the Norwegian islands which destroyed glycerine-producing factories. 'But this time,' Claude told him, casting a glance around the room before lowering his voice to a theatrical whisper, 'we'll be using anti-tank guns, landing craft, secret weapons. It'll be a declaration of war in the true sense.'

Ayral returned to Liverpool 'flattered by the attention and reassured that *Fidelity* was destined for glorious things'. Claude, who showed no sign of disquiet at the division of his crew into those who backed him and those who feared his command, now had another ally who, 'won over by the commander's gift of the gab, his highly placed connections, by having witnessed the undeniable deference accorded him by the British . . . no longer saw Claude as a danger'.

For Ayral, though, this new-won comradeship with his captain proved no longer-lasting than a 'honeymoon'. As one month lengthened into two, and work on the ship stretched out towards August, an atmosphere of 'rebellion' once more began to grow on board. 'It was a hothouse,' Ayral recollected. 'We were idle, overcrowded, the big city was temptingly close, and there were a lot of Free French sailors there whose good turn-out and discipline made us feel more than ever like pirates.'

Claude, chief Blackbeard, was given a new nickname by his crew – '*le bandit*' – which seemed daily more fitting. One afternoon, he and Madeleine were walking through the port – he in full naval commander's uniform, she in Wren officer's blazer, skirt and top – when they passed a British rating who saluted Claude but failed to register Madeleine. She made no comment. Claude, wiping his palms on his trousers, reached for the man's shoulder and spun him round.

'You didn't salute the Wren officer.'

Madeleine's eyes were lowered. She didn't see the impact when it came, but heard the dull crump, and something that sounded like a snapping. Later, when she and Claude were sitting down, she saw dried blood on his ring.

FRUSTRATED AT the delay, with SOE still undecided about *Fidelity*'s next mission, Claude presided over growing anarchy, behaviour which – while not actively encouraging – he did little to curb. When he got word one night that one of his men had been in a brawl with a Free French sailor, and moreover that his man had landed the other in hospital, he sought him out and congratulated him, handing over a five-pound note as reward. Life on board, according to Ayral, was scarcely more peaceable: 'acts of indiscipline, misappropriation of funds, thefts of belongings, arson . . . we lacked for nothing'. Before long, Claude found himself standing in the office of Liverpool's most senior admiral, a discussion which ended with Claude, like an enraged child, marching from the room and slamming the door behind him. The admiral responded by indicating that Claude's commission was now on the line.

Two days later, a posse of *Fidelity* men, acting under Claude's orders, raided an arms and ammunition warehouse on a neighbouring dock. It was night-time, under a sickle moon, and the men moved through silver shadows, silent as foxes. Forming a human chain, they passed out machine guns, grenades, revolvers, boxes of ammunition. When the police searched *Fidelity*, they found, said Ayral, a bare fraction of what was taken.

And so it went on, an escalation of hostilities designed by Claude to goad SOE into speeding *Fidelity*'s return to the action. When the navy protested at the theft of its weapons, and pressed harder still for Claude's scalp, SOE stepped in and protected him. Claude – 'emboldened', in Ayral's words – staged another raid. Breaking unannounced into the office of Liverpool's Free French naval commander, he and two crew-men pinned the other Frenchman to the wall, revolvers at his chest, and Claude rifled through the desk and wall cupboard till he'd found what he came for: three bottles of Pernod, 'piously squirreled away for important occasions'.

HOWEVER MUCH Claude's approach provoked fear and indignation, there were many among his crew, and within SOE, who sympathized. To them, Claude's volatility was born of frustration: here was a warrior, they reasoned, impatient to fight.

Hitler, the object of Claude's hatred, was now, in the summer of 1941, massing his armies along the Soviet border. His eastward ambitions, as the reader of *Mein Kampf* knew, had long been clear: 'When we speak of new territory,' he wrote, 'we must speak of Russia. Destiny itself points the way there.' Russia would provide living space, *Lebensraum*, for the expanding German *Volk*, whose faith in their leader was now euphoric. Newsreel footage of Hitler returning from France in July showed bare-chested children running alongside the railway tracks, hollering and waving; grinning farmers, pausing atop horse-drawn winnowing machines to raise a hand in salute. In Berlin, Hitler and Göring, high on a balcony, gazed down at thousands and thousands of sun-happy faces, lost in worship.

'Armies do not exist for peace,' Hitler wrote. 'They exist solely for triumphant exertion in war.' In June, three army groups crossed the Soviet border and began their advance on Moscow. A fortnight into the campaign, half a million Russians lay dead and nearly one million had been taken prisoner; within a month, the Germans had won an area nearly double the size of their own country. In one engagement alone, the Red Army lost six thousand tanks.

SOE, FOCUSED ON the occupation of Western Europe, was as restless as Claude to see the end of the Liverpool refit, and to have *Fidelity* in action. Discussions throughout June and July were constant and labyrinthine: the ship would carry agents to Gibraltar, 'act as our base [there], and . . . bring home prisoners of war and other embarkees'; rescue a group of Italian anti-fascists from Morocco, and some five hundred Polish troops from Casablanca, currently in internment camps; stop in Lisbon and 'extract a number of Poles of all kinds'; and drop more agents on the south coast of France. Finally, a date was set: *Fidelity* would be leaving Liverpool in convoy on 22 August.

Buoyed by the news, Claude and Madeleine let their guard

slip, and began to spend more nights together on board. Till now, they had maintained a professional cool, taking care not to seen as lovers by the crew or officers. This, they both knew, was a vital precaution: should rumours filter through of a sexual relationship, they would be more vulnerable to other charges of misconduct. Now, though, they began to be more carefree. Shortly before their departure, crewman Auguste Roulland overheard Madeleine quizzing her steward. One of her shoes had gone missing, she said. She was flustered. 'What have you done with it?' she demanded. 'Where is it?'

The steward retreated, began his search. Having 'hunted everywhere', he eventually returned with the shoe. Madeleine, still convinced he was to blame for its loss, could be heard some way off, fairly shouting. 'Well?' she snapped, standing in stockinged feet on the cool metal of the corridor.

The steward held out the shoe. He spoke quietly, his head lowered. 'It was in the captain's bedroom, ma'am. Under his bed.'

Determined to exploit *Fidelity*'s potential more fully, SOE had given Claude a complex series of orders. The instructions broke into six sections, the 'most important' of which concerned the handling of agents: the unnamed members of 'Autogyro' and 'Urchin', to be dropped on the French coast between Canet and Cap Leucate; the pickup of escaped prisoners of war from the same area; and the drop-off of agents in Algeria, where around one hundred and fifty prisoners of war would also be waiting. For each operation, there were prearranged coded greetings: evacuees awaiting rescue in France were to call out 'Sunday' from their fishing boat and, in response, Claude was to flash back 'Home, Home'. In Algeria, the same operation was to be prefaced by the exchange 'Royal Air Force . . . Royal Navy'.

Fidelity, bristling with new armament, would now, it was hoped, come into her own, and Claude was given orders to 'intercept, capture or destroy enemy vessels trading with Spain'. He was also permitted, at his 'discretion', to hoist any ensign he wished, 'including an enemy flag'.

Madeleine, once again, was cipher officer, responsible for the reception, decoding and transmission of secret telegraph signals. The code words that she now set about memorizing were part English slang – 'Fiddlesticks' for '*Fidelity*' – and part very personal, a sign of her and Claude's indissoluble identification with the ship and its future: '*Commandant blessé*' would be conveyed by the single word 'Madeleine'; *'commandant tué'* by 'Claude'. The 'emergency key phrase' was 'Victor Madelain', an inverted, oddly masculine approximation of Madeleine's own forenames, Madeleine Victorine.

THE NIGHTS were clear and cold, a tent of stars. *Fidelity* looked different again: 'Mediterranean blue', according to Jean Ayral, returning from an appendectomy just in time to join the sailing. Her true nature had not been disclosed to the sloops and escorts of the convoy: the floatplane on the foredeck and the speed launch were hidden, her guns were concealed. And so when a sloop passed close one morning, and Madeleine – in Wren uniform, hair spun about her face by the wind – was spotted on the open section of the bridge, leaning over the rail, the sloop's captain sent an excited message. He suggested an 'exchange' – two of his officers for Madeleine, 'that one taking the air'. No problem, Claude signalled back. 'Come alongside.'

Claude called Madeleine under cover and asked for her hat and jacket. She saw his smile, found herself laughing. She took them off and handed them to him.

A short while later John O'Neill, a young officer, emerged on the bridge. He stood in front of Claude, reporting for duty. O'Neill – 'a very small man', according to another crewman, 'whose nickname "Pipite" summed him up exactly' – listened to Claude's instructions and then, as directed, took Madeleine's hat and jacket.

Gingerly, taking care his beard was not spotted, O'Neill made his way outside, and stood at the rail where Madeleine had been just ten minutes earlier. The other boat was alongside now, and sailors were lined up along its deck, cat-calling and whistling. Claude and Madeleine remained inside, crouching down so they were invisible to everyone but O'Neill. The ships' engines idled; there was little wind, and only a gentle swell, so every cry, every lascivious holler, was audible.

Claude waited. The volume increased: two hundred males, somewhere off the west coast of Spain, the scent of a woman in the air. He waited some more and then, with Madeleine nudging him, unable to bear the tension, he gave a nod to O'Neill, who turned to face the other ship. Swift as if someone had hit the mute button, the shouting died to silence.

As THE WEATHER worsened, Claude's sense of fun was visible less often. During a storm on 2 September, *Fidelity*'s doctor, Surgeon-Lieutenant Donald Finlay RANVR – one of the few non-French crewmen – broke his leg. No foul play was suspected, ruled a one-line mention in a later report: it was 'a pure accident due to the bad weather . . . everything possible was done for his relief and comfort'.

The fate of Commandant Violet, a Free French officer being carried to the Mediterranean despite Claude's misgivings, was deemed, by comparison, worthy of a dossier all its own. Ayral, still recuperating from his operation, watched as relations between the two men grew steadily more acrimonious. '[Claude] used to openly reproach his passenger for the feebleness of his political beliefs. He was, in effect, a functionary, whose insipid personality contrasted keenly with the young sailors' around him. As the days went by he was treated more and more like a leper.'

Violet did little to make life easier for himself. Unlike the rest of the crew, who had spent many months adjusting to Claude's mercurial temperament and used tact and humour when confronted with his anger, the Free French officer took on Claude directly. Claude responded with further provocation: on one occasion, finding the lookout asleep at the masthead, Claude pulled his revolver and fired at him. Violet, unused to the delicate politics necessary to maintain a working relationship with Claude, took up the matter over dinner.

Auguste Roulland, with some understatement, described the ensuing fracas as a 'severe argument'. Claude, summoned before a naval board of inquiry on *Fidelity*'s return to Britain, reported that the venom of his exchanges with Violet – in particular their altercation over lunch on 3 September – were merely his legitimate response to a pattern of behaviour that had remained unchanged since their departure thirteen days earlier. 'Violet', he is quoted as saying, 'made allusions about the British fleet – derogatory remarks. They were definitely anti-British and very upsetting. I warned Major Violet that I would put him under arrest because of these anti-British comments.' According to Finlay, Violet's remarks were at least in part symptomatic of his shaky state of mind: 'When we left until the time he committed suicide he was very depressed and suffering from seasickness.' Finlay had prescribed Benzedrine tablets, and 'a light diet. He spent a great deal of time in his cabin.' On the 'rare occasions' Violet did appear in the wardroom, Claude described him as 'seeking quarrels with everyone': when 'reproached, [Violet's] replies did not vary: he attributed his attitude to, firstly, his health, and secondly he accused himself of having become a traitor towards his own country.'

And so it was, riven with internal conflict, that the queasy Violet joined Claude, Madeleine and *Fidelity*'s other officers for lunch. Conversation turned to the fall of France, specifically – as Sub Lieutenant G. A. Avoncour told the inquiry – 'the responsibilities for the French defeat'. Avoncour's allegiance to Britain – like many others on board – had been secured by Winston Churchill's promise of June 1940.

Prime minister for barely six weeks, Churchill had reacted emotionally to France's capitulation, sending not only aid in the form of planes, but pledging that any Frenchman who wished to fight for Britain against Germany would be offered British citizenship. In late 1941, though, none of *Fidelity*'s men had yet been given their naturalization papers.

Avoncour, to murmurs of approval, ventured the opinion 'that the offer Mr Churchill made to France was very worthy'. Violet interrupted, stating that the English should take 'a much greater responsibility' for France's defeat, a view that Avoncour – no doubt with one eye on the approval of his watching captain – was swift to challenge. 'I said do not speak like that, for you are truly wrong. I said that I had been present at the happenings at the moment of collapse and the things I saw proved that the responsibility was with the French officers.'

Violet turned, and – casting a glance at Claude – pointed at the portrait of King George VI, which Claude had hung on the wardroom bulkhead. To Claude – now Commander Jack Langlais, RN, more fiercely nationalistic than any native Briton; who had with Madeleine witnessed at first-hand one of the British royal couple's visits to the bomb-shredded East End of London; who spoke with daily reverence of the monarch's stoicism and fortitude in refusing to leave the capital, despite the falling bombs – George VI had assumed unimpeachable, godlike status.

Violet, still pointing, turned back to face Claude. 'You are making war,' he sneered, 'for that imbecile.'

Avoncour remembered further insults aimed at the king – 'mad', 'foolish', 'incapable' – which for Claude were too grievous to relate. 'He even said much worse things than that,' he told the inquiry, before adding something they already well knew; the very thing, indeed, which had triggered calls for an inquiry in the first place. 'I am a violent man.'

CLAUDE ORDERED Violet to his cabin, giving instructions to one of his gentler crewmen to act as waiter: 'I ordered Sub Lieutenant Lalande for this duty . . . as some of my crew who are very loyal [also] heard these remarks.' This uncharacteristic restraint was noted by every witness: Madeleine, in British uniform like the other French officers, recalled Claude's one-line bark, no fists, no blood: 'Leave the table and go to your room.'

The meal continued, an empty chair where Violet had sat. Claude, Finlay told the inquiry, then sat down, called his steward and ordered two bottles of champagne. He popped both corks and filled his officers' glasses. 'He said he was sorry he lost his temper, and that was that.'

Nowhere in the board of inquiry transcript is there any sense that Claude's officers were in anything but agreement with him. Sub-Lieutenant John Allen – lone among witnesses in reporting Claude's admonishment as being longer than a single instruction – gave the impression of using quotation marks to convey his own disapproval of Violet by proxy. 'The captain said, "You are onboard a British ship and I warn you to keep your sentiments to yourself. If you cannot keep them to yourself you cannot stay in my mess and you must go to your cabin." '

At half-past two that afternoon, the dull crack of a gunshot reached the bridge. Finlay, ship's surgeon, ran to Violet's cabin. The door was open, and a small crowd had gathered. As Finlay stepped over the threshold he saw Violet's body on the floor, a revolver near his open hand. His head was under the washbasin, and his hair was matted, the colour of royal velvet.

A plate lay on a side table, with some boiled potatoes pushed to one side. When Finlay bent down he could see 'powder marks' on Violet's temple, the site of the bullet's entry. The fine hairs that pushed back from Violet's temple were 'scorched', frizzed like coiled wires.

AMONG MEN who'd not seen Violet's body, a predictable rumour began to circulate: Claude had murdered Violet himself, or had had him killed; the gun had then been cleaned of fingerprints, as in crime procedurals, the victim's limp fingers pressed around the grip, and the weapon allowed to fall. Discrepancies between the different accounts only fuelled the suspicions.

Recording the sequence of events some three weeks later, Claude made no mention of hearing a gunshot – something referred to by more than one witness at the board of inquiry – and explained instead that, at five that afternoon, he'd 'given orders for Cdt Violet to be brought to my office, but no answer could be obtained to repeated knocks on the door of his cabin. This door was then forced, and Cdt Violet was discovered – dead. He had shot himself through the head with his service revolver.'

With time to reflect, Claude attempted to fit the puzzle together. Violet, he wrote, had in Liverpool 'repeatedly asked to embark as a volunteer'. On the face of it, the Free French officer seemed a promising recruit: he'd 'procured . . . plans of [Mediterranean] powder magazine and gas plants', for which Claude paid him ninety pounds. When Claude forwarded these to SOE, however, Violet became 'very frightened of an indiscretion . . . and urged me to keep him in my service; he argued that he would be able to furnish me with other plans if his request was acceded [to]'. Claude's final words to Violet

– that he would now be 'disembarked at Gibraltar' – were, Claude believed, the final blow to an already 'fatigued' and 'liverish' individual. 'The only supposition I can make is that this officer wished to make use of our ship to get back to France. On hearing that he would be disembarked at Gibraltar, and fearing an inquiry, he took the fatal decision.'

At eight forty-five that evening, Claude and Madeleine stood side by side on deck, the other officers in a semicircle around them. Violet's body lay on a trestle, shrouded in a French flag, his feet over the edge of the gunwale. Claude read the last rites and the trestle was tipped until the body fell stiffly towards the black water.

THE SUICIDE OF Violet aside, this was *Fidelity*'s most dangerous expedition yet, and the staccato entries in Claude's log testify to the growing U-boat threat. On 27 August, five days into the convoy, Claude, on the bridge at ten minutes after midnight in 'heavy seas and little visibility [had seen] to starboard a violent flame followed by a loud explosion: a ship had been torpedoed in a neighbouring column'. An hour and a half later, a second ship was sunk. Throughout the night the seas grew more mountainous, and *Fidelity* began shipping water. At nine on the morning of the 28th, a rolling wave broke over her foredeck, splintering the motor launch. The next days brought fog, another ship down, and other vessels firing blind into curtains of shifting sea mist. Come night on 3 September, with the body of Violet on the Atlantic floor, Claude ordered the first disguise: by dawn on 4 September, he was *capitán* of the Spanish merchantman SS *Iñes* of the 'Transmediterránea Compañía', flying the Spanish *tricolor*.

Fidelity, billed as an anti-aircraft escort, now split from the convoy and headed for Gibraltar. She was behind schedule,

delayed by wild seas and engines that, despite constant stok-
ing – creating furnace-room heat of one hundred and thirty
degrees Fahrenheit – would not push her any faster than ten
knots. Claude, out of sight of the convoy, began operating as
the lone wolf of his imagination. During this period, and after,
Fidelity ignored all wireless signals sent by SOE in Gibraltar:
Madeleine, cipher officer, relayed each to him. He read them,
and silently handed them back.

Such behaviour – and the only partial success of his missions – angered Gibraltar's naval commander, Vice-Admiral
G. Edward-Collins. *Fidelity*, he wrote in an extended, exas-
perated memo to London a month later, arrived unannounced
at Gibraltar in the small hours of 10 September, forty-eight
hours behind schedule. From Claude's point of view, the delay
was weather-driven, and unavoidable: the overnight stop was
intended as a shortest-possible stop-off, just long enough to
pick up four agents and – 'it is hoped', as his SOE orders put
it – Pat O'Leary, who was now understood to have escaped his
initial captors. But there was no O'Leary, and when Claude
ordered his men to raise the anchor and set off to land the
agents near Canet and pick up a party of escaped prisoners of
war, it was in the face of an even rougher sea, and gale-force,
head-on wind.

Below decks, three of Claude's men were working on an
escape plan. Auguste Roulland was frustrated by the uncertainty of life on board and the transitory nature of their
successes. 'I wanted to see the enemy face to face, and figured
that I could get to the occupied south of France via Spain
and the Pyrenees.' As likely, he was aware that his time on
board was nearing its natural end: by his own admission,
he was 'very naughty in those days. All the men were. We were
all a little bit mad on that ship. That was the way the captain

wanted us: to be tough guys like him, to care about nothing.'
Roulland's misdemeanours had mainly involved Claude's
personal wine cellar and larder. He was aided by the fact
that, as captain's steward, he held a key to both. In port, he'd
habitually engaged in a little light pilfering: 'If I went out one
night with some mates, we would normally come back and
help ourselves to the captain's wine and have a big feast.' On
other occasions it was food; at other times rum, whisky. His
punishment, when Claude and Madeleine returned from
London one time, had been very public. Claude assembled all
his officers and Madeleine, and arranged them in a semicircle
in the wardroom. He told a petty officer to fetch Roulland.

'As soon as I saw him,' Roulland recalled, anger causing
his voice to tremble, 'I could see he was grinning with rage.
"You've been naughty again," he said, and he punched me in
the face and kicked me in the stomach. Blood was pouring
down my white uniform.'

Claude snapped at Roulland to stand to attention. 'Then
he gave me another volley of punches.'

Madeleine stepped forward. 'Captain,' she said, unafraid,
looking Claude straight in the eye, 'it is not right to make a
man stand to attention and then hit him.'

'Shut up!' Claude bellowed, beyond reason. Grabbing
Roulland by the hair, he began dragging him towards the spiral
stairwell. Roulland made just one effort at retaliation – snatch-
ing at Claude's tie, ready to punch him back – when he felt a
gun at his head. He heard the voice of Lieutenant Fontenay:
firm, yet not without compassion: 'Don't do it.' He was taken
below and locked in solitary confinement for a month.

LONGING FOR RELEASE, Auguste Roulland and two others
began construction of a raft. The raft was simple: a thirty-foot

plank, stabilized by cross-struts, with a rope-hole at one end. He made oars, too, and the plan was to wait until after midnight, then lower the raft by rope through the stern hawse-hole. Once it hit the water, the fugitives would climb down the rope and paddle away. All their essentials – revolvers, knives, tobacco secreted in watertight, knotted condoms – were stowed in a gas-mask bag. The stern sentry was accomplice, and had been briefed: once they were all on the raft, he'd heave the rope back aboard.

The night of 20 September, with *Fidelity* sailing south – 'halfway between the Pyrenees and Barcelona, about three miles from the coast – ideal' – Roulland climbed over the stern to oversee the lowering of the raft. The swell was easy, the ship was progressing at a moderate speed, and the raft hit the water, rocked and settled. Roulland began to climb down the rope when 'the blooming thing suddenly went through my hand'. Flailing, the empty raft drifting off in *Fidelity*'s screwfoam wake, he managed to grab on to the hawse-hole, and heave himself back on deck.

However keen he was to escape *Fidelity*, Roulland had now been shaken. 'Frightened to death the same thing would happen again', he told the others he would henceforth be staying on board. The next night, on the second Roulland raft, another escape attempt was made. A stoker took Roulland's place. This time, Roulland himself ensured the rope was tied to the ship. With the raft on the water, the men climbed down the rope and Roulland cast them off. He heard a cry, and then the rumble of the engines and the shoosh of the wake obliterated all sound.

Shortly before dawn the next morning, Roulland was summoned to Claude's cabin. One of the escapers had been due to take the watch at four. When his bunk was found empty, Claude had ordered a roll call. Three were missing, one of whom, Claude knew, was a friend of Roulland's.

Roulland entered Claude's cabin, stood to attention, and waited. Claude stared at him in silence. For three minutes he said nothing. 'It wasn't up to me to speak,' Roulland remembered, shrugging.

Finally, Claude spoke. 'You know Morrel has disappeared?'

'Yes, sir, I've heard.'

'You work with him every day. You must know something.'

'I knew he'd been in the Spanish army, sir. That's all.'

Claude let Roulland's lie hang unanswered. Minutes of silence followed. Finally, having nothing concrete to pin on Roulland, Claude dismissed him.

Come daybreak, there was a line of men leaning over the stern, trying to gather clues about the escape. Three sets of bootprints were clearly visible down the fresh paint, the rope now swinging with the pitch of the ship: a vestigial tail, tiny as an elephant's against the vessel's broad backside.

THE RETURN OF *Fidelity* to Gibraltar occasioned another round of spluttering from Vice-Admiral Edward-Collins. The crew were all 'mountebanks', who should be court-martialled and replaced with 'personnel from the Royal Navy proper'; Claude, having been 'ordered to anchor unobtrusively in the Commercial Anchorage . . . [chose to] anchor his ship in the middle of the fairway to the northern entrance to the harbour, thereby drawing undue attention to the ship'; instructions to refrain from communicating with the shore were 'ignored'; Finlay, ship's surgeon, had disembarked in a 'temporarily unbalanced and neurotic state, [talking] of committing suicide'; and the ship itself, he added, was now under suspicion of 'smuggling valuables from France'. The sight of Madeleine, striding around the streets on Claude's arm 'heavily bedecked with jewellery' – laughing, kissing her lover, drinking till late – struck him as the final slur upon the good name of the Royal Navy. As for 'ugly rumours' about the maintenance of discipline on board, and the allegations that Claude had 'actually boasted of the fact that the temperature in part of the ship where [a] prisoner was confined was one hundred and eighty degrees Fahrenheit, and that the prisoner had been given no food whatsoever, and that such water as he had been offered had been adulterated with salt', clearly, 'an immediate inquiry [was] called for'.

The inquiry, though, exonerated Claude. He was not to blame for Violet's suicide, nor for any of the crew's other injuries. 'His methods of enforcing discipline are not orthodox', it concluded, 'but nevertheless we believe they are not resented but rather appreciated by his crew.' By the end of February, his sense of pride restored after what he considered the indignity of the board of inquiry, Claude was once again making plans for his future – plans that ran contrary to the wishes of the Admiralty. According to naval documents, it was now being proposed that *Fidelity* should become part of the Western Approaches fleet, to act as an escort vessel for transatlantic convoys. In due course, she should be 'permitted to operate independently, and on escapades in keeping with the temperament of the Commanding Officer. Lt Cdr Langlais is unquestionably loyal and we should use him properly, ie with the minimum of restraint.' Admiral Percy Noble, Commander-in-Chief Western Approaches, agreed. 'Here we have a man of great courage, determination and loyalty, although somewhat unorthodox in his methods . . .

[whose] fiery temperament has shown itself in somewhat medieval methods of punishment.' Claude, it seems, had effectively conveyed to Noble the ferocity of his allegiance to Britain: 'His principle enemies are Germany and Vichy, but I fancy that the Free French party is a close third. His ambition is to be a real British subject, and a good British naval officer in order to "clear the honour of France". Anything which will thwart this desire or cast a slur upon his own personal honour may have disastrous effects so far as he, himself, or his ship is concerned.' Claude, though, who'd dropped 'melodramatic hints as to secret orders' when Noble visited *Fidelity* in Liverpool, was now busy proving that his ship was, in Noble's words, 'a law unto herself'. He now 'believed', according to a separate communiqué, 'that he [was] going to the Far East with Admiral Somerville, having been given this impression lately at the Admiralty'. Claude had made up his mind.

SOUTHAMPTON, FEBRUARY 1942

CLAUDE AND MADELEINE'S determination to return to the Far East – and their courting of Sir James Somerville, now Commander-in-Chief Eastern Fleet – had quickened ever since the Japanese attack on Pearl Harbor on 7 December 1941. That Sunday morning, with no declaration of war, three hundred and sixty airplanes from the Japanese air force had bombed the US naval and air base at Pearl Harbor on the island of Oahu, Hawaii, killing more than two thousand people and destroying ships, planes and other military equipment. The next day, the US opened hostilities against Japan, and three days after that, Japan's allies Germany and Italy declared war on America. For Claude and Madeleine, the expansion of the Japanese empire over the next three weeks into regions they knew well – Singapore, Thailand, Indochina, Burma, Hong Kong, Malaya – felt like the call of fate.

From Liverpool, *Fidelity* sailed in February 1942 to Southampton, and it was clear from the scale of the refit that Claude and Madeleine had got their way: *Fidelity* was being prepared to sail east, into action against Japan in Burma. The ship was dry-docked and workers from Harland and Wolff shipbuilders began constructing the launch pads that would hold the Kingfisher floatplanes, the cradle of the torpedo boat which was shortly to arrive, extra accommodation for the detachment of Royal Marines commandos over which Claude would also be taking command, and the biggest job of all, the conversion of her engine from coal- to oil-burning.

Claude, pirate captain, took delivery of a jeep. 'He used to drive around the docks like a lunatic,' recalled one dockhand, 'driving across railway lines, ignoring roads, Miss Barclay always at his side.'

Madeleine, though, during these early days in Southampton, was noticeably subdued. On the sea passage south, Totoche had been lost overboard. The way Auguste Roulland remembered it, there was a certain tragic comedy to the accident. He and another crewman were sawing and hammering, making an enclosure for the pair of piglets – future cured ham, dried Serrano – that Claude had picked up on a sortie to the Isle of Man. 'We had plenty of wood and were making a lot of noise. The carpentry shop, the little cabin where we were working, was just opposite Miss Barclay's quarters, and she opened her door and asked us if we could be a bit quieter.' Madeleine gestured back into her cabin. 'It's Totoche, you see,' she told the men. 'He doesn't like the noise.'

Roulland nodded, looked past Madeleine into the darkened interior of her cabin. He heard a yip, some scuffling, and Totoche skittered past Madeleine's ankles, ran down the corridor and into the sunlight.

'He ran towards the stern,' Roulland said, shaking his head, 'and then jumped.'

Madeleine shouted for Claude. 'Stop the ship!' she screamed, her hand to her mouth. She ran for the bridge, still shouting. But the ship sailed on, the steely winter sun slanting low across her bows, through the bridge windows where Claude stood impassive. Madeleine, fists banging Claude's chest in rage and grief, lost herself to tears.

CLAUDE AND MADELEINE rented a house in Southampton, and the work began. 'It was,' remembered one dockyard hand, 'a somewhat unusual job.' The ship arrived from Liverpool in a state of chaotic organization: 'movement on board was made difficult by congestion caused by storage of cases seemingly everywhere. The crew had several pets. I remember a monkey having free run of the accommodation.' As well as the jeep, Claude had also procured a motorcycle with sidecar, in military camouflage, and for this alternative cross-town transport for him and Madeleine he ordered a custom-made landing stage.

They travelled frequently to London. As before the first Mediterranean expeditions, Claude was in salesman mode, pitching for weapons and men. This time, though, he was more ambitious. Already having secured the promise of a Thorneycroft torpedo boat and two Vought-Sikorsky VS310 Kingfisher floatplanes – single-float aircraft originally designed

Vought-Sikorsky's VS310 Kingfisher floatplane, two of which
Claude secured for *Fidelity*

for the United States Navy, intended for catapult operation from cruisers and battleships – he now wanted his own contingent of Royal Marines Commandos to carry out the amphibious raids into Japanese-occupied territory.

He'd also gone through his crew list and, returning to Southampton, dismissed ten men. Auguste Roulland was among them. 'I was told I was an undesirable. I didn't really care. Back in those days, I took things as they came.'

MADELEINE, confronted by new crewmembers, having to withstand constant muttered innuendo, withdrew into her books again. She'd been told that it would not be until they reached the Far East that her skills as an agent would be needed, and this moment seemed a long way off. Michael Pollard, who'd just begun training as a first lieutenant on the new torpedo boat, MTB 105, remembered 'the attitude towards her being one of resentment: what was she doing there? Most of us thought that there was more to it than met the eye, but we weren't party to what it was. It was clearly more than just a sexual relationship – she was his working companion, as well as his mistress – but she never said anything. She certainly never spoke about her previous life.'

It had taken little time for Claude's reputation to spread: on his call-up, Pollard was asked by the training officer at HMS *Hornet* – the Coastal Forces depot in Gosport, near Southampton – whether he 'would like to go and play pirates'. His next interview was with Captain Slocum from naval intelligence, an exchange which 'revealed little of substance about what I would be doing'. He was then posted to MTB 105, as second-in-command to Lieutenant John 'Pipite' O'Neill.

MTB 105 – one of four experimental torpedo boats built by Thorneycroft's Southampton boatyard in 1940 – had been

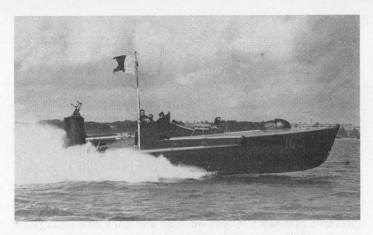

Fidelity's prized torpedo boat, MTB 105, built by
Thorneycroft's Southampton boatyard in 1940

assigned to *Fidelity* after some persuasion from Claude.
Powered by a Rolls-Royce Merlin engine, she was quick – a
potential fifty-two knots fully laden – but, with a wooden
keel, unstable at high speed. Claude loved her, and from
the moment she hit the water after her refit he visited her
regularly, taking Madeleine on high-crank sorties around
Southampton Water, kicking the boat into skidding turns, the
shallow hull hammering sideways across the water. Unlike
Fidelity, she was a craft of beauty and finesse: concave bow
lines and gunwales, low-slung cabin, pennants snapping on the
aerial mast above the captain's head. She carried four mounted
machine guns, and a torpedo tube that could be swung
through three hundred and sixty degrees. Should *Fidelity* ever
face U-boat attack, the presence of the torpedo boat – not to
mention the skirt of quick-drop anti-torpedo nets with which
Fidelity was currently being fitted – would, Claude hoped,
ensure her survival.

ISLE OF WIGHT, SPRING AND SUMMER, 1942

IN THE SPRING, Claude and Madeleine moved from Southampton to the Isle of Wight. They bought a house from Arthur Wheeler, a local fisherman – Cliff Cottage, a bungalow at the end of Chine View, a terrace of three cottages that looked south-west towards the Atlantic. It was small and access to it, down a sea-blown dead-end track, was precarious. But – with furniture donated by the villagers of nearby Chale – it became home; and, though it was bought by Claude, he made sure it was registered in her name: security, should he die and she outlive him.

It was a borderline place to have chosen as home, a house below which the yellow sandstone cliff was continually fissuring and crumbling, scoring new cracks in the approach track to the house. The inevitability of Chine View's seaward collapse – today, there is a tumble of soft cliff and wild downland grass where once Claude and Madeleine held bridge parties for the local vicar and all-night claret sessions for their favourite officers – was no secret: during peacetime, a visit to the death-ledge terrace had been a popular tourist excursion. 'The tarmac breaks off as if sliced with a knife,' wrote Patricia Sibley, who'd taught at Chale primary school in the late 1940s and, in the mid-1970s, revisited the area, researching a guidebook. 'I do not dare go right to the edge because it probably hangs out over a void. The cliff beneath falls away almost sheer in a hideous blue-black slough. Last year a house tottered on the very edge, its roof beginning to tilt: now only some rubble remains.'

This is the last Will and Testament

of me

Madeleine Victorine Barclay of Cliff Cottage Chine View Chale in the Isle of Wight Spinster **I appoint** Jack Langlais Commander in His Majesty's Royal Navy to be the sole Executor of this my Will and Subject to the payment of my funeral and testamentary expenses and my debts I give devise and bequeath to the said Jack Langlais absolutely the whole of my estate both real and personal and of whatsoever nature or kind the same may be and wheresoever situate I revoke all former Wills and testamentary dispositions at any time heretofore made by me and declare this to be my last Will **In witness** whereof I have hereunto subscribed my name to this my last Will and testament this twenty first day of October — One thousand nine hundred and forty two.

M V Barclay

Signed by the said Testatrix Madeleine Victorine Barclay as and for her last Will and testament in the presence of us both present at the same time who at her request in her presence and in the presence of each other have hereunto subscribed our names as witnesses.

G W Connor
Solicitor
Cowes I.W.

Rev Newham
Clerk to Mr G W Connor.
Solicitor
Cowes I.W.

Yet it was also a spot of thrilling natural beauty: on clear days, Claude and Madeleine could step out of their front door and see clear to the Needles, fifteen miles to the west, the furthest tip of the island. A short walk in the other direction, over tussocky rocks, through thickets of blackthorn and bramble – the overgrown archaeology of successive landslips – was St Catherine's Point, and the crenellated whitewashed lighthouse tower, out of use since the start of the war. The dangerous topography of the undercliff between Chale and Ventnor, where *Fidelity*'s commandos would soon begin training, appealed to Claude: it inspired, indeed, the kind of awestruck horror and admiration with which he enjoyed being greeted. Notices hastily erected in early 1928 – 'Caution. Drive carefully. A portion of the upper cliff is likely to fall in the near future' – might equally have been applied to him, warning of the dangers of proximity.

Within days of moving into Cliff Cottage, Claude and Madeleine had learned the area's history: how, on 23 July 1928, cracks in the upper cliff had widened to four inches; how three days later, with crowds now gathered, the rocks were on the move. At three that afternoon, wrote one observer, 'the whole cliff face became detached and swayed forward, slowly at first, then gathering impetus as it crumbled, crashed and thundered down hundreds of feet on to the road below': a hundred and twenty thousand tons of rock, which in September collapsed still further, pushing out into the sea, redrawing the shoreline and creating behind it a chaotic country park, through which Claude and Madeleine scrambled alone on orange-cast summer evenings, watching the jackdaws and rock doves hover in the updrafts thrown by the inner cliff.

It was here, too, that Madeleine accompanied Claude and the commandos on many of their training outings. Targets were set up along the bottom of the cliff. Madeleine joined the end of a line of commandos, lying on flattened wild grasses, the men in khaki, the soles of their boots black and shiny as new-laid asphalt, she in a skirt and working shirt. At the signal, they took aim and fired. When the commandos compared targets, they saw that her shots were grouped closer, a tight hole-punch around the bullseye.

Madeleine's accuracy with a rifle – and the sight of her picking off blackbirds with a double-clasp pistol grip – went some way towards softening the commandos' initial antipathy. When they first met her, they found it hard to believe that a woman would be allowed to serve on a Royal Navy warship, if not a disgrace, a by-proxy slur on their own competent maleness. Furthermore, it was clear that she and Claude were lovers. And yet she was a markswoman, a professional; she was discreet in word and action; and she brought down falcons, often with a single clean shot, that preyed on the carrier pigeons returning from occupied France.

It was wreckers' country, this southern Isle of Wight coast, and the more Claude learned of the shipwrecks and piracy, the more he felt sure he was in the right place, the fitting last training ground before the final push east. The first recorded shipwreck along this treacherous coast was 1314 – in Chale Bay, directly below Claude and Madeleine's kitchen window – when a vessel carrying wine from the king's Duchy of Aquitaine foundered on the Atherfield Ledge. The sailors escaped and sold the wine locally: Walter de Godeton, Lord of the Manor of Chale, took fifty-three casks. His punishment for knowingly receiving stolen goods was to build a lighthouse at St Catherine's Point, a construction that was so ineffective in the fog that, between 1750 and 1850, more than a hundred ships were wrecked in the bay.

SETTLING IN, they bought a car: an ageing Austin Ten with springs so exhausted and undercarriage so bone-rattly that Madeleine referred to it as '*tape-cul*': rattletrap. Like much else in their possession, its provenance was dubious: Claude had let it be known that he was looking for an old jalopy that could serve as a mobile target for commando exercises and Ben Schrôder, pilot of one of *Fidelity*'s seaplanes, told him about the Austin, which a friend of his in Southampton was offering for sale. It cost Claude ten pounds, and the moment it touched the quayside Claude decided that he wanted it.

Chrome bug-eye headlamps, forwards-opening back doors, spare tyre under the moulded rear hood, salt-streaked matt-black carriagework: it looked like a vicar's car, or the runabout of a back-country copper. And it was in this car that Claude and Madeleine drove to Ryde one summer morning to meet the Portsmouth ferry. Rumours had reached the Admiralty that some of the commandos were growing uncomfortable not only with Claude's military style – mortar-bombing a pond on the undercliff to provide fish for his dinner; suggesting that Madeleine supervise rifle training – but also with the presence of Madeleine herself. A Royal Marines captain, Peter Norcock, was sent to investigate.

Claude and Madeleine met Norcock at the pierhead. Claude introduced Madeleine: 'my second-in-command, and our explosives expert'. Norcock, for whom the scene remained vivid decades later, was led along the pier and shown to the back seat of the Austin, which was parked at the bottom of Union Street. Madeleine sat beside him, smiling. Claude powered out of town, warm dust bowling in his wake, and hit the high-hedged country lanes at fifty miles an hour. Madeleine, no longer smiling, was now yelping every time the car heaved into a tight bend, or hit a pothole. She pressed her hands to the seat, then to the window.

Norcock watched Claude, incredulous. He saw a man in the grip of a blind egotistical hedonism, seemingly oblivious to his passengers' discomfort. He saw flamboyance, of a kind unknown in the British military: a tooth, watch, bracelet and East End salesman's rings, all in gold. When they passed their first car Claude shoved his hand into the glove compartment, pulled out a light bulb and tossed it through his window. And Norcock witnessed the other driver open-mouthed, struggling to keep control, rocked by the sharp crack of the exploding bulb and by the realization that someone, for some unknown reason, thought little of their safety.

They pulled to a halt outside a cottage in Chale, the commandos' training base. Claude, eyes wide, asked Norcock if he'd like 'to see my guns'. Norcock, keener to talk to the commandos, demurred, but Claude insisted. A walk away, near the top of the cliff, was a Bofors gun, barrel pointing out to sea.

'My defence against air attack,' Claude breathed, rubbing a palm vigorously over his buzzcut. 'Want to see it fire?'

Again Norcock shook his head. Claude blew on a whistle – two short blasts – and a handful of commandos ran up the cliff towards them, readied the gun and started firing. Within five minutes the Isle of Wight, Portsmouth and Southampton were put on red alert, the highest state of readiness for imminent air attack.

MADELEINE BEGAN to entertain. First, she told Claude, she needed a chef, someone to do the catering while she welcomed guests. Claude suggested his cook, still on *Fidelity* in

Southampton: a tall Francophone African, nom de guerre Edward Brown. Madeleine's first guest was the local vicar, the Reverend Constantine Sinclair. He became a regular, and he and his wife would pair up with Claude and Madeleine – 'Monsieur le Commandant' and 'Mademoiselle' – to play bridge, the front door open to the warm summer evenings, the scent of gorse flowers, the smell of the tide.

One evening, cooler than normal, with the sun already gone, the fire began to smoke. It had never done this before, bellying woodsmoke into the room as if something had fallen into the chimney. The four of them moved to a side room, carrying the table and chairs through. They played on until it became too cold, until it was hard to tell the difference between their pluming breath and the exhaled smoke from Claude's cigarettes; until the chill made their hands shake and the cards unsteady.

THROUGH MIDSUMMER, Claude supervised the training of the commandos, Madeleine at his side. The men practised roped and free climbing on the cliffs below Claude and Madeleine's cottage, perfecting abseiling at speed, men pouring down the ropes like spiders racing to ground. Claude ordered one of *Fidelity*'s landing craft to be brought from Southampton and the commandos worked on their beach landings, crunching through surf onto the shingle. For the moment, this was as close to the action as they were going to get: on one occasion, one of the men smashed an ankle on landing. He and his party scrambled up the cliff to Chine View in soaked uniforms and were taken in by Edith Cole, Claude and Madeleine's neighbour. She handed out warm tea, sat the men down, and then they carried their injured comrade on. Some days later there was a knock at her door. She opened it to find one of the commandos standing on the threshold, carrying gifts of sugar and tinned peas.

They set up a two-inch mortar on the undercliff, on Claude's orders targeting a pond in which local men and their sons often went fishing. When they ran down to the pond to assess the damage, they could see the chainmail bellies of rainbow trout nudging the surface, some no bigger than upturned teaspoons. Later, focused more on the preparation of his men than the sensibilities of the villagers, Claude instructed the commandos to strap plastic explosive to the underside of Chad's Rock, a striking hunk of overhanging limestone in the cliff. Within the week, letters of protest were running in the *Isle of Wight County Press*.

With *Fidelity* nearly ready to leave Southampton, Claude stepped up the training. It was now August, and he stipulated dawn runs for the commando officers and men. On the undercliff he had them build a ten-foot-high wall, ordered them to carry bricks and cement down the track, through the heat-haze summer grasses. When they began their assault-course training it was Madeleine who stood sentry by the scaling wall, firing a rifle over the heads of the slower men; and when they'd finished, sweat running from the rims of their green berets, she told them they weren't yet off duty: she needed the steps to her house repaired, and required men and mortar for the job.

Waiting for the off, the commandos killed time by hunting rabbits – drilling holes in drinking troughs as they tried to bring them down with rifles – and raced each other along the lanes on new motorbikes, of which Claude had just taken delivery. Few of the commandos had ridden bikes before, and when they finally left the island for Southampton, not all of the machines made it along with them. The rest were broken-backed at the bottom of cliffs, upside-down in black-thorn hedges.

Two seaplanes, a motor-torpedo boat, two landing craft, motorbikes, a jeep, torpedo tubes, Asdic sounders, depth charges, anti-aircraft and machine guns: after three refits, and now running on oil instead of coal of uncertain quality, *Fidelity* was finally the fighting ship for which Claude had lobbied and cajoled for the last two years. The real measure of his success, however – and testament to the wary respect he was accorded within the Admiralty – was the allocation of Royal Marines commandos, a figure that, from thirty-six when they arrived on the Isle of Wight for the first time in early July, was now up to some fifty men as they travelled north to meet Claude and the rest of the crew in Loch Broom, in the far north-west corner of Scotland, for their final leg of training.

THOUGH COMMANDOS – elite troops, trained to fight without the support of artillery and other heavy weapons; who depended only on their own skill and the use of small arms – had been drawn from British army units since 1940, the first Royal Marines Commandos had been in existence only since November 1941. The first company was 40 RM Commando – composed, as with all other commando units, entirely of volunteers – and it was from this group of men that T Company had been drawn on 23 April. For the next twelve weeks, before coming under Claude's command on the Isle of Wight, T Company had undergone training at the commando training depot at Achnacarry, some ten miles north-north-east of Fort William.

Achnacarry Castle, the seat of Sir Donald Walter Cameron of Lochiel, Cameron-clan chief, is a crenellated-granite

Victorian-gothic mansion, buried in forest at the far eastern tip of Loch Arkaig; from 1942 to 1945, it was the hub of British commando training. Along lawns where once Lochiel and his friends had swung croquet mallets, despatching balls deep into the rhododendrons, now Nissen huts lay in lines. It was, according to Hilary St George Saunders, who wrote the first history of the commandos, 'a lonely glen . . . Here, amidst the wild scenery of moors and lochs, in weather which was at all times rainy, and in winter often bitterly cold, the initial training was carried out.' Claude's commandos – like Claude and Madeleine before them – learned how to handle explosives, 'the tactics of concealment and infiltration, sniping and intelligence work'. They learned how to kill using just a knife, to climb without ropes, and cross rivers on three-rope bridges. Days were long, and the pressure on their endurance intensified as the weeks of training wore on: by the end of three months, commandos were expected to be able to march fifteen miles uphill in two hours and fifteen minutes.

All exercises were carried out using live ammunition and, from a total of twenty-five thousand, some forty men lost their lives during training. Like most such training, the tougher it got, the more a battle-ready sense of humour was required. Donald Gilchrist, Achnacarry adjutant, recalled an introductory week of exercises which included climbing Ben Nevis and hiking the eighteen miles back to Achnacarry; assault courses; learning how to bake an animal on an open fire by first coating it in wet clay; erecting a 'death slide' across the River Arkaig; and a thirty-six-hour fully laden yomp across wet heather, sleeping sodden in the open, before staging a 'mock attack' upon Arkaig Bridge.

Sometime during T Company's training at Achnacarry, Claude was sent to join the men for a course on jungle training. Gilchrist, who never met Claude, later learned about his visit from Lieutenant-Colonel Charles Vaughan, depot commandant. Like so much else in the lives of Claude and Madeleine the exotic reality had quickly become blurred with equally colourful, if erroneous, myth. 'It was an incredible episode,' Gilchrist wrote in his memoir of life at Achnacarry. 'To say that the Frenchman concerned was amazingly eccentric would be an understatement. He had been a Governor of one of the French island possessions in the Pacific, and had sailed into Southampton in a yacht to offer his services to Britain. With him he had brought his attractive girl secretary. He was made a Commander in the Royal Navy, and his secretary a WRNS officer ... A rakish figure with a Van Dyck beard, he arrived [at Achnacarry] in blue battledress, the pockets of which were bulging with a weird assortment of guns and knives. At the drop of a hat, he would demonstrate his prowess with either type of weapon, regardless of safety precautions. Bullets and blades were soon flying all over the place.'

Claude was accompanied by 'a very zealous and proper young Royal Marine officer', whom he appeared to use as a kind of comic foil: Laurel to his Hardy.

' "Soon I weel be sent to the jongle," ' Claude is reported as telling his interpreter, the opening shot of a dialogue that 'became a regular feature of their relationship'.

' "Yes, sir," the young officer would agree.

' "And you will be sent weeth me, no?"

' "Yes, sir."

' "Do you know what I weel do weeth you when I get you in the jongle?"

' "No, sir."

' "I weel keel you!" the commander would hiss at him.

'And the young officer would leap to attention and in clipped tones reply, "Very good, sir!"'

On one occasion, Claude was talking to Vaughan near the mature rhododendron bushes that front Achnacarry Castle when a quarter-master approached them with a new machete to show Claude. He held it out, explaining that this was the kind of weapon used in jungle combat, when Claude tore it from his hand, turned for the shrubbery, and 'began to hack his way through Lochiel's beloved rhododendrons with wild cries of delight. Huge chunks of bush flew in all directions, and the Commander, hacking furiously, disappeared from view. Just as suddenly he reappeared again from the depths of the bush and ecstatically brandished the machete under Vaughan's nose, jabbering lyrically about its excellence as a weapon.'

When Claude left Achnacarry it was – unlike most commandos – at the wheel of a car. In Fort William, driving too fast, he knocked down a pedestrian. Stopping the car, 'the Commander lifted the man up bodily, propped him against a wall, and poured whisky down his throat. Finally he stuck the bottle in the poor man's astonished grasp and drove away before the police arrived on the scene. Mercifully, the man was not badly injured, and nothing more was heard of the matter.' And the same, Gilchrist mused, writing in the late 1950s, went for Claude. 'Perhaps he is still hacking his way through the jungle of some Pacific island to this day, accompanied by his girl secretary and the stiff-upper-lipped young Marine officer.'

MID-AUGUST, and Claude was yet to tell his officers any details about the mission for which they'd been so long preparing. Michael Pollard, first lieutenant on *Fidelity*'s torpedo boat, remembers 'a very polite afternoon tea' with

Claude, Madeleine and MTB 105's commander, Lieutenant
John O'Neill, at Claude and Madeleine's cottage on the Isle
of Wight. It was Pollard's first meeting with Claude and
Madeleine, and conversation was kept at a memorably shallow
level. All four of them spoke in English – Claude and
Madeleine were, by this time, 'quite fluent' – but no military
information was forthcoming. 'It was a social occasion. We
discussed the view, how blue the sky was. And they certainly
did have a wonderful view.'

Before the end of the month, Claude had decided that it
was no longer tenable to keep his officers in ignorance, and
summoned them to a meeting on *Fidelity*, now out of dry
dock in Southampton. For the officers billeted on the Isle of
Wight, this was the first time they had met the pilots of the
two seaplanes and the men and officers of the torpedo boat,
which was now lying athwartships in *Fidelity*'s well deck.

Claude led the way across the deck, past ranks of bicycles,
motorbikes, two landing craft. To visitors at this time,
Fidelity 'appeared to be extremely crowded with gear, boxes
and people. There were also many animals – parrots, monkeys
– running free.' Madeleine walked ahead with Claude, and
when they all gathered in Claude's day cabin, a circle of
expectancy, she stood at Claude's side.

Claude addressed his men. He seemed different: wilder,
more excited. He spoke of the commandos, the torpedo boat,
the guns. He spoke as if he were head salesman, and the officers his reps. HMS *Fidelity*, he stressed, was now capable as
any warship, kept safe from submarine strike by her torpedo
boat. And pretty soon they'd be leaving Southampton for
Scotland: their final preparations as a crew, the first time all
the disparate elements of the ship's complement would have
come together.

Finally, he broke the news. They'd be sailing to Burma, he said, to serve under Admiral Sir James Somerville, Commander-in-Chief of the Eastern Fleet. The fact that, over the past two years, *Fidelity* had been transformed from a dishevelled French merchantman to what – he now stressed – was an unrivalled fighting machine was down to the influence he held in the Admiralty. Official documents prove his case: that he was a 'good friend' of Ian Fleming, wartime personal assistant to Rear-Admiral John Godfrey, Director of Naval Intelligence, and later the creator of James Bond; that his self-made connections went all the way to Admiral Sir Dudley Pound, First Sea Lord and Chief of Naval Staff. Now, though, he threw out just one further name: Admiral Lord Mountbatten, Chief of Combined Operations. The presence on board of a dedicated Royal Marines Commando unit was, he said, down to the personal intervention of Mountbatten himself.

There is no record of the connection in any of Mountbatten's writings, nor his biographies, but it is more than likely true. As Chief of Combined Operations, Mountbatten was in charge of a force 'whose long-term function', in the words of his official biographer Philip Ziegler, 'was to prepare the way for the invasion of Europe, but which, in the meantime, was responsible for raids on the continental mainland'. His orders from Churchill made this explicit: the invasion of Europe was to be his main objective – with 'a programme of raids of ever-increasing intensity'. His weapons for such raids were the commandos – his 'test pilots' – which, by the late summer of 1942, had already secured some notable successes, most striking of which was the raid on the German submarine base at St-Nazaire in March 1942. Any detachment of commandos would have had to have been approved by him: and so he must have known and approved of Claude.

Claude turned to O'Neill. 'Isn't that so, John?' he said. 'You were there when Mountbatten promised me the best commando troops he had.'

O'Neill nodded. Claude pressed on. He loosened his tie, threw his jacket on to the back of a chair.

'My friends,' he said, the very Caesar, 'I will lead you to glory. And if we die, our end shall be noble. Heroic.'

He bent down, and from a locker pulled a bottle of whisky. He passed round glasses, and walked around the circle, filling each one.

'To destiny, my friends,' he said, raising his own glass at last. Only Madeleine looked down, her eyes on a point on the floor midway between the officers and herself and Claude. She moved one foot against the other.

'To destiny,' Claude repeated, raising his glass to his lips. 'To death. And to glory.'

THROUGH THE SUMMER, travelling to and from London with Madeleine, Claude – unbeknownst to his crew – had been trying to secure some measure of financial security for his men. Two years on from the fall of France, with still no sign of Churchill's promised British-naturalization papers, Claude was now pressing for money. The Ministry of Aviation Production, he claimed in June, still owed him £500, a sum which could easily be raised by the sale of cargo still in storage in Gibraltar. Minutes of a meeting held that month record Claude calling for 'a sum of £500 (no more) to be handed to him for the benefit of some of the necessitous members of his crew. He explained that some members of his original French crew are no longer fit for service and he has, out of his own pocket, bought a cottage in the country [Cliff Cottage, on the Isle of Wight], to which he can send these needy men. He now needs to reimburse his outlay on the cottage to spend it, I understand, for the men's benefit.'

If there was something disingenuous about Claude's plea – the cottage after all, was already occupied by him and Madeleine, and nowhere else is there any mention of disabled crew members in need of special accommodation – it is also apparent that Claude saw himself from the start as more than just a military leader to his men. He was parent, school-teacher, general, dictator, mother hen. Whether there was in fact even one 'crippled' crewman, as he put it in one of his first letters, or several who were 'no longer fit for active service', in the words of a late-August petition to government, he believed he was owed more than he had been given. As summer turned to autumn, his correspondence became shot through with frustration: 'In reply to para 3 of your letter, I should think that there must be a misunderstanding,' he wrote. 'May I recapitulate . . .'

No decision was taken. Within Whitehall, letters were drafted, typed, despatched and landed on the desks of civil servants who ruminated, consulted and deferred. For every bureaucrat who suggested that 'the position of Commander Langlais and his crew is so special that it might be desirable to consider' paying Claude 'in order that he may expend it for the benefit of his crew', there was another who regretted that, 'on the case as presented, we can't agree to a payment'. While his commandos travelled to Manchester at the end of October for two weeks' parachute training, Claude fought on for his men. When the commandos returned, and *Fidelity* sailed from Southampton for Ullapool, he was still lobbying.

SIX WEEKS FROM her departure for the Far East, *Fidelity* sailed alone up the coast of Wales and on into Scottish waters. The seaplanes flew north separately, to rendezvous in Loch Broom. The eight-strong crew of the torpedo boat, with their vessel hoisted on board, were assigned regular watch duty. On the approach to Ullapool, Michael Pollard, the torpedo boat's twenty-one-year-old first lieutenant, was asked by Claude if he'd been keeping his charts up to date.

'Being an honest chap,' Pollard recalled, 'I said, "No, not at all." We'd been issued with a complete set of the south and west coasts, which I considered to be overkill.'

Claude was 'very upset': he shouted, remonstrated, demanded to know what Pollard would have done if he'd ordered the boat into the water with no warning. He told Pollard to update his charts immediately, and stopped all shore leave until he'd seen evidence that the job was done.

Pollard, who only had 'a month or two's' annotations to include, took little time to finish the work. Claude gave him a present: 'a fantastic pistol, a Luger, as well as boxes of nine-millimetre ammunition'. To Lieutenant John O'Neill, Pollard's immediate superior, Claude gave a Mauser pistol. 'He never said where they came from, but they were beautiful presents. I suppose that meant he'd forgiven me.'

FIDELITY dropped anchor in Loch Broom, mooring in deep water on the southern side of the loch. The whitewashed harbourfront of Ullapool, the largest settlement in Wester Ross, lay half a mile due north, on the other side of the water. As the crew took their bearings – looking across the snow-frosted moorland to the peak of Stac Pollaidh, rising like a figment of the American West from the wintry tundra; glimpsing ptarmigan, pale as ice, take flight from a granite cliff edge in their winter plumage – they could see just the single dwelling on their side of the loch. It was a crofter's cottage – marked Alt na h-Airbhe on Pollard's charts – with a single-track approach road, winding down through hairpins from a mountain pass.

All the way north the barometer had fallen, and with it the easy warmth of the late-summer south coast. Loch Broom, at twenty-one miles, is the longest sea loch in north-west Scotland and, with coming winter, was doing its best to live up to the Gaelic *a'bhraoin* – 'loch of the showers' – from which its name is derived. Up here, such is the scale of the landscape and the speed of meteorological fluctuations, that it can seem as though two or three weather systems – sleet, hail, rainbow, stillness and sunshine, white water approaching across a loch calm enough to hear the outbreath of porpoises – are in operation at the same time. Westerly swells, sweeping off the Atlantic, can drive all the way through to the head of the loch: on rougher days, Pollard and the crew of the torpedo boat found themselves confined to *Fidelity*.

It was, Pollard recalled, 'quite unusual to go to that part of Scotland to do training and manoeuvres', but everything about *Fidelity* was unusual, and – if their cover was to be maintained – secrecy was key. Claude, away from the scrutiny of superior officers, set out a programme of exercises to test beach-landing techniques. He and Madeleine would stand on the bridge and watch while Milner-Gibson oversaw the lowering of the landing craft. A group of men would already

be ashore, hidden in the bracken and behind soft licheny
boulders, up to their knees in peatbog, waiting to defend
'their' territory. Obsessed by verisimilitude – and wanting to
emulate training conditions at Achnacarry – Claude insisted
on live ammunition being used, and so when the commandos
abseiled down the side of the ship into the landing craft and
began the approach to shore, they kept their heads low, the
crack and whine of incoming fire only just overhead.

Claude and Madeleine seemed playful, mischievous,
relishing moments of danger, often firing over the heads of
the commandos as they neared shore; looking back, the men
would see them laughing, as if all this really were a game; as if,
far from the theatre of war under splintering golden skies
and heather dusted with early snow, there really was no war,
no enemy. Claude, Pollard remembered, had been 'very quick
to make contact with the local laird on arrival in Ullapool', and
when not making sport of the preparations for war, he took
his officers deer stalking.

Through the end of November and into the early part of
December this was increasingly how Claude and Madeleine
spent their time. Claude left the commandos under the leadership of Captain Harry Grant-Dalton, and he and Madeleine
– and, on occasion, select other officers – spent days in the
mountains with local ghillies, getting downwind of the red-
deer sentinel stags as they stood sentry for their herds, inching
on their bellies under rock outcrops till they were close and
still enough to take a shot.

They walked the banks of the Lael and Broom and Dun-
donnell rivers – salmon kicking free of the honey-coloured
water – and, like the commandos, pulled the pins from
grenades and lobbed them into the water, scooping out the
casualties with hands slippery from fish scale. On these trips,

Claude would use the torpedo boat as his taxi transport, requesting O'Neill and Pollard to drop him and Madeleine and the rest of the hunting party at another point on the lochside, and anchor offshore till they were ready to be picked up. Pollard – the times he was the one waiting with the boat – remembered these as long days. 'One time,' he said, 'we'd taken the party to a remote part of the loch. I remained on board to look after the boat while the others went off. I soon lost sight of them. After an hour or two I was getting rather bored since there was not a lot to look at other than a shag feeding in the loch some way from the shore. I had my new Luger with me and decided on some target practice, since the whole area appeared to be clear. My shots were surprisingly close, but never hit the shag, which dived after every shot. However, the bullets richocheted off the water and whined on over the opposite shore where, out of sight, the shore party was walking.' When Claude returned at the end of the day, Pollard had to face his anger. Why had he been shooting at them? He'd seen no seabirds, no legitimate target. Placating Claude took 'a lot of explanation'.

Yet Pollard, with his rogue marksmanship, was doing no more than following Claude's lead. The live-ammunition practice landings continued and, a few days after Claude had heard Pollard's bullets whistle past his own head, a commando was brought down, hit from behind, the bullet slicing through his cervical vertebra. Most likely it was Claude who pulled the trigger, not realizing that a shot aimed low across the water – 'to add realism', in Pollard's words – would glance up again on impact, its trajectory barely slowed.

There were moments of irony, even farce. One rough day, with a sharp nor'wester blowing off the Minch, the torpedo boat was sent south to pick up a senior admiral, come to check up on *Fidelity*'s readiness for combat. O'Neill piloted the craft down the coast – past Gruinard Island, round Greenstone Point – pulling into Loch Ewe with the swell finally behind him. He boarded his passenger and turned into the wind again. The sun was flint-bright on the water and the admiral, according to Pollard, 'was full of interest to begin with, wishing to see how fast she would go'. O'Neill obliged, opening up the throttle, hammering the wooden bow up the peaks, into the lulls. The admiral grew silent, his face pale. When they pulled alongside the fishing boats on the Ullapool quay he staggered from the boat, hand to his mouth. For the way back – despite the distance, the snow-blown icy miles of Desolation Road – he ordered a car.

For Claude, the state of the torpedo boat, and the preparation and confidence of its crew, were crucial. Travelling east in convoy, slower than the corvettes, *Fidelity* would be especially vulnerable; without her seaplanes, circling for U-boats, and her torpedo boat – small enough to be a near-impossible target, yet with enough armament to see off predators – she'd stand little chance in the mid-winter Atlantic. And so he was often on board the smaller craft, encouraging, quizzing O'Neill, overseeing training. The crew became swift and light-footed, loading torpedoes at speed, launching practice warheads towards the open sea. There were hitches, though: on one occasion, a torpedo hit the water, dived, then turned through ninety degrees and ploughed for shore. 'It headed for the south bank,' Pollard remembered. 'This side of the loch was virtually uninhabited, with only one rather pretty little white house on the whole length. Our torpedo went straight for this, running up the beach, through the open garden gate and halfway up the garden path before stopping.' The recovery party stepped ashore with some trepidation, nervous lest the crofter react violently to finding a torpedo in his garden. But the house was unoccupied, and the weapon was hefted back on board as quickly as possible, O'Neill and Pollard shaking their heads as they gunned out across open water towards *Fidelity*, still laughing as they secured the torpedo boat to the stern warp and readied themselves to tell Claude.

To POLLARD, Madeleine remained enigmatic. Her quietness in the wardroom, the way she sat and listened, offering just the occasional word, a diplomatic intervention when Claude was becoming heated, impressed him. 'She was a very intelligent woman who had the knack of listening to conversations without joining in. She kept away from everyday life on board.' Yet he noticed, on occasion, a 'strong motherly streak', and a contrasting ability – when she chose to shed her reserve – 'to become the life and soul of the party in no uncertain manner'.

Much of their time in Loch Broom, Claude and Madeleine chose not to spend their evenings in the wardroom with the other officers, preferring instead the privacy of Claude's cabin. Madeleine had hinted to those officers she most trusted that the journey east, and the task that awaited them in Burma, would be their most dangerous assignment yet, and she'd spoken openly of her fears that they would not return. Alone with Claude, there was no need for pretence: here she could shed the professional front required before the other men – the steely spy, resolute as any man – and soften.

One evening, she and Claude surprised the other officers by appearing unannounced in the wardroom. Michael Pollard remembered them 'just seeming convivial: I don't think we were celebrating anything in particular'.

The drinking began: claret, whisky, champagne. Uncharacteristically, Madeleine stepped away from Claude's side to joke and talk with the other officers. There was a fluidity to the evening: men talking in groups of two and three, then joining with others to form larger packs where the conversation was more communal. It grew late.

Claude, standing in the middle of the room, held up a wine glass. He rang a fingernail against the bulb and the wardroom fell to silence.

'So,' he announced, his accent more indistinct than ever. 'What is the position of the paymaster?'

To Pollard, the enigmatic nature of this opener – and the wide-mouthed grin that accompanied it – served as warning. 'We all sat up and took notice.'

The paymaster slowly raised a hand, uncertain whether to return Claude's smile. Claude called him over and ordered him to take down his trousers and underpants. Unnoticed, Madeleine picked her way through the men and left the room.

Claude stood, hands on hips, while *Fidelity*'s paymaster unbuttoned his fly and, eyes on the ground, let his trousers fall in concertina rolls around his boots. He was just hooking his thumbs under the elastic of his naval-issue underpants when Madeleine came back in. She was carrying something in her hand: a small glass bottle, and a paintbrush.

She placed herself in front of the paymaster and – with a murmur now running around the room – unscrewed the top of the bottle. She dipped the brush, held the bristles against the rim to let the excess drain away, and then lifted it out. It was ink, scarlet and running down the handle of the brush. She bent down and, in Pollard's words, 'anointed the paymaster's testicles'.

Claude thanked Madeleine – suddenly formal, as if she'd done no more than efficiently perform some clerical duty – then nodded at the paymaster, who grabbed at his trousers.

Claude, looking around, beckoned another officer over. The other men were now whooping and calling out – half through nerves, half through relief it was not them standing there half naked in front of Madeleine and her glistening paintbrush. She 'joined in', according to Pollard, 'with great alacrity': as if only when performing the forbidden did she become fully alive. Few men, said Pollard, remained undaubed: the ceremony continued 'until everyone was pretty exhausted'.

THEY SAILED SOUTH during the first week of December and, in Liverpool, took their last leave before setting off for the Far East. Claude's instructions were now specific: documents from naval intelligence to Admiral Somerville stated that *Fidelity* was expected to 'carry out amphibious operations under your orders, in conjunction with SOE and India Combined Operations HQ as and when appropriate'. Should these tasks prove unfeasible for any reason, *Fidelity* was to act as a regional convoy escort, or 'on training duties . . . in India and Ceylon'.

Refuelling, overrun by mechanics servicing her engines one last time, by armament engineers checking her torpedo tubes, depth-charge gear, landing craft, Asdic and anti-aircraft guns, *Fidelity* received a surprise visit. Pat O'Leary, in London for a debriefing with the British escape organization MI9, had heard that Claude and Madeleine were preparing to leave for Burma, and he took the train to Liverpool to wish them well.

In the nineteen months since Claude and Madeleine had last seen O'Leary, he'd become one of the British secret service's most valued agents. Having been sprung from prison in Nîmes, following his abortive landing at Collioure on the south coast of France, he'd been involved in the setting up from Marseilles of an organization that, over the course of the war, enabled more than six hundred Allied prisoners of war and shot-down airmen – among them Airey Neave, fleeing Colditz – to return to Britain and combat. In October 1941, O'Leary – as cocktail-party charming as he was disciplined and applied – took over command, and the escape network became 'his': the 'Pat Line'. With each 'parcel' costing some £200 to get home – with his escapees' Spanish guards requiring cash not only to escort the fugitives across the Pyrenees but to buy food for them along the way – he'd become adept at fundraising from local and national French businesses. He'd dress in disguise: as a black-clad priest, travelling by train through occupied France; as a Marseilles businessman, in suit and tie, kid-leather briefcase.

On board his old ship, O'Leary was introduced by Claude to the men who'd joined since his departure in April 1941: Pollard, like the others, had 'a brief chat, but [O'Leary] spent most of the time talking to his old friends'. O'Leary was aware that the men, more than at any time in the past, were heading into extremely hazardous territory: not only the threat of U-boats, which would not likely be unaware of the forty-five-vessel convoy now assembling in ports across Britain, but the Japanese forces controlling much of the Far East.

O'Leary's feelings for Claude and Madeleine went far beyond the professional; he loved them, and felt much affinity with them; and referred to them later in terms that made his feelings unequivocal. Madeleine he found alluring – 'blonde and sophisticated', 'enchanting', with 'dancing feet and blush-red fingernails' – while, for Claude, only superlatives would do. He was, as he later told Claude's sister-in-law, 'the finest warrior I have ever known'.

Yet today he had come, in Pollard's assessment, 'to say

goodbye'. He walked the deck with Claude and Madeleine, drank coffee in the wardroom, stood quietly on the bridge with them and watched the activity below. And then he embraced them both, and walked off down the quay, waving one last time before he disappeared from view.

THE ATLANTIC OCEAN, DECEMBER 1942

THEY LEFT ON a Friday – 18 December 1942 – and as the last ship cleared the Mersey estuary, the Liverpool section of the convoy began to take shape. By the time they reached Malin Head, the most northerly point of Northern Ireland, there were forty-five vessels. On these clear first days, the sky chalky with high-altitude fishbone cirrus, and an easy rolling swell, Claude and Madeleine, on the bridge of *Fidelity* – positioned at the back of the convoy – could pick out ships all the way to the front, some six miles south. Seen from above, there would have been a pleasing symmetry to the pattern below: twelve columns of ships, a half mile separating each vessel from the fantail wake of the one in front. Forty-five vessels which had travelled from the Humber, Tyne, Firth of Forth, Bristol Channel, Merseyside and Clyde, and which would, in time, be heading for Panama, New York or North Africa or, in the case of *Fidelity*, the Far East: gunmetal specks against a beaten-steel ocean, hoping for protection in numbers, for 1942 had been the worst year of the war so far for Allied shipping lost to U-boat attack. In March, ninety-four ships were sunk; in May, one hundred and twenty-five; in June, one hundred and forty-four; and from then until now, the figure settled on around a hundred a month: twenty-three a week, three a day.

By the time *Fidelity*'s convoy – ONS154, 'O' for 'outward-bound from Britain'; 'N' for 'destined for North America'; 'S' for 'slow' – set sail, U-boat losses were mounting too. At the start of 1942, Germany had two hundred and sixty submarines at sea, and was adding to this fleet at a rate of twenty a month: at any one moment, it was possible for it to have a hundred U-boats in the Atlantic at the same time. They patrolled the convoy routes in long lines, and attacked in 'wolf packs' of ten, fifteen, twenty at a time.

The Allies, foreseeing certain defeat if this pitch of destruction continued, brought in self-contained strike forces of six or eight escort vessels – two-hundred-foot long corvettes, their low-convex whaler sterns heavy with depth-charge rails – that were kept continuously at sea, ready to run to the help of convoys that came under attack. *Fidelity*'s convoy had an escort of five corvettes and one destroyer. The escort ships occupied no fixed position, instead working the perimeter of the convoy, chivvying stragglers back into position and scanning the ocean for anything – a flash of white water, the distant speck of a conning tower – that might indicate that there were U-boats closing in. With her floatplanes and torpedo boat, it was hoped that *Fidelity* could offer the other ships an extra level of cover; and Rear Admiral Wyon Egerton, convoy commodore, had given her a position of central responsibility: as the middle ship in the last row, she was mirror-vessel to Egerton's merchantman SS *Empire Shackleton*, which sat centre of the front row, the low baritone of the racing screw palpable through every inch of her deck plating.

THE CONVOY passed north of Ireland, then on into the open Atlantic, leaving the coast of County Mayo, then County Kerry, a long way to port. Three days in, the weather began to change. The skies turned purplish, lead-bellied with rain that, with the rising wind, drove horizontally across deck. Claude spent much of his time on the bridge; Madeleine was seldom seen. Those of *Fidelity*'s officers on watch worked four-hour

By the end of 1942, convoys were protected by escort warships

shifts, followed by the same period off-duty: mealtimes, and rest. In these early days, much the most challenging task was keeping the ship in formation. The convoy, Pollard recalled, progressed 'along a predetermined zigzag course', similar to a sailboat tacking into the wind, 'except that alterations in course would be made at differing intervals of time and be of a differing number of degrees'. The object – 'to confuse any watching U-boats' – made navigation 'a complex game'.

Claude, worsening weather notwithstanding, was in exuberant spirits. *Fidelity*, he felt sure, was certain to see action en route for the Far East, and he rated her chances highly. As well as the Kingfisher floatplanes and torpedo boat, she was one of only two ships in the convoy carrying high-frequency direction-finding equipment, which enabled her radio operator – working closely with Madeleine, at the cipher desk – to pick up wireless-telegraphy signals sent by U-boats. From October 1941 – their faces lunar green before the cathode-ray display screens – radio operators had been able to gauge both the bearing and distance of enemy submarines using this new technology. Yet, as one of the outriders of the convoy, *Fidelity* was also at increased danger, more vulnerable, less protected. Most likely was that, should she at any time fall behind the rest of the convoy and be sighted by a U-boat, she'd be judged a trap, and treated accordingly. As the German Submarine Commander's Handbook put it, 'Submarine traps must be reckoned with in dealing with convoys. These have instructions to station themselves among the last steamers, and to fall behind, pretending that they have engine trouble, etc, in order thus to attract attacking submarines, to lead them away from the convoy and to be able to attack them. Be cautious, therefore, when attacking steamers sailing behind convoys.'

BY 22 DECEMBER, with the convoy well into the mid-Atlantic, the barometer was dropping fast. Henry Revely, third officer on board SS *Zarian*, a merchantman carrying six thousand tons of military stores, aircraft and bullion to Freetown and other North African ports, was finding it hard to cross from one side of the wheelhouse without 'crashing against the . . . doors as I went through . . . The sea was roughing and the wind increasing . . . *Zarian* was behaving uncomfortably now. As her head came out of the trough she tossed heavy spray aft on to the bridge and solid water was being lopped over her shoulder in heavy dollops to smash against the winches and deck fittings.'

The ferocity of the storm – gale force and rising by morning on 23 December, 'whipping the tops from the great Atlantic rollers' – forced each ship to focus on survival.

Zarian 'was battling hard to lift her head out of the troughs and climb the vicious masses of oncoming water. Mostly she climbed to the crest, but often had to slice through the last ten feet or so which viciously smashed on to her foc'sle head to thud and cascade on to her foredeck, staggering her by the sheer weight. Her stern tossed high, baring her propeller so that the engines raced madly. As the day became lighter the storm-lashed ocean revealed one other ship. Somewhere abroad almost fifty ships had lost their way in one night of dispersion.'

These kind of high seas were typical in the winter Atlantic: in December 1942, winds of force seven and above were recorded on twenty-six days. Many of *Fidelity*'s crew had never experienced such conditions before, and cowered queasily in their bunks, listening to the groaning of the bulkheads, trying to read under sputtering electric bulbs as, during the first night watch, the wind touched gale-force nine.

The ocean had now become the enemy, and Claude ordered all hatches to be bolted down. Below him on the fore-deck the landing craft and floatplanes were awash in white water, which sluiced across a submerged deck every time the ship cut upwards through the rising crest. The bridge windows streamed thrown spray. Crewmen and commandos checked their life jackets, and ran through their emergency items: photographs, miniatures of rum, plugs of tobacco, chocolate. There were three hundred and thirty-two men on board, as well as one woman – eight times the number for which *Fidelity* had been designed – and the building heat in the engine room showed that the ship was starting to feel the strain.

SOME WAY NORTH of the convoy, two packs of German sub-marines were at sea. Working on the basis of reports received from Beobachtungsdienst, or B-dienst, the German navy's signal-intelligence service, Admiral Karl Dönitz, head of the U-boat division, had been expecting a large convoy to appear off the west coast of Ireland around 23 December, and he'd issued orders for two groups of submarines – 'Spitz', literally, 'pointed'; and 'Ungestüm', 'impetuous'; a total of eighteen boats – to intercept it. The storm, though, meant the U-boat commanders – like the crew of *Fidelity* and the other ships in the convoy – were reduced to struggling for survival. On watch in the conning tower, the wind – as Oberleutnant zur See Herbert A. Werner, a longstanding U-boat commander, wrote of another, similarly ferocious gale – 'punished us with driving snow, sleet, hail, and frozen spray. It beat against our rubber diver's suits, cut our faces like a razor, and threatened to tear away our eye masks; only the steel belts around our waists secured us to boat and life. Below, inside the bobbing steel cockleshell, the boat's violent up-and-down motion drove us to the floor-plates and hurled us straight up and threw us around like puppets.'

The U-boats had come from bases all along the west coast of occupied France – Brest, Lorient, La Pallice, St-Nazaire – as well as Kiel, home of the Fifth U-Boat Flotilla. By the last week of December, most had been at sea at least a month, and their crews – forty-four officers and men in the case of a VIIC U-boat, which comprised the majority of the Spitz and Ungestüm fleets – were unwashed, bearded, already longing for shore leave. Inside, even when sailing on the surface, the interior of the hulls was humid and dank; men worked in clothes that seemed never to dry and ate bread that was often soggy and mildewed. Condensation made the cold steel of the hull beady and glistening with moisture. In the wild seas of 22 and 23 December, crewmen were smashed about the cabins as their boats raced to the rendezvous; only the routine daily trim dive brought relief, enabling the men to finish chores they'd been unable to do on the surface. At these moments, the bow compartments were transformed into workshops, the hammocks stowed and bunks raised as the torpedomen greased the torpedoes, checked hydroplane controls and oiled lubrication points. At night, the U-boats fought through the spray on the surface, the lookout men with their heavy Zeiss binoculars hanging useless around their necks.

The men dreamed of exercise. 'I'd give a lot for a half-hour's walk – or a cross-country run through the woods,' laments the narrator of Lothar-Günther Buchheim's *Das Boot*. 'My calf muscles have gone slack. My existence consists of nothing but lying down, standing up, and sitting still. Some hard physical exercise would be a big help. Felling trees, for instance.' And they pined for women. Korvettekapitän Wolfgang Lüth, commander of *U181*, felt like many U-boat commanders that female contact was essential for his crew's well-being. 'Though I know that a woman can break a man's fighting spirit, I also know that she can give him strength, and I have often observed that married men return from their leave particularly well rested for a new mission,' he told a naval officers' convention at the end of 1943. Brothels in submarine ports operated at capacity: on leave from serving in *U230* in Brest, Herbert Werner remembered nights in the Casino Bar with Suzanne, Janine, Paulette and Simone. In Lorient, recuperating from a cruise, 'if the days were long, so were the nights. Our crewmen had inherited the local *établissements*; they enjoyed the girls who had served many a sailor before them, including comrades who now lay on the ocean floor.'

Shore life could be as wild and unfettered as the weeks

of confinement on board were routine-bound and, often, alcohol-free. According to Lüth, the crew could 'take a swig from the bottle now and then on special occasions, as when a steamer is sunk or if someone gets soaked while working on the upper deck'. Entertainments were few: songs on Sunday on the gramophone, a pool of well-leafed illustrated magazines.

Yet, despite the myth of the U-boat crew as somehow the gentleman arm of Hitler's armed forces, by the end of 1942 Dönitz was coming under increasing pressure to use whatever means he could to ensure the destruction of Allied seamen and ships. At a conference in the Reich Chancellery on the afternoon of 28 September 1942, the U-boat chief listened while, in the words of the official minutes, '[the Führer called] attention to the fact that it is very much to our disadvantage if a large percentage of the crew of sunken merchant ships is able to go to sea again in new ships'. Hitler's orders to Dönitz left no room for doubt: 'It is nonsense to offer provisions to survivors in their lifeboats, or provide sailing instructions for their return home. I hereby order that ships and their crews are to be destroyed, even if the crews are in lifeboats.' Dönitz, according to an eyewitness, stood up to Hitler in a manner the leader seldom encountered. 'No, *mein Führer*. It goes against the honour of a seaman to shoot at shipwrecked survivors. I cannot issue such an order. My U-boat men are volunteers, waging a costly struggle in the belief they are fighting honourably for a good cause. Their combat morale would be undermined by this order. I must request that you withdraw it.' Hitler, extraordinarily, backed down. 'Do what you want, but no more offering assistance and sailing instructions.'

The issue, however, remained confused and open to interpretation. Dönitz's biographer Peter Padfield, working from evidence Dönitz gave at his trial at Nuremberg, has written that Hitler 'knew that behind Dönitz's ostensible orders to take Captains, Chief Engineers, Chief Officers and Navigators prisoner, lay secret instructions, given orally to Commanders, to annihilate survivors – so long as this did not endanger the boat.' This conclusion would appear to be backed up by the Nuremberg testimony of Kiel U-boat chief Korvettekapitän Karl-Heinz Möhler, in which he said that he had told commanders that 'U-Boat Command cannot give you such an order officially. Everybody had to handle this according to their own conscience.'

Yet, despite Möhler's stand, there remains only one incontrovertible and verifiable case of a U-boat crew firing upon survivors. En route to the Indian Ocean, *U852*, commanded by Kapitänleutnant Heinz Eck, sank the Greek steamer *Peleus* south-west of Freetown on 13 March 1944. Through the night, Eck cruised the wreckage, ordering his watch officer to machine-gun men who were clinging to rafts and timber beams and hatchboards. Three men survived, and it was their evidence that convicted Eck and his officers to death by shooting. Eck went to his death denying that Dönitz had any part in his decision to kill the survivors of *Peleus*.

Möhler, though, remained an influential figure until the end of the war. Between his assumption of command of the Fifth U-Boat Flotilla in June 1941 and late December 1942, when Spitz and Ungestüm assembled in the eastern Atlantic, moving south in search of the giant convoy German intelligence had promised, the men of more than half of the eighteen U-boats that comprised the two wolf packs had served time under his command. Men such as Kapitänleutnant Siegfried Strelow who, at thirty-one, was the same age as Madeleine and three years Claude's junior; who, during his career so far, had sunk seven Allied ships; and who, as Christmas Day drew near and the storms began to ease off, stood alongside his lookout men scanning the horizon for the dark etchings of smoke on the horizon that would indicate that, finally, they were within sight of their prey.

24 TO 25 DECEMBER 1942

FOR THE SHIPS IN the convoy, Christmas Eve brought relief: a rising barometer, and wind that had eased to force five. The sea was still heavy, but the ships were less endangered, and began to regroup. 'The sea had lost its viciousness,' remembered Henry Revely, SS *Zarian*'s third officer, and *Zarian*'s captain ordered full speed. By mid-morning, the merchantman was a mile off the port side of the convoy, and Revely noticed that the other ships were flying their 'convoy pennants to help identify the stations they were trying to make'. The escort ships operated like sheepdogs, harassing stragglers back into position. By three that afternoon, with *St Laurent* silhouetted against a 'low, lemon sunset' at the western head of the convoy, all the ships had been gathered. Night fell, and, for the first time since leaving Britain, the moon lay on the ocean, bright and pale as bone.

Come Christmas Day, the convoy was making good headway once more. On board *Fidelity*, the day passed without festivity. Pollard recalled that, 'in my experience, no HM ship ever drank at sea – other than rum rations for the ratings – and *Fidelity* was no exception to this. The wardroom bar was only opened when the ship was in harbour or anchored in some safe haven.' On *Zarian*, though, the cook served roast turkey, followed by Christmas pudding. 'All too soon' Revely was called back to the bridge; and 'the festivities of Christmas Day night, be they so called, had come to an end'.

26 TO 27 DECEMBER 1942

AT FOUR-TWENTY on the afternoon of Boxing Day, the lookout watch on the conning tower of *U664* reported to their commander, Oberleutnant Adolf Graef, that they'd sighted ships on the horizon. For a boat now long out of port, which had pushed itself at close to seventeen knots for the previous twenty-four hours, the sighting was cause for jubilation and relief. Graef gave instructions for the boat to steer parallel to the convoy, about six miles off its port flank. He stood in the conning tower, binoculars raised. 'At least forty ships,' he called out. 'Steering two hundred and sixty degrees, speed seven knots.' In the radio room, the news was tapped out to Dönitz at his headquarters in Paris.

So far, to plan: these were standard wolf-pack tactics, established by Dönitz in the spring of 1941: first, the laying of a patrol line of submarines along a convoy's anticipated path; then the radio report back to Dönitz or his operations chief Eberhard Godt; then the wolf-pack's race to get ahead of the convoy by nightfall, when the U-boats would attack through the heart of the formation.

Dönitz sent a one-line reply to Graef: keep contact, await orders to attack. Graef closed to four miles and, as he drew parallel once more, the soundsman reported 'propeller vibrations bearing 010 degrees'. Graef sounded the alarm and pitched the submarine into a steep dive. At one hundred metres he levelled, blew the tanks, and waited.

CLAUDE AND MADELEINE, standing together on the bridge under the broken skies of Boxing Day, saw only order: the snaking wakes of the ships running before them as they zigzagged in formation; the windblown smoke trails from the ships' funnels, identical in angle and density, in the way they blew up and then sideways and then dissolved to nothing. On board *Fidelity*, the easing of the storm had brought relief; and now, though it was starting to drizzle and though spray was still blowing from the crests of the waves like spindrift, the boat was rolling and pitching less. Men had emerged from their bunks and were sitting in small groups in the crowded cabin spaces, playing cards and talking.

They were far from home: midway between Newfoundland and the north-west tip of Portugal, in an area of the Atlantic known as the 'Black Pit', too far from North America or Europe to be reachable by Allied air support, where U-boats could travel at speed on the surface without fear of being attacked.

It had been a long, unrelenting storm, and *Fidelity*'s convoy had only caught the tail. From the second week of December, conditions in the Atlantic had been so extreme that Dönitz had called for a temporary suspension of U-boat operations: until now, December had seen the sinking of just four Allied merchantmen and one British destroyer. Ordering the two packs of U-boats into the southern section of the northern Atlantic, then, was in part the result of intelligence, part guesswork: the only way for convoys to avoid the severest weather, Dönitz figured, would be to steer a more southerly route, precisely the same conclusion that Rear Admiral Egerton, ONS154 convoy commodore, had reached.

MIDNIGHT ON Boxing Day. The ships were about five hundred miles due north of the Azores. On board *Fidelity*, Madeleine was in her cabin once again, suffering from sea-sickness. Oberleutnant Adolf Graef brought his boat to the surface. For the past two hours, jolted by the reverberations from depth charges dropped by the corvette HMCS *Shediac* – lights fusing, plates smashing in the galley, men with their hands over their ears – he'd waited at depth. Now, with silence above, and the metallic ping of the sonar having receded to inaudibility, he judged it safe to bring the boat up. Standing in the conning tower, though, he could see nothing. A cold drizzle was falling, gauzy curtains of mist sweeping from the west. Below, his soundsman reported that the hydrophone had picked up the distant drone of propeller screws. Graef scrambled down the ladder and set his course once more.

MAINTAINING POSITION in such conditions was proving difficult and stressful for the ships in the convoy. They were underway in complete darkness, all navigation lights out. 'Four hours on the bridge could be a nightmare,' recalled Henry Revely. 'The dark, shapeless loom of a ship closing on the beam quickened [our] heartbeats.' Anxiously, he came off watch. He tested the red safety bulb on his life jacket and lay down in his bunk to rest.

He did not sleep. At midnight on 26 December, the look-out post on *Shediac* sighted a U-boat some way to port of the convoy, making rapid headway as if trying to outpace the ships. To judge from U-boat records, the submarine was probably Graef's *U664*, which now found itself suddenly under a white-phosphorus sky, exposed by the carnation bursts of starshell flares. Revely, recalling the moment – the slow drift earthward of 'scores' of parachute-slung flares – saw 'the black sky of a moment before . . . filled with . . . scintillating lights, descending like an invasion from outer space'.

And then, darkness. On board *Fidelity*, Claude was standing on the bridge. Over the last four days he'd had only snatched sleep, and – while Madeleine worked in the sepulchral glow of the cipher room – he hurried between the bridge and the radio operator. Though exhausted – surviving on coffee, a mug gripped always in his hand – he was voluble, unable to sit down, wanting continual updates on submarine soundings.

Throughout the night of 26 December, into the small hours of 27 December, *Fidelity* seemed in no immediate danger. Unlike SS *Zarian*, which was sailing on the port flank of the convoy, *Fidelity* was in the back row, five columns in, protected from the rear by three corvettes. The escorts, though, seldom maintained a fixed position, and there were long hours where there was little cover. At eight in the evening of 26 December, *Shediac*, the corvette positioned immediately behind *Fidelity*, broke away from the convoy to attack *U664*, forcing Graef, its commander, to stay submerged until midnight. On *Fidelity*'s bridge, the lookouts nervously watched their stern, depth-charge crews ready.

The night passed slowly. The last of the starshell flares had hissed to darkness in the water. It took a few moments for Claude's eyesight to adjust, to begin to pick the shapes of vessels from the blackness around. The rumble and boom of exploding depth charges was becoming more frequent, and seemed to be moving closer. At 4.15 a.m., he saw an explosion of blood-orange light more than a mile to the south, fanning and rising, spreading till it seemed to melt into the underside of the clouds.

In the communications room, Madeleine heard the news from the radio operator: SS *King Edward*, a merchantman carrying forty-eight men and a cargo of slag ballast to New York, had been torpedoed. A minute after impact, the bridge had tilted backwards. Two lifeboats had hit the water, men scrambling hand over hand, their legs slipping on wet rope. Just as the captain had reached his lifeboat, the ship's engines had exploded, tearing a hole in her midriff. She had sunk like a closing book, folding the second lifeboat into the vortex of her descent, upending the boat and catapulting her men into the boiling phosphorescent water.

King Edward was the third ship to go that night. Three hours earlier, SS *Empire Union* – a freighter running at the convoy's far south-western tip, a good two miles from *Fidelity* – was struck and sunk; and, just ten minutes later, SS *Melrose Abbey*, carrying three and a half thousand tons of coal and

Depth charges in action

seven hundred tons of mail for Port of Spain, Trinidad, was holed. Both ships, close neighbours on the convoy's forward starboard tip, were victims of Kapitänleutnant Klaus Hartmann, in *U441*. In uncertain seas, and under cloud so low it seemed to obscure the ships' topmost rigging, he attacked on the surface, untroubled by the corvettes until, at a quarter to five in the morning and reloading for another volley of torpedoes, he saw a warship closing fast. He dived to one hundred and forty metres, rocked by depth charges all the way.

By dawn on Monday 28 December, in thickening fog, another ship – the Dutch cargo steamer SS *Soekaboemi* – had been sunk: four vessels lost so far, and thirty-seven men dead. The attacks through the night meant that the convoy had now surrendered its geometry: the rectangle of ships was mauled jagged at the rear, blunted at the starboard tip. Come first light, men were scattered on rafts, or adrift singly in the icy sea, the red lights on their life jackets blinking ever dimmer. Those still alive clung close in the dead flat light; and when they looked up, hoping for the looming cross-hatch of a scrambling net slung from the flank of a friendly ship, they saw only the fog of the new day. It curled over the water, cold and pale as dry ice, seeming to break open above to offer glimpses of blue, but then closing to twenty feet. It dampened all sound: the noise of lifeboat oars dropping water on their backlift echoed like a door-knock in an empty hall; and the men on the rafts found themselves whispering, watching their outbreaths plume and fade, longing for cigarettes, hot water, warm towels.

All through the night, SS *Toward* cruised the wake of the convoy for survivors. When *King Edward* was hit, the torpedo explosion that punched a steel flowerhole in her hull was felt as a shockwave by every other vessel in the convoy, and the captain of *Toward* – now designated official rescue ship – ordered his crew to stand by. With no navigation lights, and the rest of the convoy moving southwards in the darkness, she eased slowly through the water, all men on deck looking for movement, shapes, lights on the surface. They picked up a raft of men from *Melrose Abbey*, throwing and rethrowing a rope till it was caught and the raft was pulled alongside. In the swell, the raft scraped and banged at the hull of *Toward* and the men grabbed for the scramble nets and climbed. By the end of the night there were one hundred and sixty-four survivors on board; many refused the offer of bunk space, preferring to sleep on deck in the open. Provisions were running short. 'Food and water for a further eleven days will be a problem,' the captain radioed the convoy commodore.

That night, too, the convoy's refuelling ship, the tanker SS *Scottish Heather*, was hit. The submarine commander – Oberleutnant Wolfgang Leimkühler, on board *U225* – had enough time after watching his torpedo strike to observe the panicked lowering of lifeboat and launch of starshell flares. Then he moved closer.

Three of *Scottish Heather*'s lifeboats put to sea before Second Officer Douglas Crook – the most senior man remaining on board – called for volunteers to stay. There was no fire; the ship seemed stable. He shut off the engines and ran an equipment check. The steering gear was still working, and the damaged tanks' bulkheads seemed to be holding. At dawn, adrift from the rest of the convoy, Crook began his search for the boats. By dusk, fog notwithstanding, he'd found them all. Four days later, alone and still afloat, the tanker entered the Clyde estuary.

AT FOUR-THIRTY in the afternoon of 28 December, the fog lifted. Some way off the convoy, with dusk falling, three U-boats – *U659*, *U591* and *U440* – surfaced together and drew alongside each other. Their commanders discussed the battle so far, their tactics for the coming night. At around the same time, Claude received his first battle orders. One of his seaplanes was needed as a patrol aircraft – specifically, to scout ahead of the convoy for U-boats – and he was asked to get it airborne.

In a vigorous swell, this was going to be an ambitious undertaking, but Claude, characteristically, agreed. He seemed excited, running along the deck, shouting at his crane operator to hook up one of the Kingfishers. *Fidelity* hove to, and the plane – carrying pilot and observer – was lowered off the starboard gunwale. It touched the water and settled. Madeleine, joining Claude on deck with the men, saw it pitched by the swell till its propeller touched the water. It seemed too light, like a balsa craft on a windy pond. Its wingfloats dug deep into the swell, then emerged, sluicing water.

It was dark now. Claude turned to one of his officers, snapped some instructions, and the other man disappeared inside. On deck, the men watched as the plane was lifted clear of the swell. It hung from the cranelink, swaying, engine still running, the backdraft from the propeller blowing Madeleine's hair about her face, snapping at the canvas covers of the landing craft. Claude called out to the pilot, Lieutenant Commander Ben Schrôder, who nodded, checked his instruments, and gave a thumbs-up from the open cockpit.

Another ship, the destroyer HMCS *St Laurent*, drew alongside *Fidelity*. She moved just ahead of the Kingfisher and Claude shouted again at Schrôder. The plane was lowered onto the water and Schrôder gunned the engine till the plane was nosing forward, bucking and rolling, blown spray streaming from its fuselage, towards the stern of *St Laurent*.

Claude and Madeleine glanced ahead, at the low stern of the destroyer, with its ranks of gun turrets, and saw a sudden explosion of white water as the ship thrust away from them. The Kingfisher followed, and it was immediately clear to the crew of *Fidelity* that the floatplane intended to use the destroyer's wake as a runway. Once airborne, Schrôder could search for U-boats, moving low through the convoy, attacking the submarines with depth charges. It was, so Rear Admiral Egerton believed, their best protection.

As the destroyer moved away, and its wake fanned out behind it, the Kingfisher accelerated. Even in the beaten churn of the big ship's wake, though, the swell was still considerable, and the plane pitched and yawed as it approached take-off speed.

On board *Fidelity*, men were cheering, cat-calling, whooping. Madeleine stood close to Claude, watching silently. The moment seemed suddenly to freeze, jerk forward frame by frame: the crowded deck, faces all turned the same way, the rest of the convoy now far ahead, the smell of the destroyer's engines in the air.

The plane lifted, then settled again. It was nearing take-off speed now, heading away from the wake, away from the destroyer, towards the open sea. Claude and Madeleine saw it head for the outrunning wave as if Schrôder planned to use this as a final ramp into the air.

The Kingfisher hit the wave and its nose lifted, then settled momentarily as the plane came back off the crest. It approached again, but the angle was different this time, and the plane appeared to be listing. The nose was up but suddenly one of its wingfloats disappeared underwater, and the plane went over, an arc of shiny metal and howling propeller, till it lay capsized, hissing steam. The wings lay upside-down, spreadeagled across the water, the main float raised above the waves. Two figures clambered onto one of the wings.

In a strengthening wind, the plane was sinking fast. When Claude looked again, only one man remained on the plane wreckage. *St Laurent* stopped, and began to turn around. On board *Fidelity* there was silence. With the engines idling, it was possible to hear the noise of the wind in the rigging: a sound of crying seabirds that had lost their way and were calling, calling, a long way from home.

BEN SCHRÔDER, the pilot of the sinking Kingfisher, was rescued by *St Laurent*, and the destroyer then moved slowly away in search of Schrôder's observer, who'd slipped from the upturned fuselage. Lookouts were posted around the ship, men scanning for a bobbing head in waves still six or seven feet high, a small-enough object made even harder to spot with no lights of any kind. Ten minutes passed, then fifteen. After twenty – at ten minutes to eight – a sailor on the bow gave a shout. The drifting airman – shivering, taciturn – clambered on board.

With the rest of the convoy far ahead and *Fidelity* now alone, Claude watched the Kingfisher disappear, finally, under the waves. Then, with scarcely a moment's hesitation, he called for the second Kingfisher to be hoisted into the water. *Fidelity*'s crew were subdued, muttering low to each other as *St Laurent*, with Schrôder and his observer on board, swung into position once more.

According to Michael Pollard – who felt it would now only be a matter of hours before he'd be ordered to take to the water in the torpedo boat – for a destroyer to 'steam at full speed into the wind, creating a "smooth" for the aircraft to use as its runway' was 'a matter of very fine judgement between pilot and destroyer. Start your take-off run too far from the destroyer and the seas have begun to build up again;

start too close and you are not airborne by the time you reach her.' Having just seen the latter scenario come to pass – with 'the destroyer turning hard to starboard to get out of the way and the Kingfisher keeping on a steady course but just clipping the top of the destroyer's wake' – he watched, anxiously.

TWENTY SECONDS after the first Kingfisher disappeared from view a series of explosions rocked *Fidelity*. There was confusion and momentary panic as the depth charges carried by the Kingfisher detonated at a depth of fifty feet. The shockwaves hit *Fidelity*'s engine room with such force that the stokers at first thought they'd been torpedoed. Pipes ruptured, tearing through the solder; ruffs of scalding water and oil spattered walls, ceiling, floors, causing the men to crouch for safety. On deck, Claude and Madeleine felt the ship suddenly shake, as if rammed; she reached for him, held him tight; and he, oblivious, yelled up at the bridge.

'Shut the engines!'

Fidelity fell silent.

THE SECOND Kingfisher floatplane achieved what the first had not, and took to the air from the destroyer's wake, flying south towards the convoy, heading for the battle on the horizon, the burning of ships that lit up the night like city-glow. Claude surveyed the damage in the engine room, noting the broken condenser piping, the debris of tools and spilled lubrication oil across the floor. He ordered repairs to begin immediately, and went back up on deck. Their chances were uncertain, he told Madeleine, but, most likely, the U-boats would concentrate on the main body of the convoy. Once *Fidelity*'s engines were repaired, they'd be able to reach the

Azores, which were now less than three hundred miles to the south. They could, he stressed, still make the Far East.

MADELEINE RETURNED to the radio room. During the last hour, incoming transmissions had been constant, and her fellow operators looked pale, hunched forward in their chairs, not even turning at her approach. She sat down, put on her headset, and began to write.

In the two hours since the first Kingfisher had capsized and sunk – since *Fidelity* had been drifting silently, shielded for the moment by the corvette HMCS *Shediac* – U-boats had been gathering on the starboard flank of the convoy. Oberleutnant Wolfgang Leimkühler – who'd torpedoed the convoy's tanker, SS *Scottish Heather*, some twenty-four hours earlier – stood in the conning tower of *U225* and watched a night sky filled with the burning white of drifting starshell flares. Later, writing his log, he noted that the ships seemed to be firing starshell continuously, even in advance of an attack.

The convoy had every reason to be extremely jittery, not least because Leimkühler – though forced by the starshell to pull back at nine-twenty – moved in on them again shortly after ten that evening, loosing a volley of four torpedoes at three ships, then a fourth. He hit two – SS *Norse King*, a Norwegian freighter, and SS *Ville de Rouen*, a former Vichy trader, captured by the British in July 1941 – and sank a third, SS *Melmore Head*. *Melmore Head* – struck on her starboard shoulder, the bulkheads rupturing, water coming fast – went down by the head, just two minutes from first impact to the vacuum suck of the disappearing stern.

To Leimkühler's south, turning head-on to the approaching convoy, was Kapitänleutnant Hubertus Purkhold, commander of *U260*. He'd been shadowing the convoy since

By the time *Fidelity*'s convoy set sail, around 100 Allied ships
were being sunk each month

darkness and now – at ten-thirty, with the fog gone – he
watched as, ungainly and poorly synchronized, the front
riders of the convoy altered course to two hundred and
seventy degrees. Bearing down on him, apparently unaware
of his presence, was SS *Empire Wagtail*. The merchantman
seemed strangely isolated: no ship on its starboard, its port-
side companion a good mile away. Purkhold fired a salvo, and
all three torpedoes struck home.

Empire Wagtail exploded: escalating mushrooms of flame,
balling and swelling and rising. The bridge, funnel and deck
plating were shredded to shrapnel. The ship broke and sank,
taking all forty-four men down with it. Returning to the
scene some three hours later – having lost contact with the
convoy in the meantime – Purkhold reported seeing four
empty lifeboats, an oil slick, floating debris.

FIDELITY, twenty miles astern of the convoy, was still drifting, engines cut. In the engine room, men were at work repairing the small-gauge copper condenser tubes. Claude, questioned via radio by the convoy commodore, was unable to say when his ship might be underway again. Returning to deck, the battle seemed almost beyond the horizon; the noise of the destroyer's guns – even the ghastly creaking and splintering of ships breaking up that dominated the dives of Oberleutnant Hermann Kottman in *U223* that night – reached Claude as a dull crump, as echoes of the war.

THE U-BOATS were in the heart of the convoy now and, as midnight approached, ships were being hit every fifteen minutes. At seventeen minutes past eleven, Kapitänleutnant Horst Dietrichs fired a spread salvo of four torpedoes from *U406*, followed by a shot from his stern tube as he pulled away. Five torpedoes, five hits: SS *Lynton Grange*, carrying three thousand tons of army and air-force equipment and three thousand tons of high explosive to the Far East; SS *Baron Cochrane*, loaded with four thousand tons of Cardiff coal, bound for Pernambuco, now Recife, on Brazil's far-eastern coast; SS *President Francqui*, in ballast for New York; and, finally, SS *Zarian*. On board *Zarian*, Third Officer Henry Revely had been watching from the bridge as *Lynton Grange* went up in flames, as 'tiny figures rushed about in the fireglow making for the boats', feeling a rush of pity for those 'poor, unlucky bastards'. Suddenly, he was thrown across the bridge. The ship had been hit: Revely's 'world had cracked open'. *Zarian* rolled, and Revely was thrown against the bridge rails, looking down now at the water rising to meet him. Slowly, the vessel settled, listing heavily to starboard, and Revely managed to stand. He ran uphill to the chartroom, grabbed the confidential-papers box and, holding it under one arm, began the 'long, tortuous climb to the boat deck'. Flames were spewing from every door, funnel and ventilator shaft. He made the lifeboat, shredding his hands on the rope, falling into the bow onto the knees of another seaman. In the cold, with water a foot deep in the hull of the lifeboat – suddenly aware he'd left both his rum and duffel coat on board – he watched his ship burn. Since darkness, nine ships had been torpedoed; three were already at the bottom. Those still intact moved on, 'leaving behind [them] a trail of burning wrecks like distant bonfires on a rugged landscape'.

IN THE CHAOS OF the battle – with only one U-boat, Oberleutnant Günther Ruppelt's *U356*, having been lost after a concerted depth-charge attack from the destroyer and no less than four of the corvettes – Oberleutnant Wolfgang Leimkühler closed in on SS *Empire Shackleton*, in command of which, he knew, was the convoy commodore, Rear Admiral Wyon Egerton. Leimkühler moved from the convoy's port bow, homing in on *Empire Shackleton* till he was four hundred metres away, then three, before loosing his bow torpedoes.

Struck in number-one hold, the explosion tearing through the deck plating, *Empire Shackleton* was suddenly a hive of beetling men, lifeboats being lowered into a red-ochre sea. When it seemed that the ship might yet survive, the remaining officers decided to head for the Azores. And it was at this point, solitary and wounded, that the ship was attacked and sunk by *U123*, commanded by Oberleutnant Horst von Schroeter, and *U435*, under Kapitänleutnant Siegfried Strelow.

AT TWENTY-TWO minutes past one in the morning of 29 December, HMCS *Shediac* – which had shielded *Fidelity* ever since her engines had been damaged – was ordered back into the battle. This did not mean, Claude was told, that he would remain unprotected: a tugboat, *Eminent*, had been summoned from Gibraltar and would tow him to safety, if he could hold off the U-boats that long.

Shediac pulled away. *Fidelity*, still without power, yawed silently in the swell. Claude watched till he could no longer see the departing corvette, until the sound of its engines had faded and it was quiet enough on deck to hear the fizzing burn of his cigarette as he inhaled, the burning tip sharp as a pencil, the dot of red the only illumination on deck.

Meanwhile Madeleine was in her cabin. While Claude had rushed about the ship since darkness overseeing the repair work, she had retreated from company, and her absence had been noticed by the crew. She lay on her bunk, listening to the echoey hammer of men running down the steel corridors, watching her cigarette smoke drift upwards, flatten and disperse as it hit the ceiling. She tried to read, but the text blurred before her eyes, becoming meaningless hieroglyphics, black marks in white space. She tried to sleep, but every time she was about to drift into unconsciousness she came round violently, shocked upright in bed, certain she'd felt the tremors from a depth charge, or the groaning of spent architecture, of a ship breaking up, the implosion in the dark water of men and materials. But then, some time in the small hours of 29 December, came a different, friendlier noise, a thrum that she could feel in the walls, that shivered the water in her basin. *Fidelity*'s engines had been restarted and, slower now and alone, the ship was underway again.

BY DAWN, four more ships – SS *Lynton Grange*, SS *Baron Cochrane*, SS *Zarian* and SS *President Francqui*, all previously torpedoed but still afloat – had been sunk by *U225*, and where before there had been derelict silhouettes, vessels in various states of disarray and brokenness, now there were men in lifeboats or on rafts made of forty-four-gallon petrol drums lashed to planking. Men lay with their heads on each other's knees, their clothes slick and dense with oil. They longed for rest, but the waves were still six feet high, and they broke over the top of the rafts, filling the lifeboats so that men had to bail continuously. On board SS *Toward*, the convoy's rescue ship, men stood or knelt or lay in every available space: hugging their knees, staring into space. The ship was full, and Rear Admiral Egerton, before abandoning his own ship, gave orders that *Toward* should pick up no more survivors. Two destroyers – HMS *Milne* and HMS *Meteor* – were on their way from Gibraltar: from now on, the rescue of men was to be their responsibility.

At half-past five in the predawn dark of 29 December the conning officer on board HMS *Milne* reported a radar signal which suggested a lone surface vessel rather than a U-boat. The destroyer took bearings: the other ship was heading southwards, at just two knots. Guessing he'd stumbled upon *Fidelity*, the captain sent a challenge. Yes, Claude wired back, this is HMS *Fidelity*. He gave his position – 43°13´N, 26°51´W – and said he was heading for the Azores.

As HMS *Milne* moved on and past – rescuing men from *Baron Cochrane*'s boat and rafts, then survivors from *Lynton Grange*, and finally Henry Revely and his crewmates from *Zarian*, hand over hand up the destroyer's scrambling nets, giving thanks for cups of coffee and ship's biscuits in the over-crowded wardroom – Claude issued orders for the torpedo boat and floatplane to be made ready. At two knots, which was all the engines now seemed to be capable of, *Fidelity* would need every bit of available protection.

To Michael Pollard, it only seemed a matter of time before the U-boats returned. As daybreak came, and with it a 'long, low swell', Madeleine appeared on deck with the other men. There was bad news: damage to equipment in *Fidelity*'s engine room meant that the torpedo boat's torpedo could not be primed with compressed air. Their only anti-submarine weapons would be depth charges.

At least the commotion and preparations lifted the mood among Claude's men – a relief on board a ship that through the storm, and now in gentler seas, had felt unbearably crowded. With the two landing craft on the after deck, the rafts and buoyancy floats that littered her other deck space, and the long forecastle head across which water rushed in even moderate seas, even an open-air stride, the simplest form of necessary exercise, was difficult.

Now underway and still unprotected by her torpedo boat, *Fidelity* was sailing with her anti-submarine nets down. The resultant drag, Claude noted, was reducing headway to close to zero. Yet the activity – the rigging of the winch to hoist the torpedo boat overboard, the hollering and sense of purposeful optimism – meant, in Pollard's words, that 'the air of tension that was so marked the night before had subsided a little'.

With *Fidelity* rolling between five and ten degrees, the hoisting out was a delicate job. The torpedo boat's eight-man crew were put aboard and the craft was swung wide of the ship, then lowered. Claude and Madeleine, standing side by side, leaned over the gunwale, smiling together for the first time in days.

'Do you want any fishing lines?' Claude called down.

'No thanks,' came the reply. 'Hand grenades will do just fine.'

Claude and Madeleine laughed: they'd fished with grenades from the Isle of Wight to north-west Scotland, and they could recognize the affection, the subtext of a shared and valued history, behind the riposte. So, where Claude might have otherwise insisted – for if the torpedo boat should lose contact with *Fidelity*, fishing would provide crucial protein – he shrugged good-naturedly and let it pass. Besides, he knew that the torpedo boat was well provisioned: some thirty-two gallons of drinking water, a device for distilling saltwater, enough ham sandwiches for five days, tinned apples, condensed milk, dates, treacle, chewing gum and iron rations: easily sufficient, he figured.

ENCOURAGED BY the continued thrum of the engines, by the slow but definite progress the ship was now making, Claude – with the Azores now just two hundred and forty miles to the south – began to feel more confident that his separation from the convoy need not necessarily mean their destruction, that it would be possible, even in the event of attack, for the ship to defend itself. With the torpedo boat now in the water, he ordered the two thirteen-knot landing craft to be launched. When these were afloat, he called for the Kingfisher, too, to be hoisted overboard.

He watched, grinning, as men ran about the decks preparing the landing craft, checking the hoisting gear. Madeleine appeared and then withdrew to her desk in the cipher room – a peripheral presence at this time of all-male bluster. All day she and Claude had barely spoken and now, as Claude found his attention drawn to the torpedo boat, which was lying motionless off the stern, she was absent once again.

The torpedo boat, as its captain, Lieutenant John O'Neill, would later write, was struggling – its 'main engine gave trouble soon after the boat was in the water'. The fuel pump was diagnosed as broken and, since this couldn't be mended without lifting the entire engine, the auxiliary – a Ford, whose seven knots gave less than a third the speed of the main Rolls-Royce Merlin – was fired up. Idling close to *Fidelity*, their craft dwarfed by the bigger vessel, the crew of the torpedo boat watched the Kingfisher successfully negotiate take-off. It circled over them, and the men looked up, cheering and waving; and then it flew south.

Fifteen minutes later the plane was back. Two submarines, one on fire, had been spotted some sixteen miles to the north-west; nearby were two crowded lifeboats. Claude dictated a message, which his radio operator transmitted to the commander-in-chief of Western Approaches, and copied to the destroyer *St Laurent*.

'TWO U-BOATS BEARING 290 DIST 16 MILES, ONE ON FIRE. AM ATTEMPTING TO ENGAGE WITH AIRCRAFT, MOTORBOAT AND MACHINE GUNS.'

He thought a moment, and sent a second.

'AM HEADING FOR THE AZORES WITH SERIOUS ENGINE TROUBLE. I SHALL TRY TO ENSURE MY OWN PROTECTION WITH MY MOTORBOAT AND AIRCRAFT. WILL FLY THE AXIS FLAG.'

The response from the Admiralty in London, to which the message was relayed, was immediate.

'*FIDELITY* MUST ON NO ACCOUNT FLY THE AXIS FLAG.'

MOVING THROUGH the life rafts and the darksmooth soup of spilled oil, weaving through half-submerged spars, the still-floating wreckage of lost ships' superstructures, came *U225*, quiet as moonlight. Oberleutnant Wolfgang Leimkühler, her commander, had passed a profitable twenty-four hours and now, having hit four ships and sunk a further five, was heading north into open sea in search of a damaged ship he believed he'd seen shortly before midday.

He was travelling on the surface, moving at speed, when – at ten minutes to four in the afternoon – he spotted funnel smoke and mastheads on the horizon. Guessing this was the ship he was after, the limping survivor he planned to send to the bottom, he dived and moved closer.

SUMMARILY AND inexplicably prevented from flying the Axis flag – a valid-enough form of protection, Claude had figured, and a bluff that the destroyer HMS *Campbeltown* had adopted to good effect as she'd approached the St-Nazaire outer caisson earlier in the year – Claude was becoming aware that the torpedo boat, operating well below its potential, was also going to offer only partial cover. Now, as well, he had survivors to rescue, and sent out the landing craft. By mid-afternoon, seeing no reason why the torpedo boat should place unnecessary strain upon her auxiliary engine, he took her in tow.

HAVING BEEN CHASED out of the hunt the previous night by two of the convoy's escorting corvettes, Kapitänleutnant Ralph Kapitzky's *U615* was now awaiting a refuel in the chilly mid-afternoon of 29 December. U-boat command's instructions were clear: look only for damaged ships, and wait for the fuel tanker. Kapitzky lay on the surface. Suddenly, from the conning tower came news of a sighting – what looked like a seaplane, coming in to land near a merchant ship. He scrambled up the stepladder, grabbed some binoculars. He watched as the ship swung out a hoist and the plane, far off as an insect on a pond, was lifted slowly into the air. He dived, set his course, and gave orders for all torpedo tubes to be made ready.

DARKNESS FELL. Thanks to the continuous efforts of her engineers, *Fidelity* was now making reasonable headway – about five knots, Pollard estimated. At around six o'clock, the ship slowed and crewmen on deck could see two full lifeboats just ahead – men wrapped in blankets and hunched over, now shouting out and waving. Close by were the landing craft, whose crew had spotted the lifeboats and were now helping the men off the small boats and onto *Fidelity*. As they climbed on deck, they were counted out: some fifty men, all from *Empire Shackleton*, including the convoy commodore himself, Rear Admiral Wyon Egerton. *Fidelity* – a ship originally designed for a crew of no more than fifty – was now carrying three hundred and eighty-one men, and one woman.

IT WAS NOW seven-fifty in the evening and Claude – not knowing how lucky he'd been, how, unknown even to the crew of the Kingfisher, the sight of the seaplane overhead had forced Leimkühler to dive – radioed Western Approaches headquarters with news of the rescue of survivors. He was growing more confident: to judge by radio traffic, the worst of the battle ahead was over. He had already proved his worth by rescuing the convoy's most senior officer; and the torpedo boat, though underpowered, was now on circular patrol around *Fidelity*.

His confidence, however, was short-lived. Twenty minutes later, a submarine echo was picked up. Claude shouted for depth charges, and two were dropped, one to port and another off the stern. To Michael Pollard in the torpedo boat, which was cruising off *Fidelity*'s starboard flank, the force of the explosions made him guess the worst, 'that [*Fidelity*] had been torpedoed . . . we made frantic inquiries as to just what was going on. At first we thought that we were the echoes they were picking up, but that fear was soon put aside – they had a genuine submarine echo. We were told to clear off and resume our patrol, giving frequent flashes to show our position.'

AT NINE-THIRTY, *Fidelity* was being closed by both *U225* and *U615*. At nine thirty-eight, approaching on the surface, Leimkühler fired his stern torpedo. Claude's lookout, seeing a trail of bubbles snake past their stern, sounded the alarm. Claude ordered a ninety-degree change of course.

Two minutes later, Pollard, scanning the seascape from the torpedo boat, saw a submarine surface dead ahead: five hundred yards, he estimated. Although it was a moonless night, the silhouette was unmistakable: the stubby conning tower, straight-line rule of the deck, forward-deck gun like a pointing finger.

On board *U615*, Kapitzky, in his turn – who'd spent the last six hours shadowing *Fidelity*, watching from periscope depth as the ship spent long periods stationary as the float-plane was hoisted on and off and the torpedo boat was launched – caught sight of the torpedo boat. For a moment, neither craft moved. Lieutenant John O'Neill, in command of the torpedo boat, radioed Claude. On the bridge, Claude peered through binoculars into the surrounding blackness. Under low cloud, the ocean was formless, without feature, a void. Even the torpedo boat – which had now suspended its flashing – was invisible. Claude radioed back that he could see nothing, and would continue on his course.

O'Neill, with no torpedo on board, moved closer to the U-boat. The submarine was beam-on to him, and so, for the moment, the smaller craft was safe. The intention, Pollard recalled, was 'to close the submarine [and] get in a depth-charge attack'. Kapitzky, watching the torpedo boat get nearer, filled his ballast tanks and dived.

TWENTY-SIX minutes later, untroubled by another string of depth-charge explosions, Kapitzky surfaced again. *Fidelity*, having weaved and dodged as much as possible with the heavy drag of both anti-torpedo nets – zigzagging at irregular intervals to confuse her predators – now set her course once more and ordered the torpedo boat to keep pace. Kapitzky, with *Fidelity* again in his crosshairs, and the torpedo boat nowhere to be seen, fired a single bow tube. He watched, waited; *Fidelity*, untroubled, sailed on. At nine-thirty, moving in again, he fired a second; then, seven minutes later, a third. Still *Fidelity* cruised on. Kapitzky fired two more, again to no effect.

At two minutes past eleven, Claude – having been alerted to *U615*'s presence – ordered four stern depth charges to be dropped. Kapitzky, submerged and listening, felt the tremors; and then, checking his equipment, decided to go in one last time. This time, though – figuring that *Fidelity*'s flanks must be protected – he would approach from the stern.

YET THE ATTACK never came. Around midnight, fog closed in and Kapitzky, surfacing repeatedly, listening in vain for propeller soundings, failed to sight *Fidelity* again. Claude, never much in doubt as to his own invincibility, sought out Madeleine. The ship, he told her, was proving unsinkable; and within a matter of hours, whatever U-boats that remained would surely be running short of fuel and have to pull back. He radioed Gibraltar and told the base that since the ship was now making a reliable five knots he'd not need the assistance of the tug. In the event of another attack, he'd use his own defences.

Only one thing tempered his confidence. For the last half hour he'd been unable to contact the torpedo boat by radio, and in the shifting fog banks, the enveloping dark, he knew there was no chance of a sighting. He gave orders for continued calls to be made to O'Neill, and then went to his cabin and, for the first time in days, he slept.

30 DECEMBER 1942

By MORNING, with the rest of the convoy now a hundred miles to the west, there had still been no communication from O'Neill. Yet the seas remained moderate and Claude, who rated O'Neill's seamanship highly, felt confident that he and the other eight men would yet be reunited.

The morning passed. At lunchtime, Claude and Madeleine sat together in the wardroom. Talk was optimistic. Now that the battle had passed, few doubted that *Fidelity* would make the Azores and, in time, the Far East. Egerton, a veteran of eight ocean convoys, spent the morning in conference with Claude. After lunch, with the likelihood of U-boat attack growing ever more distant, Claude ordered the torpedo nets to be raised and, free of drag, the ship seemed to leap forward.

The sky began to clear and, as afternoon eased towards dusk, a low pale sun appeared through broken clouds. Men moved about on deck, talking in groups, leaning over the side. Though it was the end of December, and they were now in the mid-Atlantic, it felt mild: when the sun broke through, duffel coats no longer seemed necessary; mufflers could be removed.

At TWENTY TO FIVE, Claude and Madeleine, standing on deck, were thrown clean off their feet. The aftershock of the impact was felt as a continuous tremor through the body of the vessel. Looking up and around them, clambering to their feet on a steepening, slithery deck, everywhere a barrage of sound – men screaming, the waterfall thunder of seawater

rushing through the craterhole made by the incoming torpedo
that had struck amidships – they reached for each other, then
were hurled apart again. Flames snapped from the ventilation
shafts. The faces on the bridge, pushed against the glass, were
distended in 'O's of horror, frozen to silence by the volume of
collapsing metal all around. Men were streaming up the stairs,
stumbling as they pulled on their life vests, fumbling with the
waist ties. All around, men shouted obscenities, prayers. For
the first time in two and a half years, none of the men seemed
to notice Madeleine.

A minute later, fighting their way towards the landing craft
– Madeleine swept off her feet by the press of bodies – Claude
and Madeleine felt their legs go beneath them as a second
explosion hit forward. *Fidelity*, which had still been moving
after the first impact, now juddered to a halt. She was broken
amidships, holed in the bow, and from beneath them came
the noise of things sliding. Madeleine imagined motorbikes,
jeeps, all their stores and men in a terminal downhill collapse;
the uprush of water through bunkrooms and mess decks;
men swimming through corridors, fighting against drowning,
already in total darkness.

Overwhelming heat pressed in on them from every side.
From the communication tubes, Madeleine could hear screaming but she could also feel burning. The smell was sweet,
almost floral: diesel and charred bodies, flashing her suddenly
back to the desecrated plantation, the stoved-in manager's
villa, her murdered husband and the hollering of the intruders, bent on vengeance, a whole lifetime ago.

Men were jumping overboard, alone or in pairs, arms and
legs pummelling the air. Claude was shouting, and Madeleine
fought to stay close to him. He yelled for depth charges. He
screamed obscenities, and seemed at that moment to be fully

and gloriously alive, luminous in the darkness. Madeleine knew, finally, that, whatever else happened, she must remain with him.

Steam roared from the safety valve beside the funnel, the noise loud as a wounded elephant. The ship was going down fast, sinking by the bow and to starboard, the stern rearing up. Men were climbing aft, holding on to the mast. There were rafts in the water, and men were clambering out of the cold water onto the planking. And there were sailors without lifebelts, clawing at their clothing as they leapt for the water, shouting out for the life rafts.

Claude gripped Madeleine's hand as the angle of the deck steepened and the nose of the ship went under. When the first of the two depth charges blew, Claude and Madeleine felt the shock like a snapping in their spines; the second, moments after, threw columns of water – a sudden park fountain – a hundred feet in the air, shot through with the colour of flame. When the foam subsided, dead men surfaced in the water, floating face up, as if sleeping.

Claude and Madeleine continued their upwards climb, hauling themselves up the canvas covers as the deck approached forty-five degrees. Claude, growing wild with fear and thrill, shouted for more depth charges, even though the men on the stern had already leapt from the ship. The pair looked around for the submarine, but visibility was all close-to – they could see the fireglow on the upturned faces on rafts, all looking up at them; the circle of light from the ship's belly of flame seemed to throw the ocean beyond into impenetrable darkness, like night seen from a lighted room.

The ship was sinking at speed now and, grabbing Madeleine's arm, Claude began to climb out along the mast. Below them, waves had reached the funnel – almost horizontal, greeting the inrush of water with an explosion of steam. They could smell oil, and in patches close to the hull there were flames on the water's surface. The foremast snapped and catapulted upwards from thirty feet under, narrowly missing them, landing in a tangle of rigging near one of the rafts.

They reached the tip of the mast and, feeling it bend and crack beneath their feet, they jumped. As they swam for the rafts they felt a series of muffled explosions. Claude reached the raft first, lying on his stomach and, stretching out for Madeleine, pulled her up beside him. Shivering together, oil in their hair and their mouths, their clothes heavy and cold, they witnessed the end of *Fidelity*: her propeller aloft and motionless, a last lone figure standing screaming on the after rail, the eerie smoothness and hush after the ship was finally gone, the speed with which the ocean reasserted itself. Everywhere were rafts, men, broken spars and, in the sudden stillness, voices calling out for each other.

EPILOGUE

AT A QUARTER past five on the evening of 30 December 1942, Kapitänleutnant Siegfried Strelow brought his submarine to the surface. A wire hawser, he noticed, lay across the bows of *U435*, and he ordered men forwards to clear it. Standing in the conning tower, he scanned the ocean before him. Half a mile away were what seemed to be hundreds of men in the water. He saw no lifeboats, just rafts and wreckage and men adrift, some clinging to floats.

Strelow had shadowed *Fidelity* since shortly after one that afternoon. He'd drawn closer warily, noting in his log that the ship in his sights – well armed, with a seaplane and motorboat – resembled *Waldemar Kophamel*, a U-boat depot ship. Aware that the ship might be a trap, he moved in cautiously.

At twelve minutes to eight, at rest on the surface, with *Fidelity*'s survivors all turned his way and watching, Strelow signalled U-boat headquarters.

'U-BOAT DECOY SUNK BY TWO SINGLE HITS, AN ELECTRIC AND AN AIR TORPEDO, AFTER RUNNING 23 AND 15 SECONDS RESPECTIVELY. COURSE 180, 4 KNOTS. A SEAPLANE ON BOARD. LOOKED LIKE A SHIP OF WAR. SIMILAR TO *WALDEMAR KOPHAMEL*. HUNDREDS OF SURVIVORS AT SINKING POSITION. TWO DEPTH CHARGES AFTER TORPEDOES HIT, ONE VERY CLOSE.'

The reply came just four minutes later.

'STRELOW TO REPORT IF SURVIVORS IN BOATS OR

WHETHER THEIR DESTRUCTION IN THE WEATHER PREVAIL-
ING CAN BE COUNTED UPON.'

FOR A WHOLE WEEK – from New Year's Eve through to
6 January 1943 – six Allied warships searched the area.
HMS *Milne* – which had passed *Fidelity* on her way to
the convoy at dusk on 29 December – was now joined by
fellow Gibraltar-based destroyer HMS *Meteor*, the Canadian
corvettes *Battleford* and *Shediac* and the British corvettes
Woodstock and *Prescott*. Seven days, and not one lookout
on any of the ships spotted even a single survivor, let alone
a body. No corpse would ever make land, nor be picked up
from a raft.

Siegfried Strelow died on 9 July 1943 when *U435* was
attacked north-west of Lisbon by a Wellington bomber. He
and his crew of forty-seven were all lost. All that remains in
the way of evidence from the night of 30 December 1942, then,
is his logbook, and in the months and years following the war,
officials in British intelligence pored over it in search of clues
as to the fate of Claude, Madeleine, Rear Admiral Egerton and
their men.

Strelow's next recorded signal to headquarters – addressed
to Dönitz himself – came at seven minutes past midnight on
New Year's Eve, some thirty-one hours after he'd torpedoed
Fidelity.

'300–400 SURVIVORS ON OVERLOADED RAFTS AND DRIFT-
ING IN THE WATER. NO BOATS. PRESUMABLY SURVIVORS FROM
STEAMERS AMONG THEM. WIND SSE, FORCE 3; SEA 2; 2/10
CLOUD; TEMPERATURE 16°; BAROMETER 1032 MILLIBARS,
FALLING.'

Neither too rough, nor too cold. And yet, within hours of
the search vessels arriving, there was nothing to be seen. No

rafts, no wreckage, no survivors, no drifting corpses. Review-
ing the evidence – taking into account the brief German-radio
interview with Strelow broadcast hours after *U435* docked
at St-Nazaire on 12 January in which he spoke of 'three to
four hundred men [clinging] to overcrowded rafts . . . on the
morning after the battle the sea was covered with survivors
trying to escape to the Azores' – intelligence officials drew a
conclusion that seems all the more chilling for what remains
unsaid. 'The inference,' they stated, 'is obvious.'

LIEUTENANT JOHN O'Neill, Lieutenant Michael Pollard and
their six-man crew were picked up by HMS *Woodstock* at
one in the afternoon on New Year's Day 1943. They'd last
seen *Fidelity* shortly before midnight on 29 December. Struggling with an overheating engine, they'd spent the afternoon
of 30 December rigging up a makeshift mast and, to quote
O'Neill's report, 'set course to the NE trying to make for
[the] UK, which was our only course'. The first O'Neill knew
of *Fidelity*'s loss was when he reported to the Admiralty in
London on 16 January.

It took another two months for the Admiralty to contact
the relatives of *Fidelity*'s crew and, when it did, the statement
it issued did little to quiet the voices muttering that there had
been a cover-up, that the crew had been taken prisoner and
were now labouring as prisoners of war on farms in Portugal.
'HMS *Fidelity*,' it stated, 'was lost while on escort duty in the
Atlantic. The weather was rough at the time of her sinking and
the chances of any survivors having fallen into enemy hands
is remote in the extreme.' To this fiction – for the weather, as
Pollard still remembers, was 'not rough' the day *Fidelity* was
lost – was added, four days later on 17 March 1943, in the
Admiralty's press communiqué, the misleading description of

the ship's 'Commanding Officer [as having been] a member of the Fighting French Forces'.

The newspaper publication of this communiqué resulted in a letter of protest from Admiral Philippe Auboyneau, leader of the London-based Forces Navales Frances Libre, the Free French Navy. Declaring his 'astonishment' that 'Péri, who joined the Royal Navy at his own request under the name of Langlais, was described as "Fighting French" ', he went on to demand a 'settlement of accounts'. Claude's gift of £9,061 to the Ministry of Aviation Production to buy Spitfires was 'an act of generosity which he had no right to make with the proceeds of the sale of a cargo belonging to France', and the sum should be repaid to the Free French Navy.

The Admiralty's defence, to judge from an internal memo at the end of April, showed how delicately the subject of Claude, Madeleine and *Fidelity* was already being treated. The description of Claude as 'Fighting French' was, strictly speaking, correct: he was not, and had deliberately not been called, a member of the Free French Navy: 'it was considered that all Frenchmen fighting the common enemy could be described as "Fighting Frenchmen" '. The words had been carefully chosen, in other words, to make Claude sound as ordinary as possible. 'To have drafted the communiqué in the normal manner as "HMS *Fidelity* (Cdr J Langlais, RN)", when no biography of this officer could possibly have been issued without disclosing a lot of undesirable details, would immediately have aroused interest in the press in this ship, which was the last thing desired.'

Yet among families of the men lost, 'interest' had already reached an intense pitch, and it was clear to Admiralty officials that something more substantial than an economical press statement was required. By midway through 1943, according to internal documents, 'a number of the relatives [were] in regular correspondence, [to] arrange meetings, etc. As is only natural under such conditions, facts become distorted, rumours are magnified and the product of the two elements has now reached fantastic proportions.' The most persistent of the relatives was one Mrs Bull who, in a two-hour meeting at the Admiralty in London, laid out the various claims that were gaining currency. Depending on the source, Mrs Bull explained, there were or were not Royal Marines on board; some of the crew were now interned in Portugal; others were in hospital in Gibraltar; the ship was 'on some secret mission with Admiralty connivance'; Claude had declared '"to hell with the Admiralty" and gone off on his own, possibly deserting to the enemy'; and the ship had 'foundered being unseaworthy and the Admiralty are unwilling to admit this'.

The focus of the rumours, though, was – and remains to this day – upon Claude and Madeleine themselves. George Millar, who lost his elder brother James, still claims that 'the full story has been hidden'. Paul Young, whose grandfather George Moule was on board, states with certainty that 'the whole thing was an embarrassment to the Admiralty; they've tried to edit *Fidelity* out of the history books'. Charles Osset, who served on board and lives today in a small terraced house on the outskirts of a Midlands town, speaks in a voice quavering with feeling when he recalls the violence of Claude's methods of discipline, and the friends he lost. To Auguste Roulland, another who had suffered at Claude's hands, both the ship and Madeleine, he states with a muted bitterness, were Claude's 'toys'. And yet Michael Pollard's lasting memories are of Claude's 'strength of character, charm and personality' and Madeleine's intelligence, maternal softness and love of a good party. 'You either adored [Claude] or hated him,' he says. 'There was nothing in between. And since I certainly didn't hate him, I suppose I must have loved him.'

For many years after the war the legacy of HMS *Fidelity*, and of Claude and Madeleine, continued to be a contentious issue. Compagnie de Navigation Paquet, the Marseilles-based freight agent to which *Le Rhin* belonged, argued at length – and with no success – that, since Claude effectively stole the ship, and since the UK government then took over owner-ship and control, Britain owed it compensation. Later efforts by Claude's brother Henri to persuade the company to create a memorial were greeted, according to Claude's nephew Bernard, with a 'harsh and final [response]: deal with the English. For Paquet, the whole thing was an expensive loss.'

Claude lived on in André, the son he knew only as a baby, who – born of Claude's brief and possibly commercial tryst with the Vietnamese Do Tikem – was handed over by Claude's wife Marguerite Paire to the guardianship of his brother's family in Dijon in 1946, when André was only nine. To Bernard, eight years his junior, André became the 'elder brother of the house': stories about the exploits of 'Uncle Claude . . . influenced me throughout my childhood'. Yet for André, the shadow cast by an unknown father stretched long as dusk. 'Half-caste, orphaned, constantly pulled between his uncle and his father's second wife, he found it very hard to forge a sense of identity.'

On 8 May 1955 – 'gorgeous', remembers Bernard, 'a big sun under the chestnut trees' – André, dressed in a dark suit and tie, stood to attention at a military parade in the heart of Dijon while a senior general pinned the cross of the Légion d'honneur to his jacket. The medal was Claude's, and André –

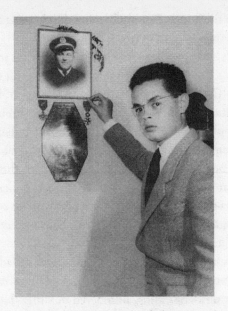

André Péri with his father's
Légion d'honneur, Dijon, 1955

who spoke of his father only rarely, and who carried just one
single photograph of Claude – seemed almost weighed down,
prematurely aged by the posthumous emblem as the family
walked home through the hot afternoon. 'I was much more
impressed than he was,' says Bernard.

Shortly afterwards, André became a soldier, a 'para-
officer' who, on home leave, would impress his little brother
with stories of his exploits: 'parachute jumps, undercover
operations, and other such things. It was pretty cool stuff.'
And then in 1967, while serving in Chad, he was killed.
André's choice of lifestyle, says Bernard, always seemed the
deliberate opposite from that of Claude and Henri. 'My father
used to bring all kinds of books on the sea, warships and naval

officers to the house. But my brother didn't want to know: he looked to the sky, and that was how he died.'

Claude's temper, Bernard confesses, still runs in the family, but it is not – as Claude often implied – the result of Corsican ancestry. 'Our great-grandfather was born in Imperia, in western Italy, twenty-five miles from the French border. Claude couldn't tell the British that he had Italian blood, so he told them he was Corsican. Corsicans are like a mafia: they are all friends and form tight-knit clans'. Péri, though, is also a Corsican name, and Bernard, a former police detective, also admits to having pretended 'on occasion' to be Corsican: warlike, independent, ruthless. 'It can help a great deal under the right circumstances.'

Claude's family remember Claude well. Madame Henri Péri, his sister-in-law, keeps photographs, certificates and letters in a series of fading, numbered box files. Henri, maybe as an act of mourning as well as remembrance, did his best, before his death, to act as archivist, sorting out papers by year; into pre- and postwar; into Vietnam, France, England; into espionage, navy, government; and, after the war, letters from admirers, fellow combatants, friends. Claude may have died when he was just thirty-four, but such meticulous cataloguing says one thing: he must live on.

Madeleine, though – in death as in life – had no biographer, no curator of her life, no companion but Claude. In her early sixties, Madeleine's mother Adèle moved from the centre of Paris to Santeny, a village on the south-eastern suburban outskirts of Paris, and it was here that she was buried in October 1957, aged sixty-eight. Yet an afternoon trip to Santeny revealed not one person who remembered her. The streets were hot and dusty, the gardens abuzz with insects, the windows shuttered. The noise of the pinball machine in the bar near the market square was audible two blocks away. There were no Bayards in the graveyard, and the town hall – even though these were working hours – was closed. An old woman who'd lived in Santeny since childhood had no memory of Adèle. Only a street-sweeper, wheeling an empty refuse cart beside a neat-striped football pitch, showed any spark of recognition, but he seemed to be responding to the idea of Madeleine, war hero, and not to that of her mother. '*Je me souviens*,' he said, lost momentarily in the romance of Madeleine's life story, and he beckoned, proffering reminiscence. There was wine on his breath.

KEY DATES

1908   *7 April* – Birth of Claude André Michel Péri in Hanoi, Vietnam

1913   François-Michel Péri, Claude's father, posted to Lyon to run France's wartime military radiocommunications base

1911   *21 February* – Birth of Madeleine Victorine Bayard in Paris

1912   *May* – Madeleine 'recognized' by her mother Adèle at the fourth-arrondissement *mairie*

1916   *March* – Madeleine's mother marries Pierre Nard, father to her younger sister Paulette

1925   Claude leaves Hanoi for naval training in Toulon

1927   Claude signs up for submarine training

1928   Claude simulates mental illness and is thrown out of the navy

1932   Madeleine marries a Frenchman, the owner of a Vietnamese rubber plantation, and leaves Paris for Vietnam

early 1930s – Claude working as insurance agent in Saigon and as an organizer of big-game hunts

1935   *13 August* – Claude marries Raymonde Fouche

1936   *12 June* – Disagreement in Saigon bar leads to Claude taking on his opponent in a handgun duel

1937   *6 April* – Claude acquitted of electoral corruption during the previous year's elections to the colonial legislature

1937   Claude meets Madeleine; they begin working together as agents for the newly inaugurated Deuxième Bureau – the intelligence section – of the French government's Colonial Ministry

1938   *21 January* – Claude's father dies at the age of sixty-seven

        28 February – Claude marries Marguerite Paire, two days before he sets sail for France; she takes care of his son André, born to another woman

        1 October – Claude leaves Paris for Berlin by car, heading overland to Vietnam

        November – Claude, itinerant spy, bags invitation to visit fellow big-game hunter Hermann Göring at his country estate, Carinhall; they lunch together in Berlin

        1 December – Claude reaches Istanbul

1939   *January* – Passes through Syria, Iraq and Iran

        March – Reunited with Madeleine in Calcutta

        24 June – Claude reaches Bangkok, meets up with Madeleine again

        June to October – Claude and Madeleine travel together back to Vietnam

        November – They sail from Saigon to Marseilles

        December – Reach Paris, report for duty to Raoul Salan, chief of the Service de Renseignements Impérial; Salan arranges for them to be trained in the use of plastic explosive

1940   *April* – Salan orders Claude and Madeleine to Marseilles, to report for service on *SS Le Rhin*, a merchantman

9/10 May – Claude destroys the *Corrientes*, a German U-boat supply ship, in Las Palmas harbour, Gran Canaria, with plastic explosive

1 June – *Le Rhin* docks at Marseilles; Claude and Madeleine travel to Paris

14 June – German infantry enter Paris; Claude and Madeleine leave the capital for Marseilles

23 June – *Le Rhin* docks at Gibraltar

26 June – Claude leads a mutiny on board; he and Madeleine remain on board, vowing to fight henceforth for Britain

27 June – Admiral Émile Muselier arrives in Gibraltar to recruit men and ships for his Free French Navy

29 June – Claude appointed commander of the Free French base in Gibraltar

21 July – *Le Rhin* joins convoy bound for Britain; attempted mutiny on board

5 August – *Le Rhin* berths in Barry Docks, south Wales

Autumn – Claude and Madeleine divide their time between London and Barry; *Le Rhin* becomes HMS *Fidelity* and is refitted and armed

1941   *January* – Madeleine enrols on the WRNS officers' training course at the Royal Naval College, Greenwich

February – Madeleine and Pat O'Leary study sabotage at SOE's training school, Aston House, in Hertfordshire

1941   *6 April* – *Fidelity* sails for the Mediterranean for spy-drop and pick-up missions

26 April – O'Leary lands his agents from a sailing boat but is captured

May – *Fidelity* in Liverpool, refitting again; in London, Claude begins lobbying for *Fidelity* to be sent to the Far East

August to September – *Fidelity*'s second Mediterranean cruise; death on board in suspicious circumstances

September – Board of Inquiry, Liverpool into the death and Claude's methods of discipline

1942   *February* – *Fidelity* in Southampton

Spring and summer – Claude and Madeleine living in a cottage on the Isle of Wight; *Fidelity*'s men and Royal Marines Commandos preparing for combat against the Japanese in the Far East

November – Training continues in Loch Broom, north-west Scotland

Early December – *Fidelity* in Liverpool; Claude and Madeleine visited by Pat O'Leary

18 December – *Fidelity* sails from Liverpool, joining 45-vessel convoy ONS154, heading for the Far East

22, 23 December – Eighteen U-boats start tracking the convoy as it heads south through the Atlantic

26 December – The U-boats have their first kill

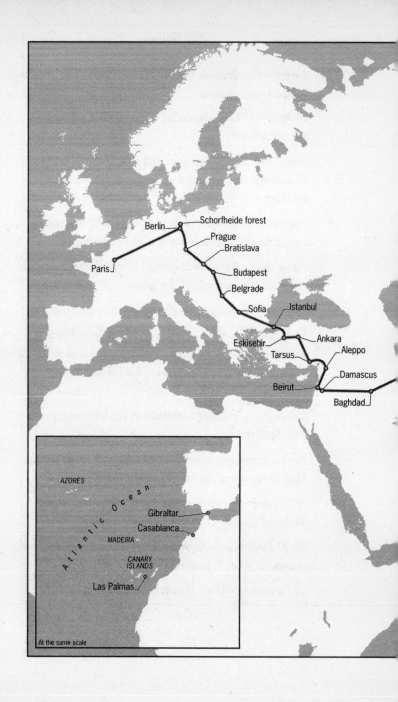

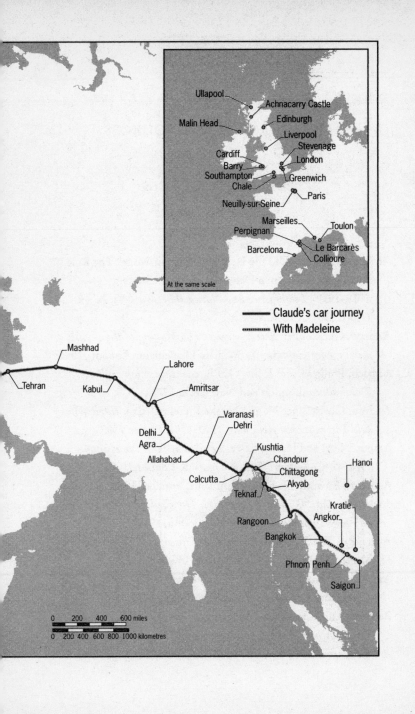

Ullapool
Achnacarry Castle
Edinburgh
Malin Head
Liverpool
Stevenage
Cardiff
London
Barry
Southampton
Greenwich
Chale
Neuilly-sur-Seine
Paris
Marseilles
Toulon
Perpignan
Le Barcarès
Barcelona
Collioure
At the same scale

—— Claude's car journey
············ With Madeleine

Mashhad
Lahore
Tehran
Kabul
Amritsar
Varanasi
Dehri
Delhi
Agra
Kushtia
Allahabad
Chandpur
Hanoi
Calcutta
Chittagong
Teknaf
Akyab
Kratie
Rangoon
Angkor
Bangkok
Phnom Penh
Saigon

0   200   400   600 miles
0 200 400 600 800 1000 kilometres

BIBLIOGRAPHY AND SOURCES

PUBLISHED SOURCES

BOOKS, ESSAYS

Alexander, Martin. 'Did the Deuxième Bureau Work? The Role of Intelligence in French Defence Policy and Strategy, 1919–1939', *Intelligence and National Security*, VI, No. 2 (April 1991), 292–333

Andrew, Christopher. *Secret Service: The Making of the British Intelligence Community*. William Heinemann, London, 1985

Altbach, Philip G. and Kelly, Gail P., eds. *Education and Colonialism*. London and New York, 1978

Andrew, Christopher M. and Noakes, Jeremy (eds.). *Intelligence and International Relations, 1900–1945*. Exeter, 1987

Arthur, Nigel and Hardy, Clive. *London at War: the Hulton-Deutsch Collection*. Hulton-Deutsch, London, 1989

Ashcroft, Edward. *De Gaulle*. Odhams, London, 1962

Auten, Harold. *'Q' Boat Adventures: The Exploits of the Famous Mystery Ship*. Herbert Jenkins, London, 1919

Ayers, Pat. *The Liverpool Docklands: Life and Work in Athol Street*. Docklands History Project, Liverpool, 1989

Azéma, J.-P. *From Munich to the Liberation, 1938–1944*. Cambridge University Press, Cambridge, 1984

Balakier, Ann S. and Balakier, James L. *The Spatial Infinite at Greenwich in Works by Christopher Wren, James Thornhill and James Thomson*. Edwin Mellen Press, Lewiston, 1995

Barbier, George et al. *Parisian Costume Plates in Full Color (1912–1914)*. Dover Publications, New York, 1982

Beadle, Major J. C. *The Light Blue Lanyard: Fifty Years with 40 Commando Royal Marines*. Square One, Worcester, 1992

Beesly, Patrick. *Very Special Intelligence: The Story of the Admiralty's Operational Intelligence Centre, 1939–1945*. Greenhill Books, London, 2000

Beevor, J. G. *SOE: Recollections and Reflections 1940 to 1945*. The Bodley Head, London, 1981

Bernier, Olivier. *Fireworks at Dusk: Paris in the Thirties*. Little, Brown, Boston, 1993

Bertrand, Régis. *Le Vieux-Port de Marseille*. Editions Jeanne Laffitte, Marseille, 1998

Bessel, Richard, ed. *Life in the Third Reich*. Oxford University Press, Oxford, 1987

Binh, Tran Tu. *The Red Earth: A Vietnamese Memoir of Life on a Colonial Rubber Plantation*. Translated by John Spragens, Jr. Edited by David G Marr. Ohio University Center for International Studies, Athens, 1985

Blackstock, Prof. Paul W. and Schaf, Frank L., eds. *Intelligence, Espionage, Counterespionage and Covert Operations: A Guide to Information Sources*. Gale Research Company, Detroit, 1978

Boyce, Fredric and Everett, Douglas. *SOE: the scientific secrets*. Sutton Publishing, Stroud, 2003

Boyce, Joan. *Pillowslips and Gasmasks: Liverpool's Wartime Evacuation*. Liver Press, Birkenhead, 1989

Breaking Our Chains: Documents on the Vietnamese Revolution of August 1945. Foreign Languages Publishing House, Hanoi, 1960

Bridgland, Tony. *Sea Killers in Disguise: The Story of Q-Ships and Decoy Ships in the First World War*. Leo Cooper, Barnsley, 1999

Brome, Vincent. *The Way Back: The Story of Lieut.-Commander Pat O'Leary*. Cassell, London, 1957

Bruge, Roger. *Juin 1940: Le Mois Maudit*. Fayard, Paris, 1980

Bulloch, John. *MI5: The Origin and History of the British Counter-Espionage Service*. A. Baker, London, 1963

Burn, Alan. *The Fighting Commodores: Convoy Commanders in the Second World War*. Leo Cooper, Barnsley, 1999

Butler, Ewan and Young, Gordon. *The Life and Death of Hermann Goering*. Hodder & Stoughton, London, 1951

Campbell, Vice-Admiral Gordon. *My Mystery Ships*. Hodder & Stoughton, London, 1928

Chaline, E. and Santarelli, P., eds. *Historique des Forces Navales Françaises Libres*, Paris, 1990. Tome 1 (*18 juin 1940 – 3 aout 1943*)

Churchill, Winston S. *The Second World War*, II, *Their Finest Hour*. Cassell, London, 1949

Cobb, R. *Promenades*. Oxford University Press, Oxford, 1980

Coffin, Judith G. *The Politics of Women's Work: The Paris Garment Trades 1750–1915*. Princeton University Press, Princeton, New Jersey, 1996

Cohen, William B. 'Colonial Policy of the Popular Front', *French Historical Studies*, 7 (1972), 368–93

Collier, Basil. *The War in the Far East, 1941–1945*. Heinemann, London, 1969

Compton-Hall, Richard. *The Underwater War 1939–1945*. Blandford Press, Poole, 1982

Contrucci, Jean and Duchêne, Roger. *Marseille: 2,600 Ans d'Histoire*. Fayard, Paris, 1998

Cooper, Nicola. *France in Indochina: Colonial Encounters*. Berg, New York, 2001

Cotton, H. E. A. *Calcutta Old and New: A Historical and Descriptive Handbook to the City*. Ed. N. R. Ray. General Printers & Publishers, Calcutta, 1909, revised 1980

Cruickshank, Charles. *SOE in the Far East*. Oxford University Press, Oxford, 1983

Cumberlidge, Peter. *Bristol Channel and Severn Pilot*. Stanford Maritime, London, 1988

Deacon, Audrey. *Diary of a Wren, 1940–45*. The Memoir Club, Spennymoor, 2001

Deacon, Richard. *The French Secret Service*. Grafton, London, 1990

—— *A History of the British Secret Service*. Taplinger, New York and London, 1970

De Beavoir, Simone. *La Force de l'Age*. Editions Gallimard, Paris, 1960

Dennis, Philip. *Gibraltar*. David & Charles, London, 1977

Dicks, Brian. *The Isle of Wight*. David & Charles, Newton Abbot, 1979

Doig, Desmond. *Mother Teresa: Her People and her Work*. Collins, London, 1976

Dugan, Sally. *Commando: The Elite Fighting Forces of the Second World War*. Channel 4 Books, London, 2001

Duiker, William J. *The Rise of Nationalism in Vietnam, 1900–1941*. Cornell University Press, Ithaca, NY, 1976

Elphick, Peter. *Far Eastern File: The Intelligence War in the Far East, 1930–1945*. Hodder & Stoughton, London, 1997

'Enseignement du 1er degré: cours moyen et cours supérieur, programme du 6è mois,' Bulletin Général de l'Instruction Publique (Indochine), partie scolaire, 3è Année, No. 6 (fév. 1924), p.2 88

Essays on Vietnamese Civilisation. Vietnamese Studies, Hanoi, 1981

Fashion in Paris: from the 'Journal des Dames et des Modes' 1912–1913. Thames & Hudson, London, 1980

Figueras, André. *Raoul Salan*. Editions La Table Ronde, Paris, 1965

Fitch, Noel Riley. *Sylvia Beach and the Lost Generation: A History of Literary Paris in the Twenties and Thirties*. W. W. Norton, New York, 1983

FitzGibbon, Constantine. *Secret Intelligence in the Twentieth Century*. Hart-Davis, London, 1976

Fletcher, M. H. *The WRNS: A History of the Women's Royal Naval Service*. B. T. Batsford, London, 1989

Folcher, Gustave. *Marching to Captivity: The War Diaries of a French Peasant, 1939–1945*. François Maspero, Paris, 1981

Fontaine, Peter. *Last To Leave Paris*. Chaterson, London, 1941

Ford, Ken. *St Nazaire 1942: The Great Commando Raid*. Osprey Publishing, Oxford, 2001

Foot, Michael R. D. *SOE: An Outline History of the Special Operations Executive, 1940–1946*. Mandarin, London, 1990

Foot, Michael R. D. *SOE in France: an account of the work of the British Special Operations Executive in France, 1940–1944*. HMSO, London, 1966

Foot, Michael R. D. and Langley, James M. *MI9: The British Secret Service that Fostered Escape and Evasion 1939–45 and its American counterpart*. The Bodley Head, London, 1979

Franck, Harry. *East of Siam: Ramblings in the Five Divisions of French Indochina*. The Century Company, New York, 1926

Fulcher, Jane F. *French Cultural Politics & Music: From the Dreyfus Affair to the First World War*. Oxford University Press, Oxford, 1999

Futura, Motoo and Shiraishi, Takashi, eds. *Indochina in the 1940s and 1950s*. Cornell University Press, Ithaca, NY, 1992

Gandy, Alain. *Salan*. Editions Perrin, Paris, 1990

Garder, Michel. *La Guerre Secrète des Services Spéciaux Français, 1935–1945*. Plon, Paris, 1967

Garstin, Crosbie. *The Dragon and the Lotus: A Description of a Journey to Indochina*. William Heinemann, London, 1928

Gauché, General Maurice. *Le Deuxième Bureau au Travail (1935–1940)*. Amiot-Dumont, Paris, 1953

Gaudel, André. *L'Indochine Française en face du Japon*. J. Susse, Paris, 1947

Gaulle, Charles de. *Speeches* Vol. I and Vol. II. OUP, London, 1942 and 1943

—— *War Memoirs*, I. *Call to Honour*. London, Collins, 1955

Gilbert, Martin. *Finest Hour: Winston S. Churchill 1939–1941*. Heinemann, London, 1983

Gilchrist, Donald. *Castle Commando*. Oliver and Boyd, London, 1960

Gillois, André. *Histoire Secrète des Français à Londres de 1940 à 1944*. Hachette, Paris, 1973

Gras, Yves. *Histoire de la Guerre d'Indochine*. Plon, Paris, 1978

Grenfell, Russell. *Main Fleet to Singapore: An Account of Naval Actions of the Last War*. Faber & Faber, London, 1951

Gritzbach, Erich. *Hermann Goering: The Man and his Work*. Historical Review Press, Decatur, Georgia, 1980

Hague, Arnold. *The Allied Convoy System 1939–1945: Its Organisation, Defence and Operation*. Chatham Publishing, London, 2000

Haine, W. Scott. *The World of the Paris Café: Sociability Among the French Working Class, 1789–1914*. The John Hopkins University Press, Maryland, Baltimore, 1996

Halls, W. D. *Politics, Society and Christianity in Vichy France*. Berg, Oxford/Providence, 1995

Hémery, Daniel. *Révolutionnaires Vietnamiens et Pouvoir Colonial en Indochine: Communistes, Trotskystes, Nationalistes à Saigon de 1932 à 1937*. François Maspero, Paris, 1975

Henri-Phillipe, *Duc d'Orléans*. Autour du Tonkin. Calmann Levy, Paris, 1894

Herbert, James D. *Paris 1937: Worlds on Exhibition*. Cornell University Press, Ithaca, NY, 1998

Hinsley, F. H. *British Intelligence in the Second World War*, 5 vols. Cambridge University Press, New York, 1979–90

Horne, Alistair. *Seven Ages of Paris*. Macmillan, London, 2002

Howarth, Patrick. *Undercover: The Men and Women of the Special Operations Executive*. Arrow, London, 1980

Humbert, A. *Notre guerre*. Editions Emile-Paul Frères, Paris, 1946

Jackson, Julian. *France: The Dark Years 1940–1944*. Oxford University Press, Oxford, 2001

—— *The Fall of France: The Nazi Invasion of 1940*. Oxford University Press, Oxford, 2003

Jackson, Sir William G. F. *The Rock of the Gibraltarians: A History of Gibraltar*. Associated University Presses, USA, 1987

Jacquin, Henri. *Guerre Secrète en Indochine*. Olivier Orban, Paris, 1979

Jamet, C. *Carnets de Déroute*. Sorlot, Paris, 1942

Jenkins, David. *Shipowners of Cardiff: A Class by Themselves: A History of the Cardiff and Bristol Channel Incorporated Shipowners' Association*. University of Wales Press, Cardiff, 1997

Johns, Philip. *Within Two Cloaks: Missions with SIS and SOE*. William Kimber, London, 1979

Jullian, Marcel. *HMS Fidelity*. Le Livre Contemporain, Paris, 1957

Karnow, Stanley. *Vietnam: A History*. Century, London, 1983

Keble Chatterton, E. *Q-Ships and their Story*. Conway Maritime Press, Greenwich, 1972

Kedward, H. R. *Occupied France: Collaboration and Resistance 1940–1944*. Basil Blackwell, Oxford, 1985

Kemp, Robert. *Irish Sea and Bristol Channel Pilot*. Granada Publishing, Frogmore, 1976 (2nd ed 1983)

Kershaw, Ian. *Hitler: 1936–45: Nemesis*. Allen Lane, London, 2000

Kertész, André. *J'Aime Paris: Photographs since the Twenties*. Thames & Hudson, London, 1974

Kingswell, Peter. *Fidelity Will Haunt Me Till I Die*. Royal Marines Historical Society, Havant, 1991

Koch, H. W., ed. *Aspects of the Third Reich*. Macmillan, London, 1985

Koestler, Arthur. *Scum of the Earth*. Macmillan, New York, 1941

Ladd, James. *Commandos and Rangers of World War II*. Macdonald and Jane's, London, 1978

—— *Inside the Commandos: A Pictorial History from World War Two to the Present*. Arms and Armour, London, 1984

Langeron, Roger. *Paris, Juin 1940*. Flammarion, Paris, 1946

Langley, Lt-Col. J. M. *Fight Another Day*. Collins, London, 1974

Langlois, Walter G. *André Malraux: The Indochina Adventure*. Pall Mall Press, London, 1966

Laughton Mathews DBE, Vera. *Blue Tapestry*. Hollis & Carter, London, 1948

Lepotier, Contre Amiral A. A. M. *Bateaux-pièges*, Paris, Editions France-Empire, 1964

Littlewood, Ian. *Paris: A Literary Companion*. John Murray, London, 1987

Logan, William Stewart. *Hanoi: Biography of a City*. University of Washington Press, Seattle, 2000

Long, Helen. *Safe Houses are Dangerous*. William Kimber, London, 1985

Lottman, Herbert R. *The Fall of Paris: June 1940*. Sinclair-Stevenson, London, 1992

Luxton, Brian C. (commentaries by). *Old Barry in Photographs*. Two volumes published by Stewart Williams, Barry, 1977 and 1978

Lycett, Andrew. *Ian Fleming*. Weidenfeld & Nicolson, London, 1995

McBride, Vonla. *Never at Sea: Life in the Wrens*. Educational Explorers, Reading, 1966

McCall, Bernard. *Barry Docks in the 1980s: A Pictorial Survey.*
    Penarth, 1989

McCormick, Donald. *17F: The Life of Ian Fleming.* Peter Owen,
    London, 1993

Macintyre, Capt. Donald. *Fighting Admiral: The Life of Admiral
    of the Fleet Sir James Somerville.* Evans Brothers, London,
    1961

McLachlan, Donald. *Room 39: A Study in Naval Intelligence.*
    Atheneum, New York, 1968

Mallmann Showell, Jak P. *U-Boat Warfare: The Evolution of the
    Wolf Pack.* Ian Allan, Hersham, 2002

Mann, Carol. *Paris: Artistic Life in the Twenties & Thirties.*
    Laurence King, London, 1996

Marr, David G. *Vietnamese Anticolonialism, 1885–1925.* University
    of California Press, Berkeley, 1971

May, Ernest R. *Knowing One's Enemies: Intelligence Assessment
    Between the Two World Wars.* Princeton University Press,
    Princeton, 1984

Melling, Phil and Roper, Jon, eds. *America, France and Vietnam:
    Cultural History and Ideas of Conflict.* Avebury, Aldershot,
    1991

Melton, George E. *Darlan: Admiral and Statesman of France, 1881
    to 1942.* Praeger, Westport, Connecticut, 1998

Mersey Docks and Harbour Board. *Business in Great Waters: An
    Account of the Activities of the Mersey Docks and the Harbour
    Board 1858–1958.* Newman Neame, Manchester, 1958

Meynier, A. *Les Déplacements de la population vers la Bretagne en
    1940–1941.* Les Nourritures Terrestres, Rennes, 1950

Miller, Lee. *Wrens in Camera.* Hollis and Carter, London, 1945

Monsarrat, Nicholas. *The Cruel Sea.* Cassell & Co, London, 1951

Moore, Donald, ed. *Barry: The Centenary Book.* Barry Centenary
    Book Committee Ltd, Barry, 1984

Moorhouse, Geoffrey. *Calcutta*. Weidenfeld & Nicolson, London, 1971

Mosley, Leonard. *The Reich Marshal: A Biography of Hermann Goering*. Weidenfeld & Nicolson, London, 1974

Mulligan, Timothy P. *Neither Sharks nor Wolves: The Men of Germany's U-Boat Arm*. Naval Institute Press, Annapolis, 1999

Musée d'Histoire de Marseille. *Marseille et les Américains, 1940–1946*. Musée d'Histoire de Marseille, Marseille, 1996

Muselier, Renaud. *L'Amiral Muselier 1882–1965: Le Créateur de la croix de Lorraine*. Librairie Académique Perrin, Paris, 2000

Nair, P. Thankappan. *A History of Calcutta's Streets*. Firma KLM, Calcutta, 1987

Navarre, Gen. Henri. *Le Service de Renseignements, 1871–1944*. Plon, Paris, 1978

—— *Le Temps des Vérités*. Plon, Paris, 1979

Neave, Airey. *Saturday at MI9: A history of underground escape lines in North-West Europe in 1940–5*. Hodder & Stoughton, London, 1969

Ngoc, Huu. *Sketches for a Portrait of Hanoi*. The Gioi, Hanoi, 1998

Nguyen, Khac Vien. *The Long Resistance: 1858–1975*. Foreign Languages Publishing House, Hanoi, 1960

Nguyen, Vinh Phuc. *Hanoi: Past and Present*. The Gioi, Hanoi, 2001

Osborne, Milton E. *The French Presence in Cochinchina and Cambodia: Rule and Response, 1859–1905*. Cornell University Press, Ithaca, NY, 1969

Ousby, Ian. *Occupation: The Ordeal of France 1940–1944*. John Murray, London, 1997

Overy, Richard. *Goering*. Routledge & Keegan Paul, London, 1984

Padfield, Peter. *Dönitz: The Last Führer*. Cassell, London, 1984

Page, Bruce, Leitch, David, and Knightley, Phillip. *The Philby Conspiracy*. Doubleday, New York, 1968

Paillol, Col. Paul. *Services Spéciaux, 1935–1945*. R. Laffont, Paris, 1975

Papin, Philippe. *Histoire de Hanoi*. Fayard, Paris, 2001

Paul, Elliot. *The Last Time I Saw Paris*. Random House, New York, 1942

Paxton, Robert O. *Vichy France: Old Guard and New Order, 1940–1944*. Barrie & Jenkins, London, 1972

Pearson, John. *The Life of Ian Fleming*. Jonathan Cape, 1966

Pedlahore, Christian. 'Constituent Elements of Hanoi City', *Vietnamese Studies*, 12 (82): 105–59

Penn, Irving and Vreeland, Diana. *Inventive Paris Clothes 1909–1939: a photographic essay*. Thames & Hudson, London, 1977

Philby, Kim. *My Silent War*. MacGibbon & Kee, London, 1968

Porch, Douglas. *The French Secret Services: From the Dreyfus Affair to the Gulf War*. Farrar, Straus, Giroux, New York, 1995

Pryce-Jones, David. *Paris in the Third Reich. A History of the German Occupation, 1940–1944*. Collins, London, 1981

Rajsfus, Maurice, *Les Français de la débâcle*. Le Cherche Midi, Paris, 1997

Revely, Henry. *The Convoy that Nearly Died: the Story of ONS 154*. William Kimber, London, 1979

Richards, Sir Brooks. *Secret Flotillas: The Clandestine Sea Lines to France and French North Africa, 1940–1944*. HMSO, London, 1996

Rigden, Denis (introduction). *SOE Syllabus: Lessons in Ungentlemanly Warfare, World War II*. Public Record Office, London, 2001

Ritchie, Carson. *Q-Ships: Britain's Secret Weapon against the U-Boats, 1914–1918*. Terence Dalton, Lavenham, 1985

Robert, Jean-Louis and Winter, Jay. *Capital Cities at War: Paris, London, Berlin 1914–1919*. Cambridge University Press, Cambridge, 1997

Roberts, Stephen H. *The History of French Colonial Policy 1870–1925*. P. S. King, London, 1929

Roskill, Stephen W. *The War at Sea 1939–1945*. HMSO, London, 1956

Sadoul, Georges. *Journal de guerre (2 septembre 1939–20 juillet 1940)*. Les Editeurs Français Réunis, Paris, 1977

Sagner-Düchting, Karin. *Renoir: Paris and the Belle Epoque*. Prestel, New York, 1996

Salan, Raoul. *Mémoires*. Presses de la Cité, Paris, 1970
—— *Indochine Rouge: Le Message d'Hô Chi Minh*. Presses de la Cité, Paris, 1975

Sarraut, Albert. *Indochine*. Firmin-Didot, Paris, 1930

Sartre, J.-P., translated by Quintin Hoare. *War Diaries: Notebooks from a Phoney War November 1939 to March 1940*. Verso, London, 1984

Saunders, Hilary St George. *The Green Beret: The Story of the Commandos 1940–1945*. Michael Joseph, London, 1949

Seaman, Mark (introduction). *Secret Agent's Handbook of Special Devices, World War II*. Public Record Office, London, 2000

Sharpe, Peter. *U-Boat Fact File: Detailed Service Histories of the Submarines Operated by the Kriegsmarine 1935–1945*. Midland Publishing, Leicester, 1998

Shennan, Andrew. *The Fall of France, 1940*. Longman, Harlow, 2000

Sibley, Patricia. *Discovering the Isle of Wight*. Robert Hale, London, 1977

Sidel, Mark. *Old Hanoi*. Oxford University Press, Kuala Lumpur, 1998

Silver, Kenneth E. *Esprit de Corps: The Art of the Parisian Avant-Garde and the First World War, 1914–1925*. Thames & Hudson, London, 1989

Smith, Graham. *Shipwrecks of the Bristol Channel*. Countryside Books, Newbury, 1991

Somerville, Admiral Sir James. *The Somerville Papers: Selections from the Private and Official Correspondence of Admiral of the Fleet Sir James Somerville, GCB, GBE, DSO*, edited by Michael Simpson with the assistance of John Somerville. Navy Records Society, Aldershot, 1996

Spiro, Edward. *Set Europe Ablaze*. Thomas Y. Crowell, New York, 1967

Stafford, David. *Britain and European Resistance: A Survey of the Special Operations Executive*. Macmillan, London, 1980

——— *Churchill & Secret Service*. John Murray, London, 1997

Stead, Philip John. *Second Bureau*. Evans Brothers, London, 1959

Steele, Valerie. *Paris Fashion: A Cultural History*. OUP, New York and Oxford, 1988

Stewart, John D. *Gibraltar the Keystone*. John Murray, London, 1967

Strong, Sir Kenneth. *Intelligence at the Top: The Recollections of an Intelligence Officer*. Doubleday, New York, 1969

Stuart Mason, Ursula. *The Wrens 1917–77: A History of the Women's Royal Naval Service*. Educational Explorers, Reading, 1977

Sweet-Escott, Bickham. *Baker Street Irregular*. Methuen, London, 1965

Thanh-Luong. *A Short History of Vietnam*. Foreign Languages Publishing House, Hanoi, 1955

Vidalenc, J. *L'Exode de mai-juin 1940*. Presses Universitaires de France, Paris, 1957

Vuilliez André : 'La Fantastique Aventure de Jean Ayral'. Article in unknown periodical, published in France

Werner, Commander Herbert A. *Iron Coffins: A Personal Account of the German U-Boat Battles of World War II*. Holt, Rinehart and Winston, New York, 1969

Werth, Alexander. *The Last Days of Paris: A Journalist's Diary*. Hamish Hamilton, London, 1940

—— *The Twilight of France 1933–1940: A Journalist's Chronicle*. Edited by D. W. Brogan. Hamish Hamilton, London, 1942

West, Nigel. *Secret War: The Story of SOE, Britain's Wartime Sabotage Organisation*. Hodder & Stoughton, London, 1992

Willmott, H. P. *The Second World War in the Far East*. Cassell, London, 1999

Wiser, William. *The Crazy Years: Paris in the Twenties*. Thames & Hudson, London, 1983

Wynn, Kenneth. *U-Boat Operations of the Second World War*. Vols 1 and 2. Chatham Publishing, London, 1997

Ziegler, Philip. *Mountbatten: The Official Biography*. Collins, London, 1985

BRITISH NEWSPAPERS

'One of the strangest stories of the war: Jacques Michel and Mlle E, secret agents' by Ronald Camp. *News Chronicle*, London, 20 October 1943

'One of the strangest stories of the war – 2: The *Rhin* gets guns and men' by Ronald Camp. *News Chronicle*, London, 21 October 1943

'Buccaneer in black bloomers' by Paul Boyle. *Sunday Pictorial*, London, 9 December 1956

'I saw her die' by Peter Kennerley. *Sunday Pictorial*, London, 16 December 1956.

'HMS *Fidelity* was a lady' by Lieutenant Commander Pat O'Leary (as told to Stanley Bonnett). *Daily Mail*, London, 17 December 1956

FRENCH NEWSPAPERS

La Fronde, Paris, 18 February 1901 (For details of seamstresses' strike of that year)
La Voix du Peuple, Paris, December 1911. 'It is unacceptable and revolting to see women hit in this cowardly way'
The International Herald Tribune, European edition, Paris. 1939–1940
Le Monde Illustré. 1939–1940

FRENCH ARCHIVES

Revue d'Histoire d'Outre-mer. 2ème semestre 2001, No. 332–333, p.148. Published by La Société française d'Histoire d'Outre-mer, Saint-Denis, France. Contains following quote: 'Claude Péri, le fils [sic] du capitaine Henri Péri qui donna en 1938 quarante-huit objets de Chine et du Tonkin (38.121), donne en 1939 cent-seize objets provenant de la 'Mission France-Asie' qu'il vient de mener à terme (39.22), puis quatre-vingt-quatorze objets de Chine (D.59.5).'

UNPUBLISHED SOURCES

Original material in this book is drawn from many different oral and written sources. I have sometimes edited, précised or modified it to suit the narrative context.

French Archives

Archives de la Marine Nationale, Ministère de la Défense de la République Française, Vincennes. Following dossiers:

CC7 4° moderne 1077/8 (PERI, Claude, André Michel)
CC7 4° moderne 3052/1 (PERI, Claude, André Michel)
CC7 4° moderne 1670/37 (BAYARD, Madeleine Victorine)
TTY 825 (SS *Le Rhin*)

The service records and some personal documents relating to Claude's father, François-Michel Péri, are kept by the Archives du Service Historique de l'Armée de Terre, Ministère de la Défense de la République Française, Vincennes.

Carré, Capitaine Claude. Les Attachés Militaires Français, 1920–1945, Université de Paris I [Panthéon-Sorbonne], 1976. Unpublished and informative *mémoire de maîtrise* about the French overseas military attachés.

Archives de l'Assistance Public Hôpitaux de Paris, 7 Rue des Minimes, 75003 Paris:

Registre des naissance, 1910–1911, coté 4 Q 3/9 (Madeleine Victorine Bayard)
Registre d'accouchements, février 1911 coté R 217 (Adèle Suzanne Bayard)

Archives of the Service Historique de l'Armée de la Terre, Ministère de la Défense de la République Française, Vincennes:

> 10H75 Dossier 3: Situation of Indochina during 1930
>
> 10H75 Dossier 1 Document 6: Instructions regarding the organization and functioning of a colonial intelligence service
>
> 10H75 Dossier 1 Document 4: Various letters regarding the SRI
>
> Weekly Intelligence bulletins 15/11/39
>
> Weekly Intelligence bulletins 30/11/39
>
> Daily Intelligence reports 21/11/39
>
> Monthly Intelligence bulletins 15/12/38
>
> Monthly Intelligence bulletins 15/11/38
>
> Monthly Intelligence bulletins 15/09/38
>
> Monthly Intelligence bulletins 15/07/38
>
> Monthly Intelligence bulletins 15/06/38

Claude Péri – unpublished family sources.

Claude Péri's archive, owned and stored by his sister-in-law, Madame Henri Péri. Private collection, Dijon. The archive includes letters to and from friends and family, photographs, Claude's journal of his 1938–1939 trans-Asia journey, a copy of the telegram sent him by Madeleine in May 1939. All quotations reproduced by kind permission of Madame Henri Péri and her son, Bernard Péri.

British archives

National Archives: Public Record Office, Kew, London:

> ADM 1/1462. Training and employment of Wren wireless telegraph officers
>
> ADM 1/11401. Recommendation of Distinguished Service Medal for Petty Office John Ford, HMS *Fidelity*

ADM 1/12062. Battle of the Atlantic: summary of convoy and escort policy, U-boat situation, air questions, etc

ADM 1/12680. Recruitment of Wrens

ADM 1/12764. Recruitment of Wren officers, 1939–1943

ADM 1/13981. Training of WRNS officers

ADM 11/14698. Centralisation of Wrens' training

ADM 12/1742. Admiralty index 1939–1940. This index contains the following reference: 'Barclay MV. 1st officer WRNS. Commissioned and appointed to HMS *Fidelity* September. MO 3537/43. W H [war history] Case 8445.' An extensive search was made for the existence of this important file; it appears however to no longer exist.

ADM 116/6359. Anglo-French agreement on reciprocal loan of warships. Including dossier on *Le Rhin*/HMS *Fidelity* and the looted cargo

ADM 178/224. Maintenance of discipline on HMS *Fidelity*. Board of Inquiry into incidents including suicide of Major Violet

ADM 199/222. Enemy Submarine Attacks on Merchant Shipping – Reports 1943, including ONS 154

ADM 199/356. ON, ONS and HX Convoys 1942–1943 – Reports of Proceedings on Nos 141–178 (incomplete)

ADM 199/583. ON Convoys, Reports 1942–1943 – Commodore's Report on Nos 122–203 (incomplete)

ADM 199/1320. War history of HMS *Fidelity* 1940 to 1944

ADM 199/2100. Individual Atlantic Convoys 1942

ADM 199/2108. North Atlantic Convoys: outward, homeward, and UC and CU tanker convoys 1939–1945

ADM 199/2111. South Atlantic Convoys

ADM 202/87. War Diary of 40 RM Commando

AIR 29/3. Air operations record book, Barry RAF

AVIA 15/1394. Sale of HMS *Fidelity*'s cargo

DEFE 2/569. Operation Sirocco

HO 192/1355. Attacks on Barry docks

HS 6/323. Planning of sabotage (SOE)

HS 6/589. Sabotage in France (SOE)

HS 6/931. Operation 'Warden': sabotage of enemy ships in Las Palmas harbour (SOE)

HS 7/27. History of the research and development section of the SOE 1938–1945 (SOE)

HS 7/28. Descriptive catalogue of special devices and supplies (SOE)

HS 7/30. Information on weapons, portable transmitting and receiving equipment (SOE)

HS 7/51. Training section 1941–45; industrial sabotage training 1941–1944 (SOE)

HS 7/53. SOE Group B training syllabus; sabotage handbook (illustrated) part I

HS 7/54. SOE Group B training syllabus; sabotage handbook (illustrated) part II

HS 7/104. History of SOE activities in Burma (SOE)

HS 8/831. Special Operations Executive file covering activities of HMS *Fidelity* January 1941 to December 1941

Imperial War Museum, Lambeth, London:

78/50/1 Commander Patrick Whinney. Two memoirs. One covers his service as an assistant to the British Naval Attaché at the French Admiralty's operation headquarters at Marceau, September 1939–1940 and gives details of the fall of France, which he witnessed at first hand. The second is a 20-page memoir of HMS *Fidelity*, in which he served as liaison officer from late 1940 until the spring of 1941.

82/24/1 Captain Frank Slocum. Photocopy of a letter, written in 1977, containing notes on HMS *Fidelity*. Slocum, as Deputy Director Operations Division (Intelligence) at the Admiralty from 1939 to 1945, was responsible for its refits.

76/151/1 Commander John Langley. Memoir of this former Royal Navy officer, seconded to the Secret Intelligence Service, containing a chapter detailing his contact with Claude and Madeleine and *Fidelity*. There are also references to his time running a sabotage school in Aston House, north of London, which Madeleine and Pat O'Leary attended.

Naval Historical Branch, London:

>German U-boat logbooks

>Claude Péri's service record in British Royal Navy

>M271. Correspondence between Dewar (NHB) and Thring (intelligence) about loss of *Fidelity*

>AB152. One-page document on loss of *Fidelity* by G. Thring. Dated 17 Jan 1946

>S4051 – document dealing with Pat O'Leary's cooperation with Marcel Jullian

>S4453 – document dealing with Henri Péri's comments on Jullian book

>'Hush – most secret' document from Admiralty to C in C Eastern Fleet 401 (Somerville), dated 11.6.42

Pollard, Michael. 'A Stage in my Education.'

Unpublished memoir. All quotations reproduced by kind permission.

Interviews/letters

Other information came from interviews and correspondence with Marie Dore, George Millar, Charles Osset, Bernard Péri, Mme Henri Péri, Michael Pollard, the late Sir Brooks Richards, Auguste 'Bob' Roulland, the late Patrick Whinney, Paul Young.

Peter Kingswell also kindly lent his own archive, containing many letters from former crew members of *Fidelity* and others, such as the late Dowager Marchioness of Cholmondeley, who knew Claude and Madeleine well.

INDEX

Acknowledgements

I would like to thank the following. Allan Adair (Naval Attaché at the British Embassy in Paris), Sarah Castleton for her editorial skills, Nicholas Crane for some crucial early encouragement, Sylvie Deroche for guiding me to Madeleine's birth records and much else besides, Marie Dore, Camilla Elworthy for coming to Dijon and being, as always, such great company, Jean-Christophe Haultecoeur for his tireless detective work, William Heap at the Foreign and Commonwealth Office in Paris, Derek Johns, Sally Kenyon at the British Embassy in Paris, Peter Kingswell for his encouragement and generous use of his archive, Graham Lambie at Glanvilles Solicitors, Isle of Wight, Ben Macintyre for pointing me towards Sylvie Deroche, the staff at the archives of the Marine Nationale at Vincennes, Patricia de Mesquita for her translation work, Léon Nyssen, Captain Derek Oakley, Bernard Péri, Madame Henri Péri, Michael Pollard, the late Sir Brooks Richards, Sophie Riché and Agnes Masson at the Archives de l'Assistance Public-Hôpitaux de Paris, Auguste Roulland, Jean and Gordon Spencer in Barry, Kate Tildesley at the Royal Naval Historical Branch in London, Des Turner and the Aston Village History Collection Trust, Mark Whinney, the late Patrick Whinney, Suzanne Whitehead at the National Maritime Museum in Greenwich and Katy Willis.

PICTURE CREDITS (*page numbers*) Regine Anania – *59*, *107*, *146*, *295*. Aston Village History Collection Trust – *165*. The saleroom at Hanoi, c.1920, French Photographer / Archives Nationales-Centre des Archives d'Outre-Mer, Archives Charmet / The Bridgeman Art Library – *24*. Corbis – *51*. Glanvilles Solicitors, Newport, Isle of Wight – *223*. Hulton/Getty Images – *123*, *141*. Imperial War Museum – *102*, *132*, *155*, *219*, *250*, *263*, *272*. Marcel Jullian – *84*, *120*, *177*, *183*. Madame Henri Péri – *31*, *34*, *45*, *57*, *70*. Michael Pollard – *221*. Time Life Pictures / Getty Images – *100*.